Latino Poverty and Economic Development in Massachusetts

Edited by
Edwin Meléndez
and
Miren Uriarte

Latino Poverty and Economic Development in Massachusetts

Latino Poverty and Economic Development in Massachusetts

Edited by
Edwin Meléndez *and*
Miren Uriarte

The Mauricio Gastón Institute for Latino
Community Development and Public Policy
The University of Massachusetts Boston

Distributed by the University of Massachusetts Press

Distributed by the University of Massachusetts Press
P.O. Box 429, Amherst, MA 01004, USA

LC 93-34381
ISBN 0–87023–894–9

Library of Congress Cataloging-in-Publication Data

Latino poverty and economic development in Massachusetts / edited by
Edwin Meléndez and Miren Uriarte.
    p.   cm.
    ISBN 0–87023–894–9 (pbk.)
    1. Hispanic Americans—Massachusetts—Economic conditions.
    2. Massachusetts—Economic conditions. I. Meléndez, Edwin.
    II. Uriarte-Gastón, Miren.
    F75.S75L38   1993
    330.9744'0089'68—dc20   93-34381
                                                   CIP

British Library Cataloguing in Publication data are available.

Contents

Part III Public Policy and Community Strategies

Preface

The Mauricio Gastón Institute for Latino Community Development and Public Policy began research concerning the economic status of Latinos in Massachusetts in early 1991 with a research competition entitled "Latinos, Poverty and Public Policy." Professor Barry Bluestone (UMass/Boston), Mr. Jose Duran (Hispanic Office of Planning and Evaluation), Professor James Jennings (UMass/Boston), Professor Edwin Meléndez (MIT), Professor Paul Osterman (MIT), Professor Miren Uriarte (UMass/Boston), and Professor Ann Withorn (UMass/Boston) evaluated the twelve research projects chosen for funding. Once the research reports were developed, the awardees were invited to share their work with other Latino scholars in a research seminar. With the feedback supplied by the seminar participants, the researchers then prepared their final reports. Many of these reports served as background information for different workshops at a policy conference held at UMass/Boston in December of 1991. The conference brought together over 200 people including researchers, community economic development activists, Latino community leaders, policymakers, and representative of the private sector. This volume and the policy recommendations contained herewith are the results of this research effort.

Our thanks to all those who participated in this enormously successful project. We especially acknowledge the distinguished work of the contributors to this volume, the Gastón Advisory Board members, the research reviewers for their steady guidance of the project, and all of the seminar and conference participants for their invaluable feedback. We are particularly indebted to the funders of this project, including The Boston Foundation, The Poverty and Race Research Action Council, and the University of Massachusetts. Finally, we want to acknowledge the contribution of all the dedicated Gastón Institute staff members, with special appreciation to Gloria Cardona, the Institute's activities coordinator, and Linda Kluz, production editor for the volume.

Contributors

RAMÓN BORGES-MÉNDEZ is a research associate at the Mauricio Gastón Institute for Latino Community Development and Public Policy. He holds a masters in city planning from the Department of Urban Studies and Planning at Massachusetts Institute of Technology and is currently a Ph.D. candidate in that same department. His research interests include urban and regional economic analysis, labor markets and industrial development in the United States and Latin America, and Hispanics in the United States.

JEREMIAH COTTON is associate professor in the Department of Economics at the University of Massachusetts Boston. He received his Ph.D. in economics from the University of Michigan and holds an M.S.W. from the University of Pittsburgh. Dr. Cotton was a doctoral fellow with the Social Sciences Research Council in 1982-83 and a minority fellow with the Council on Social Work Education in 1975-78. His publications include "Color or Culture? Wage Differences among Non-Hispanic Black Males, Black Hispanic Males and White Hispanic Males," which appeared in the *Social Science Quarter* in 1992; "A Regional Analysis of Black-White Male Wage Differences," which appeared in the *Review of Black Political Economy* in 1992; and "Labor Economics and Racial Inequality," which appeared in *Labor Economics: A Critique*, edited by William Darity, Jr. (Kluwer Academic Press, 1992).

LUIS FALCÓN is assistant professor in the Department of Sociology at Northeastern University. He received his Ph.D. in sociology from Cornell University and holds an M.S.W. from the University of Puerto Rico. Dr. Falcón's publications include "Trends in Labor Market Position for Puerto Ricans on the Mainland: 1970-1987," written with Charles Hirschman and appearing in the *Hispanic Journal of Behavioral Sciences* in February 1992; "Migration and Development: The Case of Puerto Rico," which appeared in *Determinants of Emigration from Mexico, Central America, and the Caribbean*, edited by Sergio Diaz-Briquets and Sidney Weintraub (Westview, 1991); and "Mexicans, Puerto Ricans and Cubans in the Labor Market: A Historical Overview," written with Dan Gilbarg and appearing in the *Handbook of Hispanic Cultures in the United States*, edited by Felix Padilla (Arte P'ublico Press, 1993).

PEGGY J. LEVITT is currently a MacArthur Fellow at the Center for Population and Development Studies at Harvard University. She holds a masters in urban planning and a masters in public health, both from Columbia University, and she is a doctoral candidate in the Department of Urban Studies and Planning at Massachusetts Institute of Technology.

EDWIN MELÉNDEZ is the director of the Mauricio Gastón Institute for Latino Community Development and Public Policy and associate professor of economics at the University of Massachusetts Boston. Dr. Meléndez received his Ph.D. in economics from the University of Massachusetts Amherst and his M.A. in economics from the University of California at Santa Barbara. Dr. Meléndez is coauthor of *In the Shadows of the Sun: Caribbean Development Alternatives and U.S. Policy* (Westview Press, 1990), *Hispanics in the Labor Force* (Plenum Press, 1991), and *Puerto Rico: A Colonial Dilemma* (South End Press, 1993). His most recent works include "Understanding Latino Poverty" (*Sage Race Relations Abstract*, 18, 2), "Puerto Rican Migration and Occupational Selectivity, 1982-88" (*International Migration Review*, 28, 1), and "The Effects of Local Labor Market Conditions on Labor Force Participation of Puerto Rican, White, and Black Women" (*Hispanic Journal of Behavioral Sciences*, 14[1]).

RALPH RIVERA is an assistant professor at the College of Public and Community Service, University of Massachusetts Boston and associate director of the Mauricio Gastón Institute for Latino Community Development and Public Policy. He received his Ph.D. from the Florence Heller Graduate School for Advanced Studies in Social Welfare, Brandeis University and his M.S.W. from Boston University School of Social Work. He is coeditor, with Sonia Nieto, of *The Education of Latino Students in Massachusetts: Issues, Research, and Policy Implications* (Gastón Institute, 1993).

NANETTE ROBICHEAU is special assistant to the department head at the Department of Urban Studies and Planning, Massachusetts Institute of Technology. She holds a master's in city planning from MIT where she specialized in community economic development.

MICHAEL E. STONE teaches Community Planning in the College of Public and Community Service at the University of Massachusetts Boston. He received his Ph.D. from Princeton University, and for more than 20 years he has been involved in research, policy analysis, program development, technical assistance, and advocacy on housing issues. Dr. Stone is the author of *People before*

Property: A Real Estate Primer and Research Guide (Urban Planning Aid, 1972) and *Shelter Poverty: New Ideas on Housing Affordability* (Temple Univ. Press, 1993).

MIREN URIARTE has been the acting dean of the College of Public and Community Service at the University of Massachusetts Boston and was the founding director of the Mauricio Gastón Institute for Latino Community Development and Public Policy. She holds a Ph.D. in community sociology and race and ethnic relations from Boston University. She has written articles on the entry of Latinos in the economy of South Florida and on the social and institutional development of the Latino community of Boston. Her work has appeared in the *Hispanic Journal of Public Policy,* the *Women's Studies Quarterly,* and the *Hispanic Journal of Behavioral Sciences, Social Work Research and Abstracts.* Dr. Uriarte is currently a principal investigator in the Boston portion of the Multi-City Study of Urban Inequality funded by the Russell Sage and Ford Foundation.

Latino Poverty and Economic Development in Massachusetts

Edwin Meléndez

Introduction

The Latino population in Massachusetts has grown phenomenally during the last decade, becoming the largest minority group in the state (Rivera, in this volume). The rapid growth of the Latino population of the state is characteristic of a pattern that is significantly changing the racial and ethnic composition of the nation. Despite the apparent importance of such a demographic revolution, the research and policy communities of the United States have paid little attention to the particular problems affecting Latinos at the state level and to the formulation of appropriate interventions to tackle such problems. Massachusetts is no exception. The objective of this volume is to provide a conceptual framework and background information regarding the economic problems affecting the growing Latino population in Massachusetts as well as to initiate a discussion of effective public policies and community strategies.

Massachusetts is a particularly interesting case for several reasons. To begin with, Latino poverty and growing inequality occurred despite the economic expansion of the 1980s. Latinos in Massachusetts experienced the largest intercensal increase in poverty of all racial and ethnic groups. The puzzle poised by the "Massachusetts Miracle" raises several of the key questions addressed by the authors included in this volume. Why didn't Latinos benefit from the prolonged economic growth of the last decade? What are the main factors explaining Latino poverty? How are these factors affecting other racial and ethnic groups? The answers to these questions and their implications for public policy and communities transcend Massachusetts.

Explanations of Latino poverty can be grouped into three general categories: those explanations that pertain to Latinos' immigrant status and rapid demographic change; those that emphasize the possibility of Latinos becoming an urban underclass; and those that focus on the relative disadvantage of Latinos in labor markets. Although most analysts will concede that Latino poverty results from a combination of factors, emphasis in one explanation could certainly lead community leaders and policymakers to focus on a particular set of interventions. If, for instance, policymakers believe that most labor-market problems such as unemployment and low wages are caused by poor language skills, the most appropriate intervention and the most likely programmatic emphasis will be courses on English as a second language, bilingual education, and translation services in the work place, the court, etc. However, if the opposite argument, which proposes labor-market discrimination (which induces segmentation into low-wage jobs) as the most important factor in the explanation for the above-average poverty rates of Latinos, is used, the intervention will emphasize the aggressive enforcement of affirmative-action regulations, work-place support groups for Latinos, unionization, and similar programs.

The chapters included in this volume attempt to assess the relative importance of the factors affecting Latino poverty in Massachusetts. The first section of the volume provides background information and a conceptual context for a more detailed discussion of Latino poverty in the state. In the first chapter of the volume, "Latino Poverty and Economic Development in Massachusetts," I propose that the beneficial impact of the economic expansion on Latino poverty was offset by the type of jobs created, the concentration of Latinos in those cities that suffered the brunt of blue-collar job losses, the relatively low educational attainment of working-age Latinos, and the growing number of households with only one potential wage earner. Other factors such as rapid population growth and a large proportion of immigrants among Latinos seem to have played a lesser role. Economic dislocation and labor-market disadvantage are central explanations of Latino poverty, although it is recognized in the chapter that other factors are also at play.

Ralph Rivera's chapter, entitled "Diversity, Growth, and Geographic Distribution: Latinos in Massachusetts,"[1] examines in detail the issues of diversity among Latinos, the growth of the Latino population, and the geographic dispersion of the population. He uses 1990 U.S. Census and other data to provide a detailed profile of the general demographic changes in Massachusetts during the last decades and how these profiles compare to the nation and to the New England area. One of the most important points made in Rivera's chapter is that the Latino population is comprised of diverse nationalities. In contrast to the national profile where Mexicans constitute the overwhelming majority of the Latino population, Puerto Ricans constitute about half of the Massachusetts Latino population while Dominicans, Central Americans, and South Americans constitute the next largest group. These national origin groups also differ significantly in terms of growth patterns and geographical concentration. Although the Puerto Rican population of Massachusetts doubled during the last decade, other Caribbean and Central and South American groups have grown even faster, thus inducing a decline in the proportion of Puerto Ricans from the total Massachusetts Latino population. Just as important is the fact that Latino immigrants to the state are increasing their numbers in towns with a traditionally high concentration of Latinos such as Lawrence, Chelsea, Holyoke, Lowell, Springfield, and Worcester and are dispersing throughout many other towns where they have not located in the past such as Haverhill, Everett, Framingham, Lynn, Leominster, Salem, and Waltham.

The implications of Rivera's findings are very important for our understanding of poverty and in the design of effective interventions. Foremost, it is problematic to talk about Latinos as a homogeneous population group. It is true they share a common language and many similar circumstances as recent immigrants, but Latinos are fragmented by multiple cultural backgrounds and national customs. A common identity and group solidarity is not evident in many social, economic, and political situations and in some instances there is evident competition for jobs and other social resources or clear antagonism among youths from different neighborhoods. Similarly, geographical dispersion has become an important barrier in achieving and promoting economic and political advancement. However, as population growth occurs in many places, the political influence and socioeconomic status of Latinos may improve in the next decade.

The next section of the volume examines the labor-market standing of Latinos and how employment and income outcomes are related to increased inequality. Taken together, the chapters by Jeremiah Cotton, Luis Falcón, and Ramón Borges-Méndez assess the functioning of labor markets at the state and local levels and provide comparative analyses along regional and demographic characteristics. The chapter by Cotton, entitled "A Comparative Analysis of the Labor Market Outcomes of Latinos, Blacks, and Whites in Boston, Massachusetts, and New England, 1983 to 1991," compares the labor-market standing of Latinos to that of blacks and whites in the Boston, Massachusetts, and New England labor markets. His findings strongly support the contention that Latino poverty in Massachusetts is rooted in labor-market disadvantage. Latinos fit the classical definition of the working poor. Cotton concludes that:

On virtually every indicator of labor-market success considered in this research, it appears that Latinos do worse than whites, and in many cases fare worse than blacks. Latinos have lower earnings than either whites or blacks; higher unemployment rates than whites and about the same as blacks; greater numbers of workers who experience unemployment at one time or another than either whites or blacks; more frequent periods of unemployment than whites or blacks; more instances of job losses through firings and/or layoffs than either whites or blacks; a lower probability of being employed than whites though not always than blacks; more involuntary part-time employment than whites or, for the most part, blacks; and a greater proportion of individuals in relatively lower-paying service occupations and a smaller proportion in relatively higher-paying, white-collar occupations than either whites or blacks.

Luis Falcón's chapter, "Economic Growth and Increased Inequity: Hispanics in the Boston Labor Market," analyzes in more detail the labor-market standing and other demographic characteristics of Latinos in Boston and compares the findings for this population to those of whites and blacks in the city. He uses data collected for the Boston Foundation Persistent Poverty Project between November 1988 and April 1989 and organizes the tables controlling for those near or below the poverty line. Although he acknowledges that poverty among Latinos largely result from the convergence of employment, educational, and demographic changes, he finds relatively little differences between the characteristics of the poor and the near poor. The most important issue for Latinos is not finding employment (with the exception of female heads-of-households) but rather the dead-end jobs available to them that are likely to offer low wages and no benefits beyond what is mandated by law. Like Cotton, Falcón suggests that it is their labor-market outcomes that underline Latino poverty rather than any significant difference in the characteristics of those who are poor and those who are not. Notwithstanding, Falcón finds that there is a predominance of women and female heads-of-households among Latinos living near or below the poverty line. Poverty among Latinos is primarily the poverty of women and children.

In contrast to previous chapters which focused on aggregate labor-market trends and data, the chapter by Ramón Borges-Méndez, "The Use of Latino Immigrant Labor in Massachusetts Manufacturing: Evidence from Lowell, Lawrence, and Holyoke," focuses on labor-market dynamics at the firm level, the industrial (i.e., manufacturing) sector, and the economic context in order to understand the roots of inequality. Studying manufacturing firms in three small towns in Massachusetts — Lowell, Lawrence, and Holyoke — Borges-Méndez found the analysis is much more complex than anticipated by previous work. Latino employment in Lowell's high-tech manufacturing and in Lawrence and Holyoke's labor-intensive operations resembles the general stereotype of workers segmented in secondary jobs and excluded from better paying positions, but there are a sizable number of modernizing firms in Lowell and Holyoke that offer better employment opportunities for Latinos. Firms seeking to improve their competitive position by fostering human resource development, job stability, and the modernization of equipment seem to improve the employment opportunities for Latinos. In a way, Latinos provide a labor force that can adapt to workplace changes and the implementation of new technologies without significantly increasing the cost of operations. The experience of modernizing firms in small towns offers hope that Latinos may have found a ladder of opportunity in labor markets. To what extent firms will continue to change their operations in ways that benefit the Latino population remains to be seen, but policymakers and Latino scholars should develop an understanding of such a promising phenomena and encourage its development.

The last section of the book focuses on the quest for effective interventions to alleviate poverty. The main actors participating in local area economic development are the state and city governments, community-based organizations, small business and merchants' associations, and banks and other private-sector organizations that provide financial and other resources. For the most part the economic well-being of any community is primarily determined by the labor-market participation of the residents in that area, and this makes economic activities at the neighborhood level very important. For example, government programs often implemented by community agencies provide basic education, training, counseling, and other support services necessary for residents to secure employment. Small businesses and commercial areas provide many of the amenities that make a neighborhood attractive for newcomers and a good place to stay for long-time residents. These local businesses also provide a source of employment and of revenues for local governments.

The chapter by Miren Uriarte, entitled "Latinas and the Massachusetts Employment and Training Choices Program," is an evaluation of the Massachusetts Employment and Training Choices program that served as the pilot project for what is today the state employment and training system in Massachusetts. ET Choices was generally considered an innovative and successful experiment. Most of the program's success was attributed to the availability of support services such as daycare and transportation allowances and the extension of medicare benefits to employed participants, which allowed single mothers receiving welfare to make a transition to the paid labor force. For Latinas, however, program participation outcomes were not as clearly beneficial as they were for other women.

Although Latinas were underrepresented in the program when compared to other groups participation, program participation was not the major problem. What Uriarte found is that Latinas are excluded from skills-training programs, the types of programs that lead to better job-placement opportunities and higher wages. General education and English-as-a-second-language are the programs most often offered at the community level by the contractors that recruited Latinas. This results in the lopsided participation of Latinos in educational programs, the programs that lead to the least job-placement opportunities and to the lowest wages. Another important aspect of the problem is that most Latinas job seekers are referred to employers by the employment service program without benefiting from skills development. As a result, Latinas are usually channelled into jobs that they could have obtained regardless of program participation. Uriarte's research suggests that traditional programs, even good programs designed to help those who are unable to benefit from mainstream educational institutions, may not be effective in serving the Latino population.

The role of small business development in alleviating poverty and as the agent of local economic development in poor urban areas has been the subject of heated debate since Richard Nixon's call to promote "Black Capitalism" in the 1960s.

In her chapter entitled "The Social Aspects of Small Business Development: The Case of Puerto Rican and Dominican Entrepreneurs in Boston," Peggy Levitt reframes the terms of the debate by focusing on the role of small businesses in strengthening the web of social stability in communities rather than assessing their contribution exclusively on economic criteria such as job or income generation at the local level. She finds that Latino small businesses, such as the common neighborhood *bodegas,* make a critical contribution to the community well-being. She argues that "Latino business owners consider it their responsibility to be the provider of last resort when people need food or money, thereby providing crucial social insurance. They help community members find jobs, housing, and health care. They are role models and teachers. The community conducts its social life and affirms its identity within the walls of their stores. Particularly important is their practice of selling things on credit, in small quantities, and at the local level so that a continued supply of goods to the very poor is ensured."

Levitt's arguments about the social role of Latino small business in the community lend support to the notion that assistance to small businesses might have a larger payoff than the one suggested by conventional cost-benefit evaluations. Investing in small business development could be an effective poverty alleviation strategy. However, part of the Massachusetts reality is that Latinos in the state do not have the same degree of geographical concentration that Latinos in other states have and many Latinos in Massachusetts live in very diverse neighborhoods. Consequently, Latino small businesses are located in commercial strips where many other businesses serve an ethnically diverse clientele. While Levitt's research question focused on the social role of small businesses as the unit of analyses, Nanette Robicheau's research pertains to the broader economic context in which these small businesses operate and considers the neighborhood as the unit of analysis.

Inner-city shopping districts frequently face a high level of unemployment in the immediate area, poor municipal services, inadequate financial and technical support, deteriorating infrastructure, rampant crime, and many other problems associated with inner-city neighborhoods. Nanette Robicheau has examined Uphams' Corner as a case study for commercial revitalization in a typical inner-city neighborhood, where Latinos constitute about a third of the population and where as a group they own more small businesses that any other ethnic group. In her chapter entitled "The Uphams' Corner Model: Comprehensive, Commercial Revitalization in Multiethnic, Low-Income, Inner-City Communities," Robicheau concludes that in order to overcome the many obstacles faced by small businesses in the inner city "commercial revitalization and business development must be seen in a broader context that includes other elements of economic and community development...as a community development goal in its own right, as a tool to advance other community development objectives."

The final chapter of the section tackles the issue of shelter poverty among Latinos and housing strategies. To our knowledge, Michael Stone is the first scholar to analyze the situation of Latinos in the largest metropolitan-Boston housing markets. Homeownership by Latinos is very low with renters making up four out of five households in the region. In his chapter "Latino Shelter Poverty and Housing Strategies," Stone attributes the low homeownership rate to "the low prevailing income of Latinos as well as the very high prices of houses over the past decades, during which time the region has experienced the large influx of Latinos." Whether renters or homeowners, the low income of Latinos induces severe affordability problems. According to Stone's estimates, in 1985, after paying rent, three out of five renter households did not have enough money left to meet their nonshelter needs.

What have we learned about the roots of Latino poverty and about effective intervention? The research reported in this volume begins to document the main factors contributing to the above-average poverty rate of Latinos and helps to evaluate public-policy and community interventions intended to alleviate poverty. The overall lessons of the studies raise serious concerns about the prospects of improving the economic conditions of the Latino population. Latino poverty in Massachusetts is rooted in economic dislocation and labor-market disadvantage. For the most part, Latinos are coming to Massachusetts as a contingent labor force, concentrated in secondary labor markets where working hours are long, pay is low, and opportunities for advancement are limited. These macrodynamics of the regional labor market are difficult to handle from a public-policy standpoint. Even when policymakers have the intention and the resources to promote effective programs, Latinos have, for the most part, not benefited from such initiatives.

The disadvantage of Latinos in the labor market is compounded by other factors such as their relative youth and low educational attainment whether in terms of formal schooling or labor-market experiences that provide skill enhancements, the large number of Latino households with only one potential wage earner, their geographical dispersion throughout the state, and their concentration in urban areas that have suffered great economic dislocation. This set of circumstances requires strong "transitional" support programs that will facilitate youths and female heads-of-households in participating in the labor force as well as retraining for dislocated workers. The experience of ET Choices indicates that programs that provide opportunities for other disadvantaged groups are not effective in providing employment and training programs for Latinos. However, those modernizing firms that provide opportunities for the stable employment and skills enhancement of workers constitute an example of firm-level dynamics that may help the long-term labor-market standing of Latinos. These firms often have links to local community-based organizations and received the indirect support of government programs in human resources development. To what extent these firm-level and community-based initiatives could be expanded and supported in order to improve the employment conditions of Latinos in the absence of broader labor-market policies and statewide programs remains to be seen.

Community and neighborhood dynamics are also important when analyzing the economic status of Latinos. In contrast to other areas of the country where Latinos have developed ethnic enclaves that nurture small business and provide employment opportunities for recent immigrants, the dispersion of Latinos in Massachusetts has precluded the concentration of economic activities and the development of a sizable demand for ethnic products in any given area. The evidence presented by Levitt suggest that Latino small businesses provide an important cushion, an economic survival network for the poor that deserves to be nurtured and supported. To what extent Latino-owned businesses will grow and become spatially concentrated enough to promote the development of an economic enclave remains an open questions. It is clear, however, that conditions in many multiethnic neighborhoods are ideal for promoting coalitions between ethnic groups, small businesses, and community-based organizations around the issues of commercial revitalization and community economic development.

A comprehensive economic development program for Latinos in the state must include housing strategies that are relevant to the needs of this population. The majority of Latinos are renters and do not have sufficient earning power or employment stability to become homeowners. Housing is an important component of a community economic-development strategy because homeownership, whether that ownership is individual or collective, serves to stabilize neighborhoods and to promote long-term political empowerment. As Stone suggests, neighborhood stability largely depends on labor-market outcomes, but there are many rental-assistance, community-property, and home-ownership programs that could benefit Latinos.

In sum, this volume contributes to our understanding of the causes of poverty in a region that is experiencing the rapid growth of the Latino population. To most observers, Latinos should have fared better during the 1980s, a decade of economic expansion in Massachusetts. But the concentration of Latinos in declining employment sectors and the lack of a solid economic base at the community level combined to preclude their participation in the emerging new economy. Perhaps more worrisome than the experience of the 1980s is the fact that the Massachusetts economy has entered yet another period of slow growth and economic restructuring while the economic standing of Latinos has not improved since the downturn of the state economy in the 1970s. The prospects for Latino economic development in the absence of vigorous public policy and community initiatives remains bleak to the informed observer.

Note

1. A version of this article first appeared in the *New England Journal of Public Policy* (Fall/Winter 1992), and it is reprinted here with permission from the John W. McCormack Institute of Public Affairs, University of Massachusetts Boston.

Part I
Theoretical and Contextual Considerations

Edwin Meléndez
Latino Poverty and Economic Development in Massachusetts

Massachusetts had the dubious distinction of having the highest rate of Latino poverty of any state during the late 1980s — almost twice the national average, according to a recent study (Haveman, Danzinger, and Plotnick, 1991). What makes this situation especially puzzling is that by 1987 the Massachusetts economy had reached a peak in employment after more than a decade of continuous economic growth and record low unemployment rates. While the Latino poverty rate in Massachusetts almost doubled during the 1970s, reaching 37.6 percent in 1979, poverty rates for whites and blacks remained relatively steady, at 8 and 25 percent respectively (see table 1). Then, during the 1980s, while poverty rates for both whites and blacks declined, Latino poverty remained persistently high at 36.7 percent. The tide of "the Massachusetts Miracle," as this period of economic expansion is popularly known, did not lift all boats.

Why did Latinos not benefit from the expansion as other groups did? Recent surveys on the causes of poverty have identified a small set of key factors, particularly relevant to considerations of policy issues, that can inform a discussion of differences in poverty rates at the state level. These factors include the performance of the economy, demographic and urban transition, education and skills development, government transfers, neighborhood effects and underclass behavior, immigration, and discrimination (Wilson 1987; Sawhill, 1988; Moss and Tilly, 1991; Meléndez, 1992).

One possible explanation for the paradox of Latino poverty in Massachusetts is that the Latino population grew too fast and that the region is undergoing a transitional stage in the adaptation of a new immigrant group. Indeed, the rate of population growth for Latinos in Massachusetts, 103.9 percent between 1980 and 1990, is the highest among the ten states with the largest Latino populations (U.S. Bureau of the Census, 1991). There are, however, at least two arguments against such reasoning. First, for the other two states with the largest growth in Latino population, California with 69.2 percent and Florida with 83.4 percent, Latino poverty rates during the late 1980s were among the lowest in the nation: 22.2 percent and 19.0 percent — substantially lower than the 27.2 percent average for the United States (Haveman, Danzinger, and Plotnick, 1991). A second consideration is that the sharpest increase in Latino poverty rates for the state occurred during the 1970s when the proportion of the foreign-born population among Latinos remained about the same overall (24.1 percent in 1970 and 26.9 percent in 1980) and actually declined for Puerto Ricans, the largest and poorest Latino group in the state, from 68.2 percent island-born to 58.7 percent.

Another important factor in explaining divergent trends in poverty rates in Massachusetts is geographic concentration. Latinos are concentrated in some of the largest cities of the state, and, as shown in table 1, the poverty rate for each ethnic group in these cities tends to be higher than their average at the state level. The most relevant pattern shown in these data is that between 1969 and 1979 poverty rates for whites in these cities increased substantially in a fashion similar to the increases in Latino poverty rates, despite the fact that the average poverty rate for whites in the state remained about the same during this period. This pattern is consistent with the argument that poverty increases in large urban areas more as a result of economic dislocation than of increased immigration or demographic change.

In discussing state economic trends during the 1970s and 1980s, however, it is important to take a broad look at the composition of the poor. Puerto Ricans, the largest Latino group in the state, had the highest family-poverty rate of all groups in 1979 (see table 2). Their family-poverty rate of 52.9 percent was more than twice the rate for blacks and eight times the rate for whites. Family-poverty rates for other Latino groups are substantially higher than the 6.3 percent rate for whites but somewhat lower than the 23.2 percent rate for blacks. It is important to consider that female householders and children under 18 have higher poverty rates than the average poverty rate for all families. In particular, about three-quarters of Puerto Rican female householders and two-thirds of children under 18 were poor in 1979, although poverty rates for these two demographic groups were relatively high among all Latinos.

The above discussion suggests that immigration, geographical concentration, and demographic factors may have contributed to the dramatic increase in Latino poverty during the 1970s and to the abnormally high rates of the 1980s. Nonetheless, Massachusetts' perverseness when compared to other states may very well have resulted from the convergence of economic factors particular to the region. Since the Massachusetts economy underwent changes during the early 1970s that are now common in other parts of the country, assessing the role of economic forces inducing persistent poverty among Latinos in Massachusetts may offer some valuable insights for social planners and policymakers across the nation.

The main objective of this chapter is to demonstrate that the beneficial impact of the Massachusetts economic expansion on some of the poorer strata of society was offset by the institutional context of Latinos in the state labor market — in other words, to discuss why the economic expansion did not benefit Latinos to the same extent that it benefited other groups. The following sections examine other possible explanations of Latino poverty in the state, including family structure, educational attainment, low wages, and high unemployment. The final section draws some conclusions about the relative importance of the alternative explanations.

Latinos and the "Massachusetts Miracle"

Throughout the late 1970s and the 1980s Massachusetts experienced an economic expansion that outperformed the national economy, as proven by almost all important key economic indicators. The origins of the expansion, however, can be traced to the hard years of the early 1970s. Between the years bounded by the 1970 and 1975 recessions, Massachusetts lost 8.3 percent of manufacturing employment, mostly in the nondurable-goods sector, where employment declined 15.5 percent. The durable-goods sector experienced a 1.7 percent decline as well. In contrast, during the same period, employment in nonmanufacturing industries expanded by 7.3 percent

In the late 1950s and throughout the 1960s, Massachusetts had benefited enormously from the combination of unprecedented military spending spurred by the Cold War and the scientific competition induced by the Soviet achievements in space (Economics Department, First National Bank of Boston, 1988, p. 189). During that time, federal research and development funds were instrumental in the expansion of high-technology manufacturing. However, just as the state's high-technology sector today is suffering the effects of the political realignment in the former Soviet territories, so cutbacks in the space program and the end of the Vietnam War adversely affected the manufacturing sector during the late 1960s and early 1970s. Harrison (1988) identifies the three principal causes of the state's economic problems during the early 1970s recessionary period as "the collapse in the demand for products of the defense industry, the secular decline in employment in the mill-based industries, such as shoes and textiles, and the region's precarious location at the end of the national power and transportation systems" (p. 75).

Of these three factors, probably the one of greatest significance for Latinos in Massachusetts was the employment loss in mill-based industries. According to Harrison, about one-fifth of the jobs lost during the early 1970s were unskilled labor. In 1970, 37.6 percent of Latinos were employed in manufacturing industries, including shoes, textiles and apparel, and food, which were among the hardest hit by the recession. Furthermore, manufacturing job losses were concentrated in Boston, Springfield-Holyoke, Lowell, and Lawrence, the areas with the largest concentration of Latinos in the state at that time. It is important to notice that between 1970 and 1980 these areas also showed the largest increases in Latino poverty rates.

The late 1970s were years of transition for the Massachusetts economy. Between 1975 and 1980 high technology led the economy out of the recession as employment in this sector expanded by 37.9 percent, the largest expansion of any industrial sector in the state (Economic Department, First National Bank of Boston, 1988). Employment also expanded significantly in the service industries (30.6 percent). However, the state's overall economy during this period performed about the same as the national economy. The growth of employment in many industries in the state, such as construction, transportation, wholesale and retail trade, and finance, insurance and real estate, was below the national level.   Not until the 1980s would Massachusetts outperform the national economy and many other mature state economies of the Rust Belt.

Exactly which factors contributed the most to the "Massachusetts Miracle" is the object of a heated debate. Nonetheless, most researchers agree that a few industries — high technology, new construction, and business services — played a critical role in the expansion (Gantz and Konga, 1989; Harrison and Kluver, 1989; Doeringer and Terkla, 1990; Lampe, 1988). The high-technology sector benefited by diversifying into profitable civilian applications such as computer hardware and software, a change that was induced by the decline in federal funding during the recessionary years of the early 1970s, the renewed military build-up of the Reagan administration, the availability of skilled labor, the agglomeration of educational and scientific research centers in the area, and aggressive venture capital in the region (Browne, 1988; Dorfman, 1988; Frankel and Howell, 1988; Walsh, 1988).

Evidence suggests, however, that by the mid-1980s the high-technology sector had begun to slow down (Harrison and Kluver, 1989). According to a recent report by the Massachusetts Department of Employment and Training (1989, p. 16), job losses in this sector can be attributed to the high value of the dollar during the mid-1980s, which reduced the competitiveness of U.S. exports in international markets; the higher productivity growth; the maturing of high-technology industries; a slowdown in technological change; and the decline of defense spending.

The industrial base of the economic expansion was significant in terms of the employment opportunities available to Latinos. On the one hand, Latinos were overrepresented in industrial occupations (as machine operators, assemblers, inspectors, etc.) and nondurable-manufacturing industries, which suffered the greatest losses in employment share during the 1980s. For instance, in nondurable-manufacturing industries, where the 10.3 percent rate of Latino employment is twice the proportion of total employment, the share of total employment in Massachusetts declined from 9.9 percent in 1980 to 5.9 percent in 1990. On the other hand, Latinos were underrepresented in professional occupations and high-technology and construction industries, which experienced employment growth.

Economic restructuring resulted in a sharp decline in labor-force participation for men and in higher unemployment among Latinos. Not only did Latinos have fewer employment opportunities, but the polarization of income induced by the disappearance of middle-income jobs induced a dramatic decline in Latinos' income relative to whites'. All things considered, however, economic restructuring and changes in the demand for blue-collar labor are only part of the story. The next sections include a discussion of demographic changes and other factors contributing to labor-market disadvantage that converged to produce persistently high rates of poverty among Latinos. An examination of the role of labor markets in Latino poverty then follows.

Family Structure and Educational Attainment

Among the factors most often mentioned as contributing to the above-average Latino poverty rates are the increase in the number of families headed by women and the lower educational attainment of Latinos (see Meléndez, 1992 for a detailed review of the literature concerning Latino poverty). Wilson (1987) and Smith (1988) suggest a strong association between poverty and the rise of female-headed households within the black and Latino communities, regardless of the disagreement among researchers concerning the causal links between these two variables. Obviously, fewer wage earners in a family increase the probability of lower family income. In the absence of adequate daycare institutions, an increase in the number of families headed by one parent may also increase child-rearing responsibilities, thus lowering the chances of labor-force participation.

Table 3 presents key demographic data for whites, blacks, and Latinos in Massachusetts. One particularly significant statistic revealed here is that Latinos are a much younger population than whites or blacks. In 1990, the median age of Latinos was 23.7 percent, about four years lower than blacks and eleven years lower than whites. The population's youth contributes to higher poverty rates because there are proportionally more persons relative to the number of wage earners in the family and also because those young people who have already entered the labor force have relatively little experience and few skills, and therefore they receive low wages.

The most significant demographic trend, however, is the dramatic increase among Latinos in the proportion of female-headed families.[1] While in 1970 the figure of 15.5 percent for female-headed families among Latinos was comparable to that for whites and substantially lower than the proportion for black families, by 1980 the proportion of female-headed families among Latinos had more than doubled, to 35.8 percent, and in 1990 the rate of female-headed households had increased to 42.7 percent. Although the proportion of female-headed households among Latinos remained about three percentage points below the proportion for black families, it increased at a considerably higher rate — almost three times the rate for whites.

Evidently, these changes in the characteristics of the population account for some of the increases in poverty rates among Latinos. The effect of the rise in the number of families with only one potential wage earner is compounded by the increase in the average number of persons per family. These demographic patterns have serious implications for the long-term socioeconomic well-being of the community, since neither tendency is likely to change significantly in the immediate future.

Another important factor affecting the socioeconomic status of Latinos is educational attainment. Education determines the skills that workers offer in the marketplace, and hence it determines their productivity, which in turn determines wages, employment stability, and other labor-market benefits. During the 1970s the educational achievement of Latinos eroded both in absolute terms and relative to other groups. For example, the median number of years of school completed for persons 25 years old and over, a widely used index of educational attainment, increased for whites and blacks during the 1970s but it went up only one percentage point for Latinos, to 10.9 median years of school — significantly lower than the 12.6 and 12.4 median years for whites and blacks.

A disaggregation of educational attainment by sex and highest degree earned shows that losses during the decade were greatest for Latino men. In 1970, Latino men had the highest rate of college completion among the largest ethnic groups of the state;[2] by 1980, the proportion of college completion among Latino men had declined 5.7 percentage points, to 1.0 percent, while whites and blacks gained about eight percentage points each, to 25.3 percent and 14.3 percent respectively (see table 4). A similar pattern of absolute and relative losses is observed for Latino women. Between 1970 and 1980, the percentage of Latino women who had completed high school declined from 26.3 percent to 22.1 percent, and the percentage who had completed college declined from 10.5 percent to 9.5 percent. In contrast, during the same decade, white and black women made substantial gains in educational attainment, particularly in terms of college education.

Data from the 1990 U.S. Census indicate that during the 1980s Latinos experienced a small gain (1.7 percentage points) in the proportion of persons with four years of college or more. In contrast, blacks gained 5.1 and whites gained 7.5 percentage points. Thus, although Latinos attained a slightly higher average level of education during the decade, they lost ground relative to blacks and whites.

The Role of Labor Markets

To understand Latino poverty in Massachusetts, it is particularly important to recognize the role played by labor markets. Migration and residential patterns, demographic characteristics, educational attainment, and trends in the regional economy all converge to create disadvantages for Latinos in the labor market, and these disadvantages are central to an explanation of the above-average rates of poverty for this population group. What follows is a discussion of some indicators of labor-market disadvantages facing Latinos in Massachusetts.

The decline in Latinos' relative earnings during the 1970s explains the dramatic decline in the mean income of Latino families relative to that of white families. As table 5 shows, between 1969 and 1979 the income of Latino families relative to the income of white families declined a staggering 18.2 percentage points, from 74.0 percent to 55.8 percent. This dramatic decline was induced primarily by a decline in the relative median earnings of Latino men, from 78.1 percent in 1969 to 64.5 percent in 1979, for a total loss of 13.5 percentage points during the decade. For female-headed families the relative income loss was even higher, 20.0 percentage points.

A pattern of relative income loss is also observed among black men. However, the loss of 5.4 percentage points in median earnings for black men resulted not in an absolute loss in relative standing as measured by family income but rather in a small gain, 3.1 percentage points for the decade. Black families did relatively better than Latino families because of the gains in relative earnings of black women, which grew by 7.9 percentage points with respect to the earnings of the white women during the decade. Families headed by black women gained 8.6 percentage points.

Although family-income and median-earnings data from the 1990 U.S. Census have not yet been released, available household-income data suggest that there were no significant changes in the relative status of Latinos in Massachusetts. In 1990, mean household income was $46,676 for whites, $31,360 for blacks, and $26,292 for Latinos (U.S. Bureau of the Census, 1992). That is, Latino mean household income remained at 56.3 percent of the average for whites — a proportion similar to the mean family-income ratio in 1980.

To the extent that earnings from employment in labor markets constitute the primary determinant of family income, trends in earnings are a primary determinant of family poverty. Consequently, in an explanation of poverty the determinants of labor-market earnings become critical. Since earnings are determined by the wage rate and the length of employment, it is apparent that Latinos' above-average poverty rates are directly related to lower wages and higher joblessness when compared to other groups.

Wage differences between Latinos and whites are explained on the supply side largely by differences in human capital (education and experience), the effects of immigrant background and assimilation in labor markets (English proficiency, length in the country), and other measurable characteristics (regional and residential location, marital status, and family responsibilities) (Meléndez, 1991). Certainly gaps in key variables such as lower educational attainment, a younger population, the recency of arrival, cultural and language barriers when adapting to new labor markets, the concentration of the population in fiscally strapped cities throughout the state, and the dramatic increase in families with one wage earner contribute to higher poverty rates among Latinos.

However, the severe impact of the mid-1970s recession is also related to the location of Latino workers in the industrial and occupational structure of the state. The position of Latinos in the labor market is determined not solely by human capital, immigrant background, and other measurable characteristics but by the interaction of these variables with employers' recruitment, promotion, retention, and reskilling practices. In many ways employers — particularly in industries such as manufacturing, services, and public administration where Latinos are concentrated or where advancement opportunities may exist — create or tailor their own supply of workers. Among the factors pertaining to the demand side of labor markets, those that contribute significantly to Latinos' lower earnings are segmented in low-wage occupations and racial, ethnic, and gender discrimination.

Segmentation into low-wage occupations not only made Latinos more vulnerable to the economic restructuring of the mid-1970s but also may have prevented their mobility to more stable industrial sectors. Data for the occupations of employed civilians in Massachusetts from 1970 to 1990 (table 6) show that, in comparison to whites, Latinos are underrepresented in high-wage occupational categories such as managerial, professional, and technical and overrepresented in low-wage occupational categories such as operators, laborers, and services. Indeed, the most significant changes in the occupational standing of Latinos during the last two decades have been not only the significant loss in the proportion of Latino professionals but the noticeable shift from a concentration in machine operators to a concentration in services during the 1990s. Since the jobs that Latinos hold in the service sector typically pay lower wages than those in manufacturing, it is apparent that the occupational position of Latinos is an important factor contributing to labor-market disadvantage and thus to poverty.

The clustering of Latinos in certain industries and occupations is related in part to the uses of immigrant labor in regional labor markets — i.e., to the formation of ethnic labor markets — and in part to discrimination. These are, of course, two interrelated processes. For instance, while the scarcity of nurses and doctors in certain regions or inner cities of the United States may prompt the recruitment of trained personnel from some Asian and Caribbean countries, the creation of an employment niche for immigrants in these occupation is far from an adverse or negative situation in labor markets. Ethnic labor markets — i.e., the establishment of recruitment networks and employment preference for a given group of immigrants in certain occupations and industries — may provide an opportunity for stable employment and for the adaptation of skills to the employment possibilities in a new country. On the other hand, ethnic discrimination may prevent immigrants from securing employment in other industries or from moving to other parts of the country.

It is also important to consider the role of discrimination in regional labor markets. For instance, a recent study documenting the effects of the Immigration Reform and Control Act of 1986 (IRCA) on Latinos found a substantial increase in discrimination (USGAO, 1990; Cross, 1990). This conclusion was supported by different sources of evidence, using a variety of methods, and examining national as well as regional data. Although the question remains open as to whether documented national trends in discrimination are significant at the state level, anecdotal data suggest an increase in discriminatory practices throughout the region.

Another major reason for lower earnings among Latinos is their higher rate of joblessness — that is, their generally high level of unemployment, their nonparticipation in the labor force because they are discouraged from seeking employment, and their involuntary employment in part-time or part-year jobs. Two frequently used indexes of employment opportunities are labor-force-participation rates and unemployment rates. Trends in these rates, as presented in table 7, are useful in understanding the relative importance of labor-market standing on Latino poverty.

Trends in labor-force-participation rates for Latino men and women are consistent with the industrial-restructuring explanation developed earlier. The decline in manufacturing in the state during the 1970s is reflected partially in the decline in labor-force-participation rates among men. Between 1970 and 1980, Latino men, who enjoyed the largest participation rate in 1970, perhaps because of the large number of recent immigrants among them, lost 10.1 percentage points. This decline was substantially larger than the decline experienced by white men (-2.7 percent) and slightly higher than similar losses for black men (-7.0 percent). By 1990, possibly because of the transition to service industries and occupations, participation rates for Latino men (76.0 percent) had increased to about the same rate as for white men (77.7 percent) and were slightly higher than for black men (73.2 percent).

Similarly, trends in women's labor-force participation are consistent with the explanation that the service sector expanded, but ethnic differences are important as well. The percentage of women participating in the labor force grew throughout the 1970s and 1980s; however, Latino women experienced modest increases of around three percentage points each decade, while white women experienced a staggering gain of eight percentage points during the same period.

By 1990, black women had lost their position as having the highest labor-force-participation rates. These differences in the trends among white, black, and Latino women are explained in part by the characteristics of the service sector and by the different effects of local labor conditions on their labor-force participation (Meléndez, 1992).

One of the best indicators of how macroeconomic conditions at the regional level affect employment opportunities is the unemployment rate. Between 1970 and 1980, the unemployment rates for blacks and Latinos increased more than the rate for whites. Unemployment rates increased about three percentage points for black and Latino men, to 9.7 percent and 9.5 percent respectively in 1980; and the rates for black and Latino women increased by 1.2 and 3.5 percentage points, to 7.6 percent and 9.8 percent. However, because of the economic expansion of the 1980s and a modest increase in average unemployment rates for whites, differences in unemployment rates have declined during the 1990s. The exception to those trends is the case of black women, for whom the unemployment rate jumped by a significant four percentage points.

Overall, trends in labor-force participation and unemployment rates portray a Latino labor force that responds to economic opportunity while remaining vulnerable to changes in the demand side of regional labor markets. The adverse effects of industrial change during the 1970s, as relative earnings data suggest, seem to have outlasted the increases in labor-force participation and employment of the 1980s. The expansion of Latino employment in services and the persistently higher poverty rates for this group indicate that finally Latinos were unable to benefit from the economic expansion of the 1980s.

Conclusions

In many ways Latino poverty in Massachusetts is not unique. While it is true that Latinos remained the poorest group in the state despite the economic expansion of the 1980s, the factors inducing above-average rates of poverty for Latinos are largely similar to the factors that induce poverty among other groups: the concentration of this segment of the population in cities that suffered the brunt of urban transition, the rise in families with one wage earner, low educational attainment, the effects of economic restructuring on employment opportunities, and low wages and joblessness. Other factors, such as rapid population growth or a large proportion of immigrants, may have played a role, but the available evidence suggests that such a role was not prominent. Perhaps what is unique about Latino poverty in Massachusetts is the combination of circumstances that led to the sharp increase in poverty during the 1970s and the convergence of factors that prevented Latinos from sharing the benefits of the economic expansion of the 1980s. In other words, not only did Latinos suffer the adverse impact of the economic dislocation of the 1970s, but the type of jobs created, employers hiring preferences, educational attainment, and demographic trends combined to preclude Latinos from participating in the employment and income gains of the 1980s.

While the previous analysis provides a framework for understanding Latino poverty in Massachusetts, much remains to be done. In particular, it is important to establish the relative importance of each factor and to establish more specific links between demographic changes, individual attributes such as age and sex, labor-market outcomes, and poverty for the different racial and ethnic groups. One would expect that poverty for different population subgroups (men and women, Puerto Ricans and Dominicans, foreign-born and natives) might have different causes. Generalizations about the "cause" of Latino poverty in this context therefore seem precipitous. It is also important to explore the relevance of alternative hypotheses, such as the rise in discrimination, that remain as plausible explanations.

Notwithstanding the difficulties involved in dissecting the causes of poverty for Latinos in Massachusetts, it is of foremost importance that researchers continue to pursue these important questions. From a public-policy perspective, we need to know whether human-capital strategies or industrial policies are more likely to have a positive impact on the labor-market standing of Latinos, and whether social policies targeting support services for families will have a stronger impact than economic development or labor-market interventions. Most likely it is a question of targeting a given strategy to a particular segment of the population. What researchers and policymakers can clearly not afford is to continue to design interventions to alleviate poverty based on analyses that are not specific to the circumstances of Latinos in the state.

Notes

I would like to thank Carmen Pinero and Kim Stevenson for their research assistance and for compiling the data for this study. I am also indebted to Ramon Borgés, Luis Falcón, Luis Prado, and Miren Uriarte for commenting on an earlier draft. Remaining errors or omissions are my sole responsibility.

1. For several reasons, the proportion of female-headed families among Latinos could be overstated by figures published by the Bureau of the Census. For instance, nonmarried consensual relations are common among Latinos. Standard survey instruments may not capture these couples as married and may therefore force them into the female-headed category. Also, fear of reporting information to government agencies, particularly among recent immigrants or any households receiving some type of government assistance, may affect the accuracy of the figures.

2. One possible explanation for the high proportion of college completion in 1970 is the high concentration of students coming from Puerto Rico who attended universities in

Massachusetts. However, the significance of this population declined as new Puerto Rico state residents came from other regions in the United States, particularly New York City, a smaller proportion of them being college-educated.

References

Browne, L. E. (1988). High Technology and Business Services. In D. Lampe, (Ed.), *The Massachusetts Miracle: High Technology and Economic Revitalization.* Cambridge, MA: MIT Press.

Cross, H. (1990). *Employer Hiring Practices: Differential Treatment of Hispanic and Anglo Job Seekers.* Washington, DC: The Urban Institute Press.

Doeringer, P. B., and Terkla, D. G. (1990). How Intangible Factors Contribute to Economic Development. *World Development, 18*(a), 1295-1308.

Dorfman, N. (1988). Route 128: The Development of a Regional High Technology Economy. In D. Lampe, (Ed.), *The Massachusetts Miracle: High Technology and Economic Revitalization.* Cambridge, MA: MIT Press.

Economics Department, The First National Bank of Boston. (1988). The Dilemma of a Mature Economy and Excessive Government Spending. In D. Lampe, (Ed.), *The Massachusetts Miracle and Economic Revitalization.* Cambridge, MA: MIT Press.

Frankel, L., and Howell, J. (1988). Economic Revitalization and Job Creation in America's Oldest Industrial Region. In D. Lampe, (Ed.), *The Massachusetts Miracle: High Technology and Economic Development.* Cambridge, MA: MIT Press.

Gantz, A., and Konga, L. F. (1989). Boston in the World Economy. *Urban Affairs Annual Reviews, 35.*

Harrison, B. (l988). The Economic Development of Massachusetts. In D. Lampe (Ed.), *The Massachusetts Miracle: High Technology and Economic Revitalization.* Cambridge, MA: MIT Press.

Harrison, B., and Kluver, J. (1989). Deindustrialization and Regional Restructuring in Massachusetts. In L. Rodwin and H. Sazanani, (Eds.), *Deindustrialization and Regional Economic Transformations.* Boston, MA: Urwin Hyman.

Haveman, J. D., Danzinger, S., and Plotnick, R. D. (1991, Spring). State Poverty Rates for Whites, Blacks and Hispanics in the Late 1980's. *Focus, 13*(1).

Lampe, D. (1988). Introduction. In D. Lampe, (Ed.), *The Massachusetts Miracle: High Technology and Economic Revitalization.* Cambridge, MA: MIT Press.

Massachusetts Department of Employment and Training. (1989). *Employment 2000: Massachusetts Employment Projections by Industry.* Boston, MA: Author.

Meléndez, E. (1991). Labor Market Structure and Wage Differences in New York City. In E. Meléndez, C. Rodriguez, and J. B. Figueroa, (Eds.), *Hispanics in the Labor Force.* New York: Plenum Press.

Meléndez, E., and Figueroa, J. B. (1992, February). The Effects of Local Labor Market Conditions on Labor Force Participation of Puerto Rican, White, and Black Women. *Hispanic Journal of Behavioral Sciences 14*(1), 76-90.

Moss, P., and Tilly, C. (1991). *Why Black Men Are Doing Worse in the Labor Market.* New York: Social Science Research Council.

Sawhill, I. (1988). Poverty in the U.S.: Why Is It so Persistent? *Journal of Economic Literature, 27*(3), 1073-1119.

Sum, A., Harrington, P., Fogg, N., and Goedicke, W. (n.d.). *Family Poverty in the New Boston Economy.* Boston, MA: Northeastern University, Center For Labor Studies.

United States Bureau of the Census. (1972, April). *1970 Census of the Population: General Social and Economic Characteristics*, PC(1)-(23). Washington, DC: Government Printing Office. U.S. Bureau of the Census. (1983, June). *1980 Census of the Population: General Social and Economic Characteristics*, PC80-1-C23. Washington, DC: Government Printing Office.

U.S. Bureau of the Census. (1990a). *Census of Population and Housing Massachusetts*, Summary Tape Files 1A and 3A. Washington, DC: Government Printing Office.

U.S. Bureau of the Census. (1990b). *Census.* Washington, DC: Government Printing Office.

U.S. Bureau of the Census. (1991, October). *The Hispanic Population in the United States: March 1991*, Series P-20, No. 455. Washington, DC: Government Printing Office.

U.S. Bureau of Labor Statistics. (1991). *Geographic Profile of Employment and Earnings.* Washington, DC: Government Printing Office.

U.S. General Accounting Office. (1990, March). *Immigration Reform: Employer Sanctions and the Question of Discrimination*, GAO 1 GGD-90-62. Washington, DC: Government Printing Office.

Walsh, D. (1988). War Stories: Defense Spending and the Growth of the Massachusetts Economy. In D. Lampe, (Ed.), *The Massachusetts Miracle: High Technology and Economic Revitalization.* Cambridge, MA: MIT Press.

Wilson, W. J. (1987). *The Truly Disadvantaged.* Chicago, IL: University of Chicago Press.

Table 1

Percentage of Persons in Massachusetts and Select Cities with Incomes below
Poverty Level, by Race/Ethnicity, for 1969, 1979, and 1989

| | | 1969 | |
LOCATION	WHITES	BLACKS	LATINOS*
Massachusetts	8.0	25.6	22.4
Boston	16.2	28.4	34.4
Holyoke	14.7	41.5	27.3
Lawrence	11.4	19.7	20.4
Lowell	11.6	39.5	22.0
New Bedford	15.3	31.7	48.7
Springfield	12.7	25.7	39.8
Worcester	10.7	28.5	23.6
		1979	
LOCATION	WHITES	BLACKS	LATINOS*
Massachusetts	8.4	25.3	37.6
Boston	15.7	28.6	41.9
Holyoke	13.1	43.5	59.9
Lawrence	15.6	21.5	45.4
Lowell	12.5	24.7	47.9
New Bedford	14.6	26.1	34.9
Springfield	12.1	26.5	58.0
Worcester	13.1	20.7	54.3
		1989	
LOCATION	WHITES	BLACKS	LATINOS*
Massachusetts	7.0	23.0	36.7
Boston	13.9	24.2	33.9
Holyoke	13.7	42.8	59.1
Lawrence	18.5	33.0	45.8
Lowell	12.0	29.8	45.5
New Bedford	14.0	35.7	52.1
Springfield	12.6	25.9	53.5
Worcester	11.7	30.5	46.8

*Persons of Latino origin may be of any race.
SOURCES: Massachusetts Institute for Social and Economic Research, University of
Massachusetts. (1992, April). Report 92-07. Amherst, MA: Author; U.S. Bureau of the
Census. (1972, April). *1970 Census of the Population: General Social and Economic
Characteristics,* PC(1)-C23. Washington, DC: Government Printing Office; U.S. Bureau
of the Census. (1983, June). *1980 Census of the Population: General Social and Economic
Characteristics,* PC80-1-C23. Washington, DC: Government Printing Office.

Table 2

Percentage of All Families, Female-Headed Households, and Children under 18 in Poverty, in Massachusetts, by Race/Ethnicity, for 1979 and 1989

Race/ Ethnicity	All Families	Female Hshlders	Children under 18
		1979	
Whites	6.5	24.1	10.8
Blacks	23.2	43.0	33.7
Latinos*	36.4	68.8	48.7
Mexican	17.6	51.6	22.6
Puerto Rican	52.9	77.4	62.7
Cuban	11.3	32.8	16.8
Other Latinos	18.7	49.2	25.7
		1989	
Whites	5.0	19.5	—
Blacks	20.6	36.1	—
Latinos*	35.7	62.8	—

*Persons of Latino origin may be of any race.
SOURCES: U.S. Bureau of the Census. (1983, June). *1980 Census of the Population: General Social and Economic Characteristics,* PC80-1-C23. Washington, DC: Government Printing Office; Massachusetts Institute for Social and Economic Research, University of Massachusetts. (1992, April). Report 92-07. Amherst, MA: Author .

Table 3

Demographic Characteristics of the Population in Massachusetts, by Race/
Ethnicity, for 1970, 1980 and 1990

Characteristics	Whites	Blacks	Latinos*
		1970	
Total population	5,477,624	175,817	64,680
Median age	29.3	21.9	20.5
Total families	1,342,084	38,319	13,995
% husband-wife	85.4	61.8	81.3
% female-head	11.5	34.3	15.5
		1980	
Total population	5,378,400	221,029	141,380
Median age	31.8	24.7	21.3
Total families	1,363,990	50,572	31,847
% husband-wife	82.4	51.4	59.2
% female-head	14.2	43.0	35.8
		1990	
Total population	5,280,920	274,464	287,549
Median age	34.6	27.4	23.7
Total families	1,390,109	68,136	62,105
% husband-wife	80.8	46.8	49.5
% female-head	15.1	45.6	42.7

* In 1970 and 1980, Latinos are included in other racial categories in total population
figures. In 1990, Latinos are counted separately in total population figures.
SOURCES: U.S. Bureau of the Census. (1972, April). *1970 Census of the Population:
General Social and Economic Characteristics*, PC(1) C23. Washington, DC: Government
Printing Office; U.S. Bureau of the Census. (1983, June). *1980 Census of the Population:
General Social and Economic Characteristics*, PC80-1-C23. Washington, DC: Govern-
ment Printing Office; U.S. Bureau of the Census. (1990). *Census of Population and
Housing Massachusetts*, Summary Tape Files 1A and 3A. Washington, DC: Government
Printing Office.

Table 4

Years of School Completed for the Population 25 Years Old and Over in Massachusetts, by Race/Ethnicity and Gender, for 1970, 1980, and 1990

Category	Whites	Blacks	Latinos
		1970	
Median age	12.2	11.6	12.0
		Male	
Total	1,403,034	34,863	12,001
% 4 years high school, no college	30.2	31.0	20.3
% 4 years college or more	16.7	6.8	22.7
		Female	
Total	1,644,604	42,817	13,317
% 4 years high school, no college	39.1	34.9	26.3
% 4 years college or more	9.2	4.7	10.5
		1980	
Median age	12.6	12.4	10.9
		Male	
Total	1,505,673	49,315	27,250
% 4 years high school, no college	32.1	36.1	22.3
% 4 years college or more	25.3	14.3	15.0
		Female	
Total	1,783,535	59,936	31,990
% 4 years high school, no college	40.5	38.4	22.1
% 4 years college or more	15.9	10.0	9.5
		1970	
% high school graduate	35.0	33.1	22.4
% 4 years college or more	12.7	5.6	15.6

Table 4 (Cont.)

	1980		
% high school graduate	36.7	37.4	22.2
% 4 years college or more	20.2	11.9	12.0

	1990		
% high school graduate	30.1	28.3	22.0
% 4 years college or more	27.7	17.0	13.7

SOURCES: U.S. Bureau of the Census. (1972, April). *1970 Census of the Population: General Social and Economic Characteristics*, PC(1)-1-C23. Washington, DC: Government Printing Office; U.S. Bureau of the Census. (1983, June). *1980 Census of the Population: General Social and Economic Characteristics*, PC80-1-C23. Washington, DC: Government Printing Office; U.S. Bureau of the Census. (1990). *Census.* Washington, DC: Government Printing Office.

Table 5

Mean Family Income and Median Earnings for Males and Females in Massachusetts, by Race/Ethnicity, for 1969 and 1979

Category	Whites	Blacks	Latinos
		1969	
Mean family income	$12,424	$7,715	$9,190
% of whites	100.0%	62.1%	74.0%
Female-head	$7,946	$4,482	$4,939
% of whites	100.0%	56.4%	62.2%
Median earnings			
Male	$7,989	$5,965	$6,239
% of whites	100.0%	74.7%	78.1%
Female	$3,760	$3,653	$3,426
% of whites	100.0%	97.2%	91.1%
		1979	
Mean family income	$24,578	$16,021	$13,717
% of whites	100.0%	65.2%	55.8%
Female-head	$11,632	$7,561	$4,904
% of whites	100.0%	65.0%	42.2%
Median earnings			
Male	$12,181	$8,630	$8,044
% of whites	100.0%	69.3%	64.5%
Female	$5,332	$5,586	$4,549
% of whites	100.0%	105.1%	85.6%
		Change 1969 to 1979	
Mean family income	$12,154	$8,306	$4,527
% of whites	0.0%	3.1%	-18.2%
Female-head	$3,686	$3,079	($35)
% of whites	0.0%	8.6%	-20.0%
Median earnings			
Male	$4,473	$2,665	$1,805
% of whites	0.0%	-5.4%	-13.5%
Female	$1,557	$1,933	$1,123
% of whites	0.0%	7.9%	-5.6%

SOURCES: U.S. Bureau of the Census. (1972, April). *1970 Census of the Population: General Social and Economic Characteristics*, PC(1) C23. Washington, DC: Government Printing Office; U.S. Bureau of the Census. (1983, June). *1980 Census of the Population: General Social and Economic Characteristics*, PC80-1-C23. Washington, DC: Government Printing Office; U.S. Bureau of the Census. (1990). *Census of Population and Housing Massachusetts*, Summary Tape Files 1A and 3A. Washington, DC: Government Printing Office.

Table 6

Occupations of Employed Civilians in Massachusetts, by Race/Ethnicity, for 1970, 1980, and 1990

Occupations	Whites	Blacks	Latinos
		1970	
Total	2,229,180	56,686	21,000
	100.0%	100.0%	100.0%
Executive, admin., and managerial	8.5	3.5	5.9
Professional	13.8	7.9	14.1
Technicians and related support	3.7	3.7	2.8
Sales	7.2	2.9	3.9
Clerical and other administrative support	20.0	19.8	15.2
Services	12.2	23.0	12.8
Precision production, craft, and repair	13.2	9.7	10.6
Machine ops., assembls., and insps.	14.4	20.2	27.1
Transportation and material moving	3.0	3.5	1.7
Laborers, handlers, and helpers	3.5	5.2	4.1
Farming, forestry and fishing	0.5	0.5	1.8
		1980	
Total	2,540,530	84,876	44,982
	100.0%	100.0%	100.0%
Executive, admin., and managerial	11.1	7.6	5.2
Professional	15.4	11.5	11.0
Technicians and related support	3.6	3.7	2.6
Sales	9.4	4.9	4.6
Clerical and other administrative support	18.7	21.8	14.4
Services	12.9	22.6	15.9
Precision production, craft, and repair	11.5	8.6	10.4

Table 6 (Cont)

Machine ops., assembls., and insps.	9.8	12.1	26.3
Transportation and material moving	3.2	3.4	3.1
Laborers, handlers, and helpers	3.5	3.4	5.5
Farming, forestry and fishing	0.9	0.4	1.2

		1990	
Total	2,826,000	83,000	83,000
	100%	100%	100%
Executive, admin., and managerial	15.1	8.8	5.5
Professional	17.5	11.4	8.4
Technicians and related support	3.5	3.0	3.4
Sales	12.9	8.9	8.1
Clerical and other administrative support	16.4	18.2	12.6
Services	11.9	27.8	28.4
Precision production, craft, and repair	10.2	7.2	10.6
Machine ops., assembls., and insps.	5.5	7.3	14.5
Transportation and material moving	3.1	4.6	2.4
Laborers, handlers, and helpers	2.7	2.8	5.3
Farming, forestry and fishing	1.2	0.2	0.9

SOURCES: U.S. Bureau of the Census. (1972, April). *1970 Census of the Population: General Social and Economic Characteristics*, PC (1)-C23. Washington, DC: Government Printing Office; U.S. Bureau of the Census. (1983, June). *1980 Census of the Population: General Social and Economic Characteristics*, PC80-1-C23. Washington, DC: Government Printing Office; U.S. Bureau of the Labor Statistics. (1991). *Geographic Profile of Employment and Earnings*. Washington, DC: Government Printing Office.

Table 7

Employment Status of Civilian Population in Massachusetts, by Race Ethnicity and Gender, for 1970, 1980, and 1990

Status	Men			Women		
	Whites	Blacks	Latinos	Whites	Blacks	Latinos
1970						
Civilian labor force	1,384,209	32,902	14,120	931,616	27,844	8,371
Labor-force participation rate	78.2%	72.8%	78.9%	44.9%	47.6%	43.3%
Unemployment rate	3.6	7.0	6.8	3.9	6.4	6.3
1980						
Civilian labor force	1,480,734	46,937	28,049	1,189,130	46,099	21,730
Labor-force participation rate	76.1%	68.0%	70.2%	52.9%	55.6%	46.0%
Unemployment rate	5.2	9.7	9.5	4.4	7.6	9.8
1990						
Civilian labor force	1,596,000	46,000	54,000	1,406,000	46,000	37,000
Labor-force participation rate	77.7%	73.2%	76.0%	61.0%	56.8%	48.9%
Unemployment rate	6.5	8.7	7.5	5.2	11.6	9.4

Table 7 (Cont)

Change 1970 to 1980

Civilian labor force	96,525	13,945	13,929	257,514	16,255	13,359
Labor-force participation rate	-2.7%	-7.0%	-10.1%	8.0%	8.0%	2.7
Unemployment rate	1.6	2.7	2.7	0.5	1.2	3.5

Change 1980 to 1990

Civilian labor force	115,266	(847)	25,951	216,870	1,901	15,270
Labor-force participation rate	2.2%	7.4%	7.2%	8.1%	1.2%	2.9%
Unemployment rate	1.3	-1.0	-2.0	0.8	4.0	-0.4

SOURCES: U.S. Bureau of the Census. (1972, April). *1970 Census of the Population: General Social and Economic Characteristics,* PC(1)-C23. Washington, DC: Government Printing Office; U.S. Bureau of the Census. (1983, June). *1980 Census of the Population: General Social and Economic Characteristics,* PC80-1-C23. Washington, DC: Government Printing Office; U.S. Bureau of Labor Statistics. (1991). *Geographic Profile of Employment and Earnings.* Washington, DC: Government Printing Office.

Ralph Rivera
Diversity, Growth, and Geographic Distribution: Latinos in Massachusetts

Massachusetts has undergone radical changes in its racial/ethnic composition in the last 10 years. Mirroring the population shifts that occurred throughout the United States in the past decade (Barringer, 1991), the population of racial/ethnic minorities in the Commonwealth increased at a significantly faster rate than that of whites.[1] The Latino[2] population, due to its extraordinary growth rate during the last two decades, is the group most responsible for making Massachusetts significant in the national trend toward greater ethnic diversity. Moreover, Latinos are now the largest racial/ethnic minority group in the state.[3]

The size and phenomenal growth of the Latino population has been the subject of discussions in the media and the business community throughout the United States. However, recognition of Latinos as a significant population that warrants such attention in Massachusetts has come very slowly. Unlike blacks, who are concentrated in Boston (50 percent of all blacks in Massachusetts live in Boston compared to 21.5 percent of all Latinos), Latinos are dispersed geographically throughout the state (U.S. Census Bureau, 1991). Their geographic distribution combined with very limited economic and political power have made Latinos victims of indifference and neglect in the Commonwealth.

This treatment has been fueled by the "information gap" on Latinos in the state.[4] The information gap is the lack of basic information and analysis of the problems and needs of this population. Data readily available for whites and blacks is often nonexistent for Latinos. This gap "extends from ... the participation and outcomes for Latinos in public programs, such as employment and educational programs, ... to the understanding of the complex dynamics of Latino communities in the State" (Uriarte, 1990, p. 3). Furthermore, even when adequate data is available, it is often not analyzed fully and comprehensively.

This chapter focuses on the diversity, growth, and geographical distribution of Latinos in Massachusetts as documented by the 1990 U.S. Census. The chapter begins with a brief discussion of the undercount of Latinos. An examination of the growth of Latinos in the Commonwealth from a national perspective and an assessment of the increase of Latinos in the New England states follows. Next, the growth of Massachusetts Latinos is explored within the context of changes in the racial/ethnic composition of the state's population.

Finally, the diversity, growth, and geographic distribution of this population in cities and towns with the largest concentrations of Latinos throughout the Commonwealth are examined.

The Latino Undercount

The U.S. Census Bureau has acknowledged that the differential undercount[5] of Latinos was a problem in the 1970 and 1980 U.S. Census (Alonso and Starr, 1986). Reasons given for the undercount include (Choldin, 1986; Hispanic Policy Development Project, 1990):

Resistance from some Latinos to government inquiry into their lives,

Prevalence of Spanish language usage among Latinos,

Paucity of Latino census enumerators,

Low educational levels and illiteracy, and

Presence of a significant number of undocumented Latinos who are reluctant to complete a census form.

In spite of Census Bureau efforts to improve the counting of Latinos in 1990, there is evidence that a substantial differential undercounting of Latinos again took place nationally as well as in many urban centers in Massachusetts (Puente, 1991). According to a post-enumeration survey conducted by the Census Bureau to determine the accuracy of the original count, the 1990 U.S. Census may have missed up to 1.7 million Latinos nationwide, which represents a 7.3 percent undercount for this group compared to a 6.2 percent undercount for blacks, and a 2.5 percent overall undercount (Census Tally, 1991). Furthermore, the Census Bureau acknowledges a minimum Latino undercount of 4.2 percent or 973,000 (Census Tally, 1991). For Massachusetts, these undercount estimates (4.2 percent to 7.3 percent) represent an undercount of between 12,077 and 20,991 Latinos.

A group traditionally perceived as greatly undercounted are the Latinos who are undocumented. The number of undocumented Latinos in Massachusetts is unknown; however, in the mid-1980s, the Massachusetts Commission on Hispanic Affairs estimated that there were between 15,000 and 25,000 undocumented Central American refugees alone (no date, p. 2). Some estimate that presently there are at least 25,000 undocumented Central Americans (Gordan, 1991). Evidence from organizations that serve undocumented Latinos in the state indicate that most are Central Americans from El Salvador and Guatemala, and Dominicans. There are also significant numbers from South America, particularly from Colombia.

The undercount of Massachusetts Latinos in the 1990 U.S. Census seems particularly severe in Chelsea and Boston. The 1990 U.S. Census reports only 9,018 Latinos in Chelsea, or 31.4 percent of the city population. Estimates of the Latino community produced by other sources, however, suggest a significantly larger Latino community. Figures developed by the Center for Community Planning at the University of Massachusetts at Boston show 11,800 to 12,700 Latinos in Chelsea, or 44 percent of the total population.[6]

Additional evidence that suggests a serious undercount of Latinos in Chelsea is found in data on the percentage of Latino students enrolled in Chelsea public schools. In 1989, 54.6 percent of the student body was Latino. Part of the variation between the 1990 U.S. Census figures on the percentage of Latinos in the total population (31.4 percent) and the Latino percentage of students (54.6 percent) can be attributed to larger families among Latinos. The sizable 23-point differential, however, suggests that an undercount is responsible for a part of this discrepancy.

In Boston, municipal officials have expressed serious concerns over the general undercount in the city in 1990. The National Association for the Advancement of Colored People and the Black Legislative Caucus also have voiced their distress over the undercount nationally within communities of color (Census Missed 6m, 1991).

Boston city officials have quarreled with the Census Bureau over the mailing list used for the census. They argued that it did not account for between 12,000 and 20,000 housing units (Coakley, 1990; Marantz, 1990; Rezendes, 1990). According to city of Boston administration officials, this resulted in an undercount of between 42,350 and 50,000 Boston residents.[7] Given that Latinos represent 11 percent of the Boston population, their share of the undercount attributed to the missing housing units would be between 4,659 and 5,500. It is important to note, however, that although Boston city officials have expressed concerns that go beyond the undercounting of housing units, they apparently did not seek remedies to address these other problems in their discussions with the Census Bureau (Coakley, 1990). Seemingly, the fact that undercounts have been historically greatest in low-income, inner-city minority neighborhoods has been neglected by Boston city officials.

According to the 1990 U.S. Census, there are 61,955 Latinos in Boston. This number represents a growth rate of 70.1 percent between 1980 and 1990 for the Boston Latino population, a growth rate extremely modest compared to Latinos in other cities and towns across the state.[8] However, as early as 1981, the Hispanic Office of Planning and Evaluation, using data from the Center for

Survey Research, had already estimated Boston's Latino population at over 55,000, i.e., 53 percent higher than the official 1980 U.S. Census count of 36,068 (Hispanic Office of Planning and Evaluation, 1981). Moreover, the Massachusetts Commission on Hispanic Affairs had also estimated the Boston Latino population at 55,000 in 1985 (Commission on Hispanic Affairs, 1986). If the Latino population of Boston was at 55,000 by 1981 or 1985, it is safe to assume that by 1990 it would have grown to significantly more than the 61,955 counted by the census.

In July, 1991, U.S. Commerce Secretary Robert A. Mosbacher announced that the 1990 U.S. Census figures would not be statistically adjusted to compensate for the undercount (Perez, 1991). The debate is not yet over since five cities[9] and several groups (including the Mexican American Legal Defense and Educational Fund) will reopen a lawsuit in a New York federal court seeking a new count. Past experiences with the census undercount, however, suggest that it is highly unlikely that an adjustment will occur. The Census Bureau has never adjusted to compensate for the undercount (U.S. General Accounting Office, 1991). It is important, nonetheless, for policymakers to understand that while the official 1990 U.S. Census data document the dramatic growth of the Latino population, these figures are very conservative estimates of the actual size of this population.

National Perspective

The United States continued to experience a dramatic growth in its populations of color during the 1980s. A significant amount of that surge was among Latinos who increased by 7.7 million people or 53 percent during that decade. The Latino population has been, and is expected to continue, increasing significantly faster than the non-Latino population. Moreover, their growth is so rapid that they are projected to become the largest ethnic group in the country by the year 2010 (Hispanic Americans, 1988). While Latinos reside in every state in the nation, they are geographically concentrated in five states. California, Texas, New York, Florida, and Illinois contain almost three-quarters of all Latinos in the United States. Furthermore, the first three states account for 64 percent of the Latino population in the country.

A salient characteristic of the Massachusetts Latino community in the national context is its rapid rate of growth. As seen in table 1, the Massachusetts Latino population grew at a faster rate between 1970 and 1980 (113.2 percent) and again between 1980 and 1990 (103.9 percent) than did its counterparts in any of the other 14 states with the highest concentration of Latinos in 1990. The 103.9 percent Latino growth rate in the last decade is almost twice the growth rate of

Latinos nationwide (53 percent). With 287,549 Latinos, Massachusetts has the tenth largest Latino population in the United States; however, it constitutes only 1.3 percent of the national Latino population.

New England

While New England continues to be one of the least diverse regions of the United States, the growth of people of color in this area of the country during the 1980s was dramatic. As a result of interstate migration and the fact that many new immigrants are choosing to settle in different states and smaller cities then their predecessors, the New England states experienced among the highest rates of growth of Latinos, blacks, and Asians of any area in the United States.

A look at the increase of Latinos in the New England states between 1970 to 1980 and 1980 to 1990 shows spectacular growth for almost all states during both periods (see table 2). The exceptions are Maine and Vermont during the 1980-1990 decade where Latinos grew by only 36.4 percent and 10.8 percent respectively after each grew by 105 percent in the previous 10-year period.

The Latino population in the other four New England states continued to swell at a rate significantly higher than the national rate of 53 percent between 1980 and 1990. The Rhode Island Latino population, the fastest growing in the country in terms of growth percentage, increased by 132.2 percent between 1980 and 1990, while Massachusetts Latinos grew by 103.9 percent. Although the New Hampshire Latino population is still quite small (11,333), it increased by an impressive 102.8 percent during the last decade. The Connecticut Latino population expanded by 71.2 percent.

It is important to note that the high growth rates for Rhode Island and New Hampshire are a function of the relatively small number of Latinos in each state in 1980. Conversely, Massachusetts had the fastest growing Latino population in the country when compared to states with more than 100,000 Latinos in 1980.

Three of the five fastest growing black populations were also in New England. New Hampshire had the highest growth rate for blacks (80.4 percent) of all states, while Vermont (71.9 percent) ranked third, and Maine fifth (64.3 percent). The two fastest growing Asian populations were Rhode Island (245.6 percent) and New Hampshire (219.0 percent), whereas Massachusetts ranked sixth (189.7 percent).

Massachusetts

RACIAL/ETHNIC DIVERSITY

During the past 20 years, Massachusetts has gone from one of the least racially and ethnically diverse states in the United States to one of medium diversity (Allen and Turner, 1990). While racial/ethnic minority groups represented only slightly more than 4 percent in 1970, they grew to over 12 percent in 1990 (see table 3). In 1980, racial/ethnic minority groups represented 7.5 percent of the total state population of which 3.7 percent were blacks, 2.5 percent were Latinos, and 0.9 percent were Asians. In 1990, this population expanded to 12.2 percent of the total population. Blacks increased to 4.6 percent, Latinos to 4.8 percent, and Asians to 2.4 percent of the population.

As stated previously, Latinos in the Commonwealth doubled in size from 1970 to 1980 and again between 1980 and 1990, and they are now the largest minority group in the state. During these same periods, the non-Hispanic white population of the Commonwealth decreased by 3.1 percent and 0.5 percent respectively, and the non-Hispanic black population increased by 20.9 percent and 29.1 percent. Clearly, the modest growth in the Massachusetts total population (4.9 percent) is due to the increase of Latinos and blacks, as well as to the Asian population that increased by a remarkable 189.7 percent in the last 10 years. While most cities and towns throughout the Commonwealth remain primarily white, the dramatic growth of the Latino, black, and Asian populations in the state's larger cities, coupled with a decrease in the white population, has resulted in a significantly more diverse population in these areas.

In 1980, people of color represented less than 20 percent of the population in the cities of Lawrence, Chelsea, and Holyoke. By 1990, 45.3 percent of the Lawrence population, 41 percent of the Chelsea population, and 34.7 percent of the Holyoke population were people of color. Furthermore, people of color constitute 41 percent of the Boston population, 36.4 percent in Springfield, 23.5 percent in Lowell, 19.8 percent in Lynn, and 16.7 percent in Worcester.

The racial/ethnic group composition of the Massachusetts counties, however, shows extremely low rates of diversity. Only two counties, Suffolk and Hampden, have populations of color that significantly exceed 10 percent. Suffolk County is the most diverse in the Commonwealth and, according to Allen and Turner (1990), the seventeenth most diverse county in the United States, with nearly 38 percent of its population comprised of people of color. Almost 19 percent of the Hampden County population consists of racial/ethnic minority individuals. Conversely, the least diverse counties in the state are Franklin County (97.1 percent white) and Berkshire County (96.3 percent white).

LATINO DIVERSITY

While holding a common language, shared ethnic heritage, and an intertwined history, the Latino population in Massachusetts is comprised of individuals of diverse nationalities. Moreover, this population's national origin composition is significantly different than that of Latinos throughout the United States. Nationally, Mexican Americans (60.4 percent) are the predominate group, followed by "other Hispanics"[10] (22.7 percent), Puerto Ricans (12.2 percent), and Cubans (4.7 percent). However, as seen in table 4, in Massachusetts, Latinos of Puerto Rican origin are the largest group (52.6 percent), followed by "other Hispanics" (40.2 percent), Mexican Americans (4.4 percent), and Cubans (2.8 percent).

Given that "other Hispanics" is a substantial portion of the state Latino population, it would be valuable to determine what specific groups comprise this category. The Massachusetts Department of Public Health's birth data allows us to draw some conclusions about this because it disaggregates Latino births into groups, i.e., Puerto Rican, Cuban, Dominican, Mexican, Central American, South American, and "other Hispanics." The Latino birth data strongly suggests that the major "other Hispanics" groups statewide are, in descending order by size of the population, Dominicans, Central Americans, and South Americans.[11]

Central America, of course, is comprised of six Spanish-speaking countries, while South America encompasses nine Spanish-speaking countries.[12] Relying again on evidence from the organizations that work with these groups, it appears that most Central Americans in Massachusetts are from El Salvador and Guatemala, and that most South Americans are from Colombia.

There are significant variations in the composition of the Latino communities in cities and towns across the state. For example, Puerto Ricans constitute the majority of Latinos in cities and towns such as Holyoke (94 percent), Springfield (89 percent), Worcester (75 percent), Lowell (74 percent), New Bedford (73 percent), Leominster (70 percent), Brockton (53 percent), Chelsea (51 percent), Framingham (50 percent), and Lawrence (50 percent). On the other hand, the "other Hispanics" group predominates in Somerville (79 percent), Lynn (64 percent), Cambridge (55 percent), Boston (51 percent), and Waltham (47 percent).

In addition, the particular national group that dominates the "other Hispanics" category varies quite markedly by city and town. Again, the Latino birth data suggests which group represents the largest portion of this population in selected cities and towns. Dominicans seem to be the major "other Hispanics" group in Lynn, Lawrence, and Boston, and there are also large numbers in Cambridge.[13] However, Central Americans appear to dominate this category in Somerville, Chelsea, and Cambridge. There are also significant communities of Central Americans in Boston, Framingham, and Waltham.[14] Finally, South Americans seem to predominate in Framingham, Leominster, and Lowell, with large concentrations in Somerville, Cambridge, Waltham, and Boston as well.[15]

GROWTH

The Massachusetts Latino population registered growth rates in all cities and towns where they reside between 1980 and 1990 with the sole exception of Fall River (see table 5). The fast growth of Latinos is a result of a young population (the median age of Latinos is 23.7 years compared to 34.6 for whites, 27.4 for blacks, and 27 for Asians) with high birth rates and immigration (both legal and undocumented). According to a recent report by the Massachusetts Department of Public Health (1989), 6.5 percent of the total births in the state were to Latino mothers during a period when it was estimated that Latinos represented only 3.8 percent of the total population (Commission on Hispanic Affairs, 1986).

The immigration of Latinos to Massachusetts, primarily from Central America and the Dominican Republic, and migration from Puerto Rico continued at an accelerated rate throughout the 1980s (Commission on Hispanic Affairs, 1986; Massachusetts Department of Public Health, 1989; Center for Community Planning, 1990). Furthermore, a significant number of Latinos migrated from other states to Massachusetts, particularly during and because of the economic boom.

While the Latino population in some cities and towns represents a somewhat smaller percentage of the total population, they increased at an extraordinary rate during the last decade as seen in table 5. The most dramatic Latino growth occurred in Revere (381 percent), Lynn (272 percent), Marlborough (271 percent), and Fitchburg (261 percent). In addition, Latinos in the following cities and towns expanded by more than 200 percent, i.e., at more than twice the state Latino growth rate: Chicopee (226 percent), Methuen (225 percent), and Somerville (213 percent). Other cities and towns whose Latino population also increased substantially include: Everett (192 percent), Haverhill (192 percent), Salem (185 percent), Lawrence (184 percent), Brockton (174 percent), Malden (168 percent), and Chelsea (154 percent).

The explosive growth rates for most of these cities and towns is primarily a function of the relatively small numbers of Latinos in each area in 1980. These growth rates clearly indicate, however, that this population is growing very rapidly in areas where it had not previously grown.

The Latino groups in Massachusetts had quite different growth rates between 1980-1990. The fastest growing Latino group was the "other Hispanics" category that increased by 128.4 percent, and the Puerto Rican population that grew by 97.8 percent. Mexicans increased by 72 percent, followed by Cubans at 22.5 percent. The "other Hispanics" group, however, experienced extraordinary growth rates, actually more than twice its state average in various cities and towns such as Chelsea (536 percent), Haverhill (359 percent), Everett (349 percent), Framingham (306 percent), Lynn (303 percent), Leominster (286 percent), Marlborough (281 percent), Salem (268 percent), Methuen (263 percent), Waltham (260 percent), Salem (257 percent), and Fitchburg (255 percent). Puerto Ricans also experienced phenomenal growth rates in various cities and towns including Chicopee (459 percent), Quincy (385 percent), Medford (277 percent), Fitchburg (268 percent), Marlborough (240 percent), Lynn (233 percent), and Methuen (228 percent).

GEOGRAPHICAL DISTRIBUTION

The Massachusetts Latino population also evidenced notable changes in its geographic distribution in the past 10 years. Latinos reside in every city and town of the state, and although they are concentrated significantly in the larger cities, they have clustered in many towns as well.

In 1980, there were only four cities where Latinos represented more than 8 percent of the total city population (Lawrence, 16.3 percent; Chelsea, 14.0 percent; Holyoke, 13.8 percent; and Springfield, 9.1 percent). According to the 1990 U.S. Census, there are now 12 cities and towns where the Latino population represents more than 8 percent of the total population. These are Lawrence (41.6 percent), Chelsea (31.4 percent), Holyoke (31.1 percent), Springfield (16.9 percent), Southbridge (12.8 percent), Boston (10.8 percent, Lowell (10.1 percent), Worcester (9.6 percent), Fitchburg (9.6 percent), Lynn (9.1 percent), Leominster (8.3 percent), and Framingham (8.1 percent). While these municipalities contain almost two-thirds of all Latinos in Massachusetts, they are scattered throughout the Commonwealth. The highest concentration of Latinos is in Lawrence, where four out of every 10 residents are Latino, and in Chelsea and Holyoke, where one of every three residents is Latino.

While the state's largest Latino community is still in Boston, the 1990 U.S. Census reveals that between 1980 and 1990 the proportion of all Massachusetts Latinos living in Boston decreased from 25.8 percent to 21.5 percent. On the other hand, Lawrence experienced the largest increase in proportionate share of the Massachusetts Latino population during the same period (7.3 percent to 10.2 percent).

Conclusion

One of the primary characteristics of the Latino population in Massachusetts is its rapid growth. We move into the 1990s and the twenty-first century with the knowledge that the Latino population, the largest racial/ethnic group in Massachusetts, has doubled in size each of the last two decades, and it is expected to continue to grow at a significantly faster rate than the white and black populations throughout the next decade. The explosive growth and geographic dispersion of the Massachusetts Latino population, as well as its diversity, justifies immediate attention by state and local policymakers in the public as well as private sectors.

Indeed, while the Latino population of Massachusetts is comprised of distinct national groups, they share common social problems and needs and pose formidable challenges to policymakers. Latinos are the most disadvantaged ethnic minority group in the state, and they have the highest poverty rate — 47 percent — of all state Latino populations (Haveman, et al., 1991).[16] The benefits of the Massachusetts Miracle that accrued to whites, and to some extent blacks, were not shared with the Latino community (Boston Foundation, 1989). Clearly, the Latino population will require expanded attention by state and local policymakers during the 1990s to enable this community to gain full participation in the Commonwealth's social, economic, and educational life.

While the issues and needs of the Latino population in Massachusetts are not new, what is new is the large numbers of Latinos affected by these issues. The implications of their accelerated growth and geographic dispersion are numerous. In the years ahead, Latinos are virtually guaranteed to have an increasing impact on the economic structures, politics, public services, and the social and civic life of many cities and towns throughout the Commonwealth. Their political and economic influence will also, undoubtedly, increase and spread.

Like previous immigrants to Massachusetts, Latinos come here seeking, among other things, economic opportunity for themselves and their families. Like earlier immigrants they seek peace and a better life for their children, and they are willing to work hard to achieve this quality of life. Expanded economic opportunities, however, are essential for the rapidly increasing Latino labor force to contribute to the present and future viability and competitiveness of the Massachusetts economy. Moreover, it will be extremely difficult for Massachusetts to have an economically competitive economy without an economically competitive Latino work force. Consequently, policymakers must seek ways to assure a full participation in the state's economy for this population. Clearly, the success of the Latino population is not only a selfish community concern, but also a matter of self-interest for the Commonwealth as a whole.

Notes

This chapter originally appeared in the *New England Journal of Public Policy*, Fall/Winter 1992, Volume 8, No. 2, published by the University of Massachusetts, John W. McCormack Institute of Public Affairs, Boston, MA.

1. White, black, or Asian will be used throughout this paper to refer to "non-Hispanic" whites, "non-Hispanic" blacks, or "non-Hispanic" Asians, unless otherwise noted.

2. Latino will be used throughout this paper to refer to a person living in the United States who are of Puerto Rican, Cuban, Dominican, or Mexican ancestry as well as other Spanish-speaking people from Central or South American countries. However, the terms "Hispanic origin" and "non-Hispanic" will be used in the tables to maintain consistency with the U.S. Census Bureau's terminology.

3. The growing population diversity in the United States and in Massachusetts makes it more important than ever to understand the meaning of the terms "race" and "ethnicity." While these terms are often used interchangeably, they are not synonymous. According to the Census Bureau, there are only four racial groups: white, black, Asian and Pacific Islanders, and native Americans. There are, however, hundreds of ethnic categories, i.e., religious, cultural, or national groups. Hispanic is an ethnic category, not a racial group, and the term refers to Latino heritage. Latinos may be of any race.

Recent reports of the 1990 U.S. Census data give figures for whites, blacks, Asians, and native Americans (all of which include Latinos) and contrast these with figures of people of Hispanic origin. The appropriate comparison and presentation should be of mutually exclusive groups. This is achieved by disaggregating Latinos from the racial groups to produce the "non-Hispanic" white population, "non-Hispanic" black population, "non-Hispanic" Asian population, etc. This comparison shows that Latinos are the largest ethnic group in Massachusetts.

4. For more information on this topic see: Uriarte, M., (1990), *Latinos, Data and Public Policy: The Latino Information Gap in Massachusetts,* Boston: University of Massachusetts, Mauricio Gastón Institute; Hayes-Bautista, D. and Hernandez, J., (1985), *Improving Data: A Research Strategy for New Immigrants,* New York: Russell Sage; and The Ford Foundation, (1984), *Public Policy Research and the Hispanic Community: Recommendations from Five Task Forces,* New York: The Ford Foundation.

5. An undercount is the portion of the "real total population" that a census fails to count. A differential undercount is produced when a census misses more of one group in the population than of another (Choldin, 1986). Historically, undercounts have been greatest in low-income, inner-city neighborhoods.

6. The Latino percentage of total Chelsea population range is generated by computations utilizing the estimated total Latino population range and the final 1990 U.S. Census figures for the total Chelsea population.

7. These figures are based on a city estimate of 2.5 persons per dwelling unit (Marantz, 1990).

8. It is also important to note that the accuracy of the 1980 U.S. Census in enumerating Latinos in Boston has been questioned. The estimated Latino undercount in Boston in 1980 was 10 percent according to the Hispanic Policy Development Project (1990).

9. The cities are Chicago, Houston, Los Angeles, Miami, and New York.

10. The U.S. Bureau of the Census utilizes "Other Hispanics" as a residual census category that primarily comprises Central and South Americans and Dominicans.

11. According to the Massachusetts Department of Public Health (1991), of all Latino births in 1989, 60.4 percent were of Puerto Rican origin, 15 percent were Dominican, 9.1 percent were Central Americans, and 15.5 percent were "other Hispanics." Moreover, unpublished 1989 Latino birth data from 18 selected cities and towns that comprise 84 percent of all Latino births during that year show that 63.8 percent of the births were to Puerto Ricans, followed by Dominicans (15.8 percent), Central Americans (8.5 percent), South Americans (7 percent), "other Hispanics" (2.2 percent), Mexicans (1.6 percent), and Cubans (1.2 percent).

12. The Spanish-speaking Central American countries are: Guatemala, El Salvador, Honduras, Nicaragua, Costa Rica, and Panama. The Spanish-speaking South American countries are: Colombia, Venezuela, Ecuador, Peru, Bolivia, Chile, Paraguay, Uruguay, and Argentina.

13. According to Massachusetts Department of Public Health unpublished 1989 Latino birth data, Dominicans represent 48.7 percent of all Latino births in Lynn, 39.1 percent in Lawrence, 21.2 percent in Boston, and 15.7 percent in Cambridge.

14. The same Massachusetts Department of Public Health data shows that Central Americans represent 48 percent of all Latino births in Somerville, 34.4 percent in Chelsea, and 24 percent in Cambridge. Moreover, they represent significant births in Boston (14 percent), Framingham (13 percent), and Waltham (13 percent).

15. The 1989 Latino birth data shows that South Americans represent 23 percent of all Latino births in Framingham, 15.5 percent in Leominster, and 10 percent in Lowell. They also represent a significant percentage of Latino births in cities such as Somerville (24.8 percent), Cambridge (18.2 percent), Waltham (15.7 percent), and Boston (11 percent).

16. According to a study by the Institute for Research on Poverty at the University of Wisconsin at Madison, the national Latino poverty rate was 27.2 percent, and the Latino poverty rates for the other state Latino populations reported were: Texas, 35.4 percent; New York, 35.0 percent; Idaho, 31.8 percent; Michigan, 30.5 percent; Colorado, 29.0 percent; New Mexico, 27.6 percent; Arizona, 26.6 percent; New Jersey, 26.6 percent; Illinois, 24.0 percent; California, 22.0 percent; and Florida, 19.0 percent.

References

Allen, J. P., and Turner, E. (1990, August). Where Diversity Reigns. *American Demographics,* 34-38.

Alonso, W., and Starr, P. (1986). *The Politics of Numbers.* New York: Russell Sage.

Barringer, F. (1991, March 11). Census Shows Profound Change in Racial Makeup of Nation. *The New York Times,* p. 1, 8.

Boston Foundation. (1989). *In the Midst of Plenty.* Boston: Boston Foundation Persistent Poverty Project.

Census Missed 6m, US Says. (1991, May 19). *The Boston Globe,* p. 1.

Census Tally May Be Short 1.7 Million. (1991, April 29). *Hispanic Link Weekly Report,* p. 1.

Center for Community Planning and the Collaborative for Community Service and Development. (1990). *The Hispanics of Chelsea: Who Are They?* Boston: University of Massachusetts, College of Public and Community Service.

Choldin, H. M. (1986). Statistics and Politics: The "Hispanic Issue" in the 1980 Census. *Demography,* 233, 403-418.

Coakley, T. (1990, September 4). City Says Census May Be Under by 50,000. *The Boston Globe,* p. 25.

Commission on Hispanic Affairs. (1986). *Hispanics in Massachusetts: A Demographic Analysis.* Boston: Commonwealth of Massachusetts, Commission on Hispanic Affairs.

Commission on Hispanic Affairs. (no date). *Report on Central American Refugees in Massachusetts.* Boston: Commonwealth of Massachusetts, Commission on Hispanic Affairs.

Gordan, A. (1991, September 17). Telephone conversation with Gordan who is documentation coordinator at Centro Presente, Cambridge, MA.

Haveman, J. D., Danzinger, J., and Plotnick, R. D. (1991). State Poverty Rates for Whites, Blacks, and Hispanics in the Late 1980s. *Focus,* 131. Madison, WI: University of Wisconsin-Madison, Institute for Research on Poverty.

Hispanic Americans: An Emerging Group. (1988, October-December). *Metropolitan Life Insurance Company Statistical Bulletin,* 2.

Hispanic Office of Planning and Evaluation. (1981). *Boston's Hispanics and the 1980 Census: Where We Live.* Boston: Author.

Hispanic Policy Development Project. (1984). *The Hispanic Almanac.* Washington, DC: Author.

Hispanic Policy Development Project. (1990). *The Hispanic Almanac,* Edition Two. Washington, DC: Author.

Marantz, S. (1990, May 2). Census May Undercount Hub by 42,000, Official Says. *The Boston Globe,* p. 25, 32.

Massachusetts Department of Public Health. (1989). *Hispanic Births in Massachusetts Volume 1: Facts and Figures.* Boston: Bureau of Health Statistics, Research and Evaluation.

Massachusetts Department of Public Health. (1991). *Advance Data: Births 1989.* Boston: Bureau of Health Statistics, Research and Evaluation.

Perez, F. (1991, July 22). Census Decision Promises More Uncertainty. *Hispanic Link Weekly Report,* p. 1, 2.

Puente, T. (1991, March 18). Latino Population Grows 53 percent, to 22.4 Million: 1980-90. *Hispanic Link Weekly Report,* p. 2.

Rezendes, M. (1990, May 6). U.S. Census Bureau Denies City of Boston's Charge of Undercount. *The Boston Globe,* p. 86.

Uriarte, M. (1990). *Latinos, Data and Public Policy: The Latino Information Gap in Massachusetts.* Boston: University of Massachusetts, Mauricio Gastón Institute.

U.S. Bureau of the Census. (1973). *Census of the Population: 1970, Volume 1, Characteristics of the Population, Part 23, Massachusetts.* Washington, DC: U.S. Government Printing Office.

U.S. Bureau of the Census. (1982). *Census of the Population: 1980, Volume 1, Characteristics of the Population, Massachusetts.* PC80-1-B23. Washington, DC: U.S. Government Printing Office.

U.S. Bureau of the Census. (1983). *Census of the Population: 1980. General Population Characteristics, United States Summary.* PC80-1-B1. Washington, DC: U.S. Government Printing Office.

U.S. Bureau of the Census. (1991). *Census of Population and Housing, 1990: P.L. 94-171 Data File.* Washington, DC: U.S. Government Printing Office.

U.S. General Accounting Office. (1991). *1990 Census Adjustment: Estimating Census Accuracy — A Complex Task.* Report to the Chairman, Committee on Post Office and Civil Service, House of Representatives, GAO/GGD-91-42. Washington, DC: U.S. Government Printing Office.

Table 1

Latino Population Growth in the 15 States with Highest Concentration of Latinos, for 1970, 1980, and 1990*

State	1970	1980	1990	Growth 1970-1980 (percent)	Growth 1980-1990 (percent)
California	2,368,748	4,544,331	7,687,938	91.8	69.2
Texas	1,840,862	2,985,824	4,339,905	62.2	45.4
New York	1,352,302	1,659,300	2,214,046	22.7	33.4
Florida	405,037	858,158	1,574,143	111.9	83.4
Illinois	393,347	635,602	904,446	61.6	42.3
New Jersey	288,488	491,883	739,861	70.5	50.4
Arizona	265,006	440,701	688,338	66.3	56.2
New Mexico	308,340	477,222	579,224	54.8	21.4
Colorado	225,506	339,717	424,302	50.6	24.9
Massachusetts	66,146	141,043	287,549	113.2	103.9
Pennsylvania	108,893	153,961	232,262	41.4	50.9
Washington	57,358	120,016	214,570	109.2	78.8
Connecticut	65,468	124,499	213,116	90.2	71.2
Michigan	151,070	162,440	201,596	7.5	24.1
Virginia	40,222	79,868	160,288	98.6	100.7

*States are ranked by the size of their Latino population in 1990.
SOURCES: Hispanic Policy Development Project. (1984.) *The Hispanic Almanac.* Washington, DC: Author; U.S. Bureau of the Census. (1983). *Census of the Population: 1980. General Population Characteristics, United States Summary.* PC80-1-B1. Washington, DC: U.S. Government Printing Office; and U.S. Bureau of the Census. (1991). *Census of Population and Housing, 1990: P.L. 94-171 Data File.* Washington, DC: U.S. Government Printing Office.

Table 2

Growth of the Latino Population in the New England States, 1970-1980 and 1980-1990

State	1970	1980	1990	Growth 1970-1980 (percent)	Growth 1980-1990 (percent)
Connecticut	65,468	124,499	213,116	90.2	71.2
Maine	2,433	5,005	6,829	105.7	36.4
Massachusetts	66,146	141,043	287,549	113.2	103.9
New Hampshire	2,281	5,587	11,333	144.9	102.8
Rhode Island	7,596	19,707	45,752	159.4	132.2
Vermont	1,611	3,304	3,661	105.1	10.8

SOURCES: Hispanic Policy Development Project. (1984.) *The Hispanic Almanac.* Washington, DC: Author; U.S. Bureau of the Census. (1983). *Census of the Population: 1980. General Population Characteristics, United States Summary.* PC80-1-B1. Washington, DC: U.S. Government Printing Office; and U.S. Bureau of the Census. (1991). *Census of Population and Housing, 1990: P.L. 94-171 Data File.* Washington, DC: U.S. Government Printing Office.

Table 3

Massachusetts Population Changes, by Racial/Ethnic Group and Total Population, for 1970, 1980, and 1990

Racial/ Ethnic Group	1970 Population (percent)	1980 Population (percent)	1990 Population (percent)	1980 Change (percent)	1990 Change (percent)
Non-Hispanic white	5,477,624 (95.8)	5,305,963 (92.5)	5,280,292 (87.8)	-171,661 (-3.1)	-25,671 (-0.5)
Non-Hispanic black	175,817 (3.1)	212,608 (3.7)	274,464 (4.6)	+36,791 (+20.9)	+61,856 (+29.1)
Hispanic origin	66,146 (1.2)	141,043 (2.5)	287,549 (4.8)	+74,897 (+113.2)	+146,506 (+103.9)
Non-Hispanic Asian	20,766 (0.4)	49,501 (0.9)	140,338 (2.4)	+28,735 (+183.4)	+90,837 (+183.7)
Total Population	5,719,587	5,737,037*	6,016,425†	+17,450 (+0.3)	+279,388 (+4.9)

* The 1980 total population includes 27, 922 persons who are of other races and not of Hispanic origin.

†The 1990 total population includes 30,728 persons who are of other races and not of Hispanic origin.

SOURCES: Commission on Hispanic Affairs. (1986). *Hispanics in Massachusetts: A Demographic Analysis*. Boston: The Commonwealth of Massachusetts, Commission on Hispanic Affairs; U.S. Bureau of Census. (1982). *Census of the Population: 1980, Volume 1, Characteristics of the Population, Massachusetts*. PC80-1-B23. Washington, DC: U.S. Government Printing Office; and U.S. Bureau of the Census. (1991). *Census of Population and Housing, 1990: P.L. 94-171 Data File*. Washington, DC: U.S. Government Printing Office.

Table 4

Composition of the Latino Population in the State of Massachusetts and Selected Cities and Towns, for 1980 and 1990

Location	Year	Total Latino	Mexican (%)	Puerto Rican (%)	Cuban (%)	Other Latino (%)
Massachusetts	1990	287,549	12,703	151,193	8,106	115,547
			4.4	52.6	2.8	40.2
	1980	141,043	7,385	76,450	6,617	50,591
			5.2	54.2	4.7	35.9
Boston	1990	61,955	2,179	25,767	2,483	31,526
			3.5	41.6	4.0	50.9
	1980	36,068	1,301	19,379	2,505	12,883
			3.6	53.7	6.9	35.7
Brockton	1990	5,860	295	3,104	188	2,273
			5.0	53.0	3.2	38.8
	1980	2,142	182	1,137	109	714
			8.5	53.1	5.1	33.3
Cambridge	1990	6,506	801	1,875	254	3,576
			12.3	28.8	3.9	55.0
	1980	4,536	496	1,583	279	2, 178
			10.9	34.9	6.2	48.0
Chelsea	1990	9,018	185	4,581	250	4,002
			2.1	50.8	2.8	44.4
	1980	3,551	83	2,592	247	629
			2.3	73.0	7.0	17.7
Framingham	1990	5,291	267	2,668	143	2,213
			5.0	50.4	2.7	41.8
	1980	2,186	120	1,402	119	545
			5.5	64.1	5.4	24.9
Holyoke	1990	13,573	84	12,687	60	742
			0.6	93.5	0.4	5.5
	1980	6,165	48	5,764	14	339
			0.8	93.5	0.2	5.5
Lawrence	1990	29,237	165	14,661	463	13,948
			0.6	50.1	1.6	47.7
	1980	10,296	92	5,726	417	4, 061
			0.9	55.6	4.1	39.4

Table 4 (Cont.)

Leominster	1990	3,161	149	2,209	34	769
			4.7	69.9	1.1	24.3
	1980	1,347	74	1,062	12	199
			5.5	78.8	0.9	14.8
Lowell	1990	10,499	153	7,732	100	2,514
			1.5	73.6	1.0	23.9
	1980	4,585	117	3,528	91	849
			2.6	76.9	2.0	18.5
Lynn	1990	7,432	299	2,285	90	4, 758
			4.0	30.7	1.2	64.0
	1980	1,998	98	686	33	1,181
			4.9	34.3	1.7	59.1
New Bedford	1990	6,653	164	4,864	39	1,586
			2.5	73.1	0.6	23.8
	1980	4,497	125	2,099	43	2,230
			2.8	46.7	1.0	49.6
Somerville	1990	4,784	233	635	147	3,769
			4.9	13.3	3.1	78.8
	1980	1,530	114	270	91	1,055
			7.5	17.6	5.9	69.0
Springfield	1990	26,528	306	23,729	199	2,294
			1.2	89.4	0.8	8.6
	1980	13,804	253	12,298	127	1,126
			1.8	89.1	0.9	8.2
Waltham	1990	3,239	204	1,423	87	1, 525
			6.3	43.9	2.7	47.1
	1980	1,417	50	842	101	424
			3.5	59.4	7.1	29.9
Worcester	1990	16,258	397	12,166	380	3,315
			2.4	74.8	2.3	20.4
	1980	6,877	167	5,433	228	1, 049
			2.4	79.0	3.3	15.3

SOURCES: U.S. Bureau of the Census. (1992). *1990 Census of Population and Housing Summary Tape File 1A*. Washington, DC: U.S. Government Printing Office. U.S. Bureau of the Census. (1982). *Census of the Population: 1980, Volume 1, Characteristics of the Population, Massachusetts*. PC80-1-B23. Washington, DC: U.S. Government Printing Office.

Table 5

Growth of Massachusetts Latino Population, by Selected Cities and Towns, for 1970, 1980 and 1990

Cities/Towns	1970	1980	1990	1980-1990 Change (%)	% Latino of Total
Boston	17,984	36,068	61,955	71.8	10.8
Brockton	936	2,142	5,860	173.6	6.3
Cambridge	1,954	4,536	6,506	43.4	6. 8
Chelsea	1,098	3,551	9,018	154.0	31.4
Fitchburg	335	1,095	3,957	261.4	9.6
Framingham	1,237	2,186	5,291	142.0	8.1
Holyoke	1,870	6,165	13,573	120.2	31.1
Lawrence	2,327	10,296	29,237	184.0	41.6
Leominster	634	1,347	3,161	134.7	8.3
Lowell	1,079	4,585	10,499	129.0	10.1
Lynn	953	1,998	7,432	272.0	9.1
New Bedford	1,144	4,497	6,653	47.9	6.7
Somerville	701	1,530	4,784	212.7	6.3
Southbridge	305	1,033	2,278	120.5	12.8
Springfield	5,456	13,804	26,528	92.2	16.9
Waltham	527	1,417	3,239	128.6	5.6
Worcester	1,674	6,877	16,258	136.4	9.6

SOURCES: U.S. Bureau of the Census. (1973). *Census of the Population: 1970, Volume 1, Characteristics of the Population, Part 23, Massachusetts.* Washington, DC: U.S. Government Printing Office; U.S. Bureau of the Census. (1982). *Census of the Population: 1980, Volume 1, Characteristics of the Population, Massachusetts.* PC80-1-B23. Washington, DC: U.S. Government Printing Office; and U.S. Bureau of the Census. (1991). *Census of Population and Housing, 1990: P.L. 94-171 Data File.* Washington, DC: U.S. Government Printing Office.

Part II
Dimensions of Inequality and Labor Markets

Jeremiah Cotton
A Comparative Analysis of the Labor-Market Outcomes of Latinos, Blacks, and Whites in Boston, Massachusetts, and New England, 1983 to 1991

The major determinants of the ongoing economic well-being and progress of a given demographic group are the outcomes of their labor-market experiences. Among the most important of these outcomes are earnings; labor-force partici- pation; employment and unemployment rates (and the underlying number of spells of unemployment experienced and the duration of an unemployment spell); instances of job losses, job leavings, rates of entry and reentry; number of hours worked; and occupational and industry distributions.

The data presented in this chapter strongly suggest that the labor-market experiences of Latinos in the city of Boston and the state of Massachusetts in particular, and in New England and the Northeast in general, result in signifi- cantly less favorable outcomes on most of these indicators than occur for either their white or black counterparts.

Latinos are the fastest growing demographic group in the United States and are predicted to become the country's largest "minority" by century's end. They are also entering the country's labor forces at an even faster clip than their population growth. Over the principal years covered by this study, the Latino population increased dramatically, far outstripping commensurate changes in either the black or white populations.

Between 1983 and 1990, the Latino civilian noninstitutional population in the United States increased by over 48 percent, while the Latino, civilian labor force increased by nearly 56 percent. In New England, Massachusetts, and Boston the increases were even more remarkable. The New England Latino population grew by 87 percent and the Latino labor force by 123 percent. In Massachusetts the two Latino growth rates were 60 percent and 90 percent, respectively; and in Boston they were 61 percent and 93 percent, respectively. By contrast the black population and the black labor force in the United States grew by about 13 percent and 16 percent, respectively, and the white population and white labor force increased by about 6 percent and 11 percent, respectively. In New England, Massachusetts, and Boston the black and white populations and their labor force increases were even less than they were nationally.[1]

Thus, the national and regional work forces are "Latinoizing" at an even faster pace than the population itself, and the outcomes associated with these rapidly changing compositions of the labor forces are of critical importance both for Latinos themselves and the rest of the society as well. Labor-market policies will have to undergo significant alterations in the coming days in order to accommodate the influx of skills, perspectives, and needs of these new workers.

Earnings

Perhaps the most widely appreciated indicator of comparative economic well-being is earnings or income. Unfortunately, the data available to this study contained very little direct information on earnings during the period considered. What little information that does exist, however, suggests that Latinos in Boston fared worse than either blacks or whites. In a 1985 household survey conducted for the Boston Redevelopment Authority (1987) by the Center for Survey Research of the University of Massachusetts at Boston, the median 1984 household income reported for whites was $22,550; for blacks, it was $13,800; and for "other minorities," of whom Latinos comprised the significant proportion, it was $11,300. While 22 percent of the white and 36 percent of the black respondents had incomes of less than $10,000, some 44 percent of the "other minority" category had such incomes. And at the other end of the income scale, while 27 percent of whites and 14 percent of blacks had incomes in excess of $35,000, "other minorities" had only 10 percent of their income in that range.

Unemployment

Another easily accessible and quite important statistic that gauges labor-market performance is the unemployment rate. The unemployment rate measures the percentage of the civilian labor force that is without a job and seeking one. Table 1 gives comparative unemployment rates for Latinos, blacks, and whites in the Boston Primary Metropolitan Statistical Area (PMSA), the state of Massachusetts, the New England division, the Northeast region, and the nation.

Between 1983 and 1987, the unemployment rates for all three groups fell sharply, no doubt occasioned by the economic good times generated by the so-called "Massachusetts Miracle." In 1987, the year most analysts now mark as both the high and end points of the Miracle, the Latino unemployment rate in Boston at 4.7 percent, though quite low indeed, was nevertheless higher than both the black rate at 4.1 percent and the white rate at 2.8 percent. Over the next two years the Latino and black rates began a steady, somewhat brisk climb up to 1990. Then, during the short interval from the end of 1990 to March 1991, both rates skyrocketed, with the Latino rate more than doubling and the black rate nearly doubling.

By contrast, both the fall and rise in the white unemployment rate in Boston was much more muted. It appears that the consequences of the Miracle's demise did not actually hit whites until almost three years after the fact, while Latinos and blacks were put on notice almost immediately. The infamous "first-hired, last-fired syndrome" appeared to be operating once again in fine form.

As the data in table 1 attest, the sharp decrease-increase pattern, though not as pronounced as in Boston and Massachusetts, is repeated in New England and the Northeast and, to a lesser extent, in the nation at large. One notable difference in the Boston and Massachusetts unemployment rates is the fact that the Latino rates are generally higher in these two areas than they are in the other larger areas. In Boston, for example, in four of the six years shown in the table the Latino/white unemployment ratios were higher than the black/white ratios. On the other hand, the black/white ratios in the United States, the Northeast, and in four of the six New England years were greater than the Latino/white ratios.

DIMENSIONS OF UNEMPLOYMENT

Although the unemployment rate is usually expressed as a single number or percentage, it is actually made up of three separate dimensions. Calculating the actual number of unemployed is not just a matter of how many people are unemployed on any particular date; it is also a matter of how many people become unemployed at one time or another during the course of the year and how long the average persons stays unemployed. And even when the *same number* of people are determined to be unemployed by the census takers, they are not the *same people*. Some of those who were counted as unemployed in last month's survey will have found jobs by the time this month's survey is taken. Others will have become discouraged and dropped out of the labor force, and their places will have been taken by others who were laid off, or quit jobs, or left school to find work, or returned to the job market after having been out of it for some time.

The percentage of different individuals who become unemployed at some-time during a given period is termed the "incidence of unemployment." As will soon be shown, the annual incidence of unemployment is generally about three times greater than the unemployment rate itself. In 1987, for example, while an average of 5.3 percent of the Massachusetts Latino labor force was reported unemployed in the monthly survey, some 15 percent of the Latino labor force experienced unemployment at one time or another during the year.

Another important aspect of unemployment is its "frequency," or the number of spells of unemployment per unemployed person in a given period. Long periods of unemployment are not always the result of a single uninterrupted spell. For many, unemployment is a constantly recurring problem. Many individuals suffer a long duration of unemployment in the form of a succession of spells of alternating work and idleness. Nearly 30 percent of the workers in Massachusetts who became unemployed in 1987 reported at least two spells of unemployment during the year.

The third crucial dimension of unemployment is its "duration" or the average number of weeks a given spell of unemployment lasts. There is a substantial difference between the difficulties encountered by a worker who is laid off and called back to work after a week or two and those of a worker who remains out of work for six months or more. In Massachusetts, between 1983 and 1991, most spells of unemployment were less than 14 weeks in duration and the majority lasted less than five weeks.

It is to be expected that the length of a spell of unemployment will be affected by the business cycle, with longer spells occurring during downturns and shorter spells during upswings. This pattern was sustained as Latinos, blacks, and whites experienced a noticeable shift toward longer duration spells as the economies of Massachusetts and New England nose-dived after 1987. The shift for whites, however, did not become pronounced until 1990. This is in keeping with the observation made earlier that Latinos and blacks felt the brunt of the downturn much before whites did. After the relatively benign years of 1987 through 1989, the white average duration of unemployment increased sharply.

THE UNEMPLOYMENT CALCULUS

Some time ago Daniel Suits and Richard Morgenstern (1967) showed that incidence, frequency, and duration are mathematically related to the unemployment rate. During a year in which the monthly unemployment surveys report an average of one million people unemployed, the total number of people experiencing unemployment at one time or another during the year would also be one million only if each person stayed unemployed for the entire 52 weeks. On the other hand, if the average spell of unemployment lasted only one week, it would take 52 million spells spread over the year to make the surveys show an average of one million unemployed. Mathematically, the incidence of unemployment, N, the average number of spells per person, S, and the average number of weeks per spell, D, are related to the unemployment rate, U, such that:

(1) $U = (N \times S \times D)/52$

Thus, as table 2 shows, during 1988 when 20.9 percent of the entire Massachusetts Latino labor force experienced at least one bout of unemployment and when the average number of spells of unemployment was estimated at 1.75 per unemployed person,[2] and the average duration of a spell was 10.5 weeks, the Latino unemployment rate was:

(2) $U = (20.9 \times 1.75 \times 10.5)/52 = 7.385$, or 7.4

Nancy Barrett and Richard Morgenstern (1974) defined the product of incidence and frequency as the "turnover rate," or the flow rate of individuals into unemployment. It is the probability that a person will experience unemployment in a given period:

(3)   turnover rate = incidence x spells

Referring again to table 2, a Latino worker in Massachusetts had a 26 percent probability of being unemployed in the relatively good year of 1987; close to a 37 percent probability in 1988; and probabilities of 38.5 percent and 39 percent, respectively, in the relatively bad years of 1989 and 1990. The Massachusetts Latino turnover rates were greater in each year than those for either blacks or whites.

Despite the higher Latino than black unemployment incidence in all years and higher turnover rates in most, the Latino average duration of an unemployment spell was less than that of blacks and even lower than that of whites in some years, notably 1990. This somewhat counterintuitive result has been noted before in other studies (DeFreitas, 1985). One explanation might be the greater willing- ness (and need) of Latinos to take lower-paying, less desirable jobs than either blacks or whites — or in the parlance of labor economese, Latinos may have lower reservation wages.

As the above discussion suggests, the differences in unemployment rates among racial and ethnic groups may be the result of a larger number of different members of one group than another having a spell of unemployment that lasts for only a short time, or different groups having a relatively few members who remain unemployed for long stretches. And because the underlying problems of the former differ from those of the latter, labor-market policies designed to address the one problem will differ from those required for the other.

Several analysts have argued that the high turnover rates among Latinos and blacks are due to their concentration in the secondary labor market where the jobs and occupations require little or no skills and pay low wages (Piore, 1972; Gordon, 1972; Cain, 1975; Dickens and Long, 1985). Job satisfaction and, therefore, job attachments are low in this sector, and both employers and employees expect only a short-term relationship, with workers moving on in search of other opportunities, possibly in the primary sector. The benefits from working in the secondary sector do not greatly exceed the costs of being unemployed, and many individuals frequently shuttle between working and not working.

High Latino and black turnover rates may also be observed in the primary or high-wage sector of the labor market because, whatever the sector, Latinos and blacks typically suffer high layoff rates during periodic business downturns — the "first-fired, last-hired phenomenon" previously noted. These high turnover rates are also due to the unfavorable occupational distributions of Latinos and blacks discussed below. Even within relatively skilled occupational categories, Latinos and blacks are crowded at the lower ends of the categories in jobs that are more sensitive to changes in business activity. Labor-market policies aimed at promoting occupational advancement and intersectoral mobility, such as affirmative action, fair employment legislation, and job-skills training, must address this aspect of differential unemployment.

Differences among demographic groups in the duration of unemployment spells tend to reflect differential returns to job search activity for members of a given group. Some groups, white males for example, are more successful than others at finding jobs. They have better access to information about job markets, more extensive and influential contacts, and networks of employed relatives and friends who can bring them to the attention of a prospective employer. They also receive more favorable evaluation of their skills and potential productivity than do other groups. Policies aimed at improvements in employment and job placement services are recommended to solve this differential along with better labor-market information both for employers and Latino and black job seekers.

REASONS FOR UNEMPLOYMENT

There are four immediate causes for the occurrence of a spell of unemployment: (1) job loss, (2) job leaving, (3) new entry into the job market, and (4) reentry into the market. Job losers are persons who lost their jobs involuntarily or are on layoff. They account for the majority of the unemployed. Job losers in the primary labor market are most often adult, prime-age males with strong attachments to the labor force. Thus, their numbers are quite sensitive to the business cycle, rising during recession and falling during recovery. Job losers in the secondary labor market are mainly concentrated among the young, minorities and women, and the separations that occur are as much due to the unstable nature of employment in this sector as to the business cycle itself. Primary-sector job losers will most likely remain unemployed for longer periods than job losers in the secondary sector since the turnover rate in the latter generally exceeds that of the former.

Younger workers and women are most likely to be unemployed because of being first-time job seekers or reentrants to the market after a period of withdrawal. Reentrants are the second largest group of the unemployed, and their numbers are also sensitive to business conditions. Unlike job loss, however, reentry is expected to fall with recessions and rise with recoveries. Groups with particularly high rates of discouraged workers (those who have "dropped out" and are no longer looking for work because they do not believe they can or will find it) can be expected to have many reentrants among their unemployed since such workers are more apt to leave the labor force during recessionary periods and drift back during expansions.

It is not as easy predicting the behavior of new entrants during recession as it is during recovery. Their ranks might decrease in the downturn because of lack of job opportunities, or their ranks might increase if many are attempting to replace a job loser in the family by seeking work themselves. In such distress one might expect them to take whatever work that is available at whatever wage and thus to have short spells of unemployment.

As a rule, job leavers, those who quit or terminate their employment voluntarily, are the smallest of the categories. And as might be expected, their numbers decline during the fall off in business activity and increase when it picks up. They make up a significant portion of what is called the "frictionally unemployed," or workers who are between jobs — usually leaving a lower-paying job for a higher-paying job — or who are seasonal workers.

During the years between 1987 and 1990, a greater proportion of the Latino unemployed were job losers in Massachusetts and New England than were blacks or whites. And as the economy continued to sour the percentage of job losers grew unambiguously among Latino and whites, but not so clearly among blacks. Blacks had generally higher reentry rates than Latino and whites, and whites followed the expected behavior pattern of reentrants, declining as the economy turned down. In several cases Latinos and black reentrants appeared to have actually increased with the downturn.

The high rates of Latino job loss is in keeping with their high turnover rates noted in table 2. Since Latinos, even more than blacks, are disproportionately clustered in the secondary labor market, most of their job loss can be assumed to derive from the inhospitable conditions in that market. The increase in Latino job loss between 1987 and 1990, the post-Miracle period, was smaller than the white increase. This would seem to be consistent with the notion of the relative cyclical insensitivity of secondary market job loss rates.

In Massachusetts, New England, and the Northeast, blacks had a lower proportion of job losers among their unemployed than either Latinos or whites. A ready explanation for this finding is not available. The fact that blacks, like Latinos, have high turnover rates and are heavily represented in the secondary labor market, as well as concentrated in jobs in the primary sector that are most prone to layoff when recession begins, would predict job loss as somewhat more significant a contributor to black unemployment.

Another anomalous finding for blacks concerns the job leaving rates. It is to be expected that voluntary quits would diminish during bad economic times as people try to hang on to what they have already got, and there are fewer opportunities to do better. This pattern seems to have held for Latinos and whites, but not for blacks. Their job leaving rates appear to have increased as the economy worsened. Again no ready explanation for this finding is available.

Labor-Force Participation Rates

While unemployment statistics are solely measures of joblessness, labor-force participation rates subsume unemployment rates and measure the proportion of the labor force that is both employed and unemployed. Thus it is something of a proxy for labor-force attachment. Table 3 shows that Latino labor-force participation grew much faster than that of whites and blacks in New England, Massachusetts, and Boston — in fact, in the latter two labor markets, the black rates fell.

The data for Boston clearly indicate that the three groups had fairly diverse patterns of changes in their rates over the 1983 — 1990 period. The Latino rates climbed steeply; the white rates less steeply; and, as noted, the black rates fell. Between 1987 and 1988, the first post-Miracle year, the three groups' experiences were the most diverse. Latino rates declined, black rates held steady, and white rates rose.

Typically, adult workers, particularly men, have higher labor-force participation rates than do younger workers and women. Although their lower rates have to do with the lingering tradition of society's view of women as attached to the home (and society's myopic refusal to consider home work as part of the gross national product), changes are afoot. The labor-force participation rates of women have increased dramatically in recent years, pushed by the changing roles women are casting for themselves and pulled by the recent economic necessity for the two-paycheck family.

The labor-force participation rates for men, though, have either declined or remained flat of late. However, this was not the case for Latino men in New England, Massachusetts, or Boston. In all of these labor markets, the labor-force participation rates of Latino men increased significantly while those of black and white men have followed the national path of decline or stagnation. Even in the face of the severe fall off in the Boston and Massachusetts economies, the labor-force participation rates of Latino men continued to climb. Slowdowns in business activity presumably should lower participation rates as workers become discouraged in the face of dwindling job prospects. This did not happen with Latino men.

Table 1 showed that the unemployment rates for Latino men rose between 1987 and 1990, so one might conclude that most of the increase in their labor-force participation was absorbed into their unemployment rolls. This was not the case. Table 4 shows the employment/population ratio for Latinos, blacks, and whites. This ratio indicates the percentage of the civilian population — not labor force — who are employed. This ratio measures the probability of being employed, making it, in a sense, a superior statistic to either labor-force participation rates or unemployment rates. The latter two statistics, by ignoring discouraged workers, tend to understate the degree of labor-force attachment of a given group. The employment/population ratio gives a clearer, simpler picture of labor-market activity — you are either employed or not employed, period.

As can be seen in the table 4, the probability of being employed increased for Latino men between 1987 and 1990 in all areas. For Latinos in Boston the probabilities increased sharply between 1983 and 1987, fell as did the labor-force participation rates between 1987 and 1988, and then rose again sharply despite the downturn in the economy. The white probabilities rose slightly between 1983 and 1988, and then ever so slightly fell over the next two years. The black rates fluctuated between 1983 and 1989, and then fell precipitously the next year.

It would be quite useful to know precisely what types of jobs constituted the employment gains made by Latinos, especially Latino men who experienced relatively more gains than Latinas. Certainly, as will be soon revealed, many of them occurred in the low-wage service sector.

The most spectacular increases in labor-force participation rates took place among Latinas. Their rates increased by an average of 10-plus percentage points between 1983 and 1990. No doubt this is closely associated with the remarkable growth in the Latino population and labor force noted in table 1. Their employment/population ratios in Boston and Massachusetts, however, increased somewhat more modestly. Thus, relatively more of the Latina increased labor-force participation was absorbed into unemployment than occurred for their male counterparts.

Full-Time, Part-Time Status

A concept that has gained currency among labor-market analysts is that of "underemployment" or "subemployment." The underemployed as defined by researchers at the U.S. Commission on Civil Rights (1982) consist of workers with intermittent employment (employment occurring between frequent spells of unemployment); workers with marginal jobs (jobs with little prospects for advancement); the working poor (individuals who work steadily all year long but still have household incomes below the poverty level); overqualified workers (those whose education and skills are greater than the jobs they perform require); inequitably paid workers (victims of wage discrimination); and involuntary part-time workers (those who work part-time due to circumstances beyond their control and who would work full time if they could).

The only one of these groups we are able to observe clearly with the data at hand is the involuntary part-time workers. The overwhelming majority of Latino, black, and white employed workers worked full time. Latinos and blacks, however, appear to have had a greater proportion of full-time workers than whites, and, as expected, a generally greater proportion of involuntary part-timers. As the economy declined, so did the percentage of full-time workers decline and the percentage of involuntary part-time workers increased somewhat in most cases.

In 1990, the worse year of the decline, involuntary part-time percentages more than doubled among Latinos in Massachusetts, but fell significantly for Latinos in New England as a whole. This pattern also occurred to a somewhat lesser extent among blacks and whites. The percentage of the unemployed seeking full-time jobs increased among all three groups. This is also to be expected since those who lost full-time jobs would naturally seek to replace them.

There were proportionally more voluntary part-time white workers than either Latino or black, and generally more Latino voluntary part-timers than black.

Hours of Work

There is a large body of literature in labor economics on the significance of the determinants of and changes in hours of work. Indeed, the traditional labor supply curve is derived from a framework that has hours of work as the dependent variable and the hourly wage as the main independent variable. The undergirding theory models the choices made by workers between how much labor or hours of work to supply in response to, say, an increase in the wage and how much leisure to buy with the increased income resulting from the wage increase. Two opposing effects are assumed to attend the wage increase. One, called the "substitution effect," implies that when the wage goes up leisure becomes more expensive, and therefore workers tend to "buy" less of it by working more. The other effect, called the "income effect," implies one of two things. On the one hand, an increase in wage rates could cause the worker to work less since she or he has more income and is thus able to buy more of all goods including leisure. On the other hand, if leisure is considered by the worker to be an inferior good, she or he might not wish to buy very much of it and therefore work more.

The substitution effect is always positive and therefore can be counted on to increase hours of work when wages increase. The income effect is more ambiguous. It could either be negative and therefore decrease hours of work offered, or positive and thus increase work effort.

A great deal of research energy has gone into attempts to determine whether or not the income effect is negative, and if so how negative. The sensitivity of these effects to wage changes and, by extension, changes in business activity helps explain the difference in, say, men and women's labor-force participation. For women the substitution effect tends to be more positive than for men, and so they supply more hours of work than men for a commensurate wage increase. Women's income effects tend to be negative but smaller in absolute value than that of men, and thus their substitution effects exert more influence.

Minorities such as Latinos and blacks might also be assumed to be more responsive to wage increases than white males because of their generally lower incomes and wages. In order to enjoy the full utilization of the leisure at one's command, one must have a certain threshold level of income and/or wealth to go with it. White males typically have more such incomes than either Latinos or blacks. Therefore, it is not surprising that Latinos and blacks work on average as many, and in some instances more, hours than whites. And in all probability it is the increasing hours supplied by white women rather than white men that is buoying up the white averages.

Latinos and blacks had a greater percentage of their employed working 35 hours or more than whites and a smaller percentage working less than 35 hours. These data are in keeping with the full-time/part-time results discussed previously. Whites do have a greater proportion working over 40 hours than do Latinos or blacks, no doubt due to the fact that white males predominate in jobs that offer opportunities to work overtime.

Occupations

The first thing to note about the Latino and black occupational distributions are the large increases in the service occupations that took place between 1987 and 1990. In Boston in 1987, only 22 percent of Latinos worked in the lower-paying service occupations such as cleaning, food service, busboys, dishwashers, hospital orderlies, short-order cooks, guards, and watchmen. Nearly 18 percent worked in the higher-paying precision production, craft, and repair occupations, which included mechanics, carpenters, electricians, masons, painters, plasterers, plumbers, sheet metal workers, and heavy equipment operators. Another 17 percent worked in occupations that included machine operators, assemblers, welders, stationary firemen, garage workers, gas station attendants, meat cutters, butchers, laundry and dry cleaning operators, and wholesale and retail trade.

By 1990, only 8 percent of Latinos worked in the production and craft occupations and 7 percent worked in machine operators and assemblers occupations. By contrast 36 percent worked in service. This represented a most profound and rapid shift in the occupational fortunes of the Latino work force. While at the same time Latinos did experience some increases in white-collar occupations, the decline in blue-collar occupations and the rise in service occupations dominated the changes. Blacks also had increases in service occupations and declines in blue-collar jobs, but their changes were not nearly so far-reaching as those of Latinos. Thus, it is suspected that the increasing labor-force participation rates and employment/population ratios witnessed earlier landed Latinos for the most part in low-level service jobs.

These shifts in the Latino and black distributions were echoed in the Massachusetts data and to a lesser extent in the New England data. Whites also experienced some slight declines in blue-collar occupations, but most of these were offset not by increases in service occupations but rather increases in white-collar jobs.

Industry

The very broad industry categories given in the data used in this study do not cast much light on the relative situations of Latinos, blacks, and whites. The decrease in durable and nondurable goods manufacturing among Latinos was most probably associated with the declines in their blue-collar occupations referred to in the previous section. Latinos also experienced increases in service industries. However, service industries differ from service occupations. Service industries also include professional services, educational services, and medical services. These are performed mainly by white-collar professionals. This is why whites are heavily represented in the service industry, but not service occupations.

The major increase for Latinos was in wholesale and retail trade industries. These industries also differ from wholesale and retail trade occupations. The industry is populated by sales types, while the occupation is a blue-collar one. Trade as an industry is pursued through stores, warehouses, and other sales outlets.

Part of the demise of the boom times in Boston and Massachusetts resulted in the considerable downsizing of government. Such changes are reflected in the decrease in government employment among Latinos and blacks. Whites, however, were relatively unaffected, for as has been said before, the Massachusetts bubble burst for Latinos and blacks long before whites got the news.

Conclusion

This chapter has sketched in some of the features of the recent labor-market experiences and outcomes for Latinos in the Boston, the Massachusetts, and the New England labor market by comparing them with the corresponding situations of blacks and whites. The general picture that emerges from these investigations and comparisons is that of a rapidly growing population with even more rapidly increasing labor-force participation and attachment, who for one reason or another have been and are being routed into occupations and industries with relatively high levels of turnover rates and relatively low levels of pay and advancement.

On virtually every indicator of labor-market success considered in this research, it appears that Latinos do worse than whites, and in many cases fare worse than blacks. Latinos have lower earnings than either whites or blacks; higher unemployment rates than whites and about the same as blacks; greater numbers of workers who experience unemployment at one time or another than either whites or blacks; more frequent periods of unemployment than whites and about the same as blacks; a greater probability of being unemployed than either whites or blacks; more instances of job losses through firings and/or layoffs than either whites or blacks; a lower probability of being employed than whites though not always than blacks; more involuntary part-time employment than whites or, for the most part, blacks; and a greater proportion of individuals in relatively lower-paying service occupations and a smaller proportion in relatively higher-paying, white-collar occupations than either whites or blacks.

There appears to be many barriers in the labor markets of this region to the economic advancement and development of Latinos, and there is no doubt that Latinos suffer from much the same institutional and structural labor-market discrimination that has operated to retard the economic progress of blacks. The society in which these labor markets are embedded is a racially and ethnically conflicted one, and there is no reason to suppose that labor markets would be immune from the social virus. Latinos share with blacks the stereotypes of "lazy, present-oriented and undependable." Such myths do not easily succumb to either facts or reason, and so the independent growth in the Latino labor force observed here — even in the face of economic decline and the implied willingness and desire of Latinos to work even at low wages — cannot be expected by itself to put the stereotypes to rest. Government antidiscrimination and affirmative action policies will have to be firmly interposed.

Latinos, like blacks, also suffer from a lack of opportunity to obtain the same levels of educational and job-skills training as whites, and here again labor-market policies must be inaugurated to fill these needs.

Unlike blacks, however, Latinos are further penalized by the special biases of a willfully monolingual society. Many labor-market avenues are closed to or narrowed for Latinos because of this bias.

Another labor-market problem of profound and unforeseeable consequences is the fact that the rapid entry of Latinos into the New England, Massachusetts, and Boston labor markets is occurring at a time of great regional stagnation and decline and governmental retrenchment. All of this is taking place as the macroeconomy itself is undergoing a technological and structural transformation wherein the production processes are becoming more and more automated through the computerization and robotization of the means of production. The resulting flow of jobs created consists of a relatively few high-paid, highly technical positions at one end of the spectrum and a host of low-paid, service-oriented jobs at the other end. The great middle set of blue-collar jobs that once were the bedrock on which the dreams of prosperity of the American, mainly white, working class were based are fast disappearing.

At the same time that the work processes are changing and working-class jobs are shrinking, there is an enormous amount of work that needs to be done. The national and regional infrastructure of streets, roads, highways, bridges, waterways, and underground mains are in desperate need of repair and replacement. There are pressing needs for health care workers of all types, education and educational workers at all levels, and environmental clean-up projects of every kind. Both the work force and the work to be done are here; what is missing is the social and economic will and good sense to put them together.

What all of this portends for the Latino population and labor force is not at all clear. What is clear, however, is the fact that the region's labor forces along with the society itself are becoming more Latinoized, and the society's labor markets will have to adjust, or be made to adjust, to that fact.

Notes

1. See U.S. Department of Labor, Bureau of Labor Statistics, various years, Geographic Profile of Employment and Unemployment, Bulletins 2216, 2305, 2327, 2361, 2381, Washington, DC: Government Printing Office. These data and subsequent data used in this report are taken from this source unless otherwise specified.

2. The average number of spells of unemployment is estimated from data given in the Bureau of Labor Statistics, 1989, August, Handbook of Labor Statistics, No. 2340, Washington, DC: Government Printing Office, and other studies (see, e.g., Hamermesh, D., and Rees, A., 1988, The Economics of Work and Pay, New York: Harper and Row, Chapter 8). These calculations and sources indicate that the average number of spells for blacks nationally are approximately 1.75 and those for whites around 1.50. These estimates are used in the absence of data on New England, Massachusetts, or Boston.

References

Barrett, N., and Morgenstern, R. (1974). Why Do Blacks and Women Have High Unemployment Rates? Journal of Human Resources 4, 452-464.

Boston Redevelopment Authority. (1987, May). Boston at Mid-Decade: Results of the 1985 Household Survey — II Income and Poverty. Report No. 290, Table 3. Boston, MA: Author.

Cain, G. G. (1975, May). The Challenge of Dual and Radical Theories of Labor Market Segmentation. American Economic Review, 16-22.

DeFreitas, G. (1985). Ethnic Differentials in Unemployment among Hispanic Americans. In G. Borjas and M. Tienda (eds.), Hispanics in the U.S. Economy. New York: Academic Press.

Dickens, W. T., and Long, K. (1985, September). A Test of Dual Labor Market Theory. American Economic Review, 792-805.

Gordon, D. M. (1972). Theories of Poverty and Underemployment. Lexington, MA: D. C. Heath.

Piore, M. J. (1972). Notes for a Theory of Labor Market Stratification. Working Paper No. 95. Cambridge, MA: Massachusetts Institute of Technology.

Suits, D., and Morgenstern, R. (1967, Winter). Duration as a Dimension of Unemployment. Paper presented at the Econometric Society Annual Meetings, New York, NY.

United States Commission on Civil Rights. (1982, November). Unemployment and Underemployment among Blacks, Hispanics and Women. Clearinghouse Publication 74. Washington, DC: Government Printing Office.

Table 1

Unemployment Rates* for Latinos, Blacks, and Whites in Boston, Massachusetts, New England, the Northeast, and the Unites States (Persons 20 years and older)

Race/Ethnicity	1983	1987	1988	1989	1990	1991†
Boston						
Latinos	18.5	4.7	6.6	8.6	9.7	21.3
Blacks	13.6	4.1	6.5	9.3	11.2	20.2
Whites	6.1	2.8	2.9	3.3	5.5	7.9
Latino/White Ratio	3.03	1.68	2.28	2.61	1.76	2.70
Black/White Ratio	2.23	1.46	2.24	2.82	2.04	2.56
Massachusetts						
Latinos	17.3	5.3	7.4	8.5	8.3	20.5
Blacks	13.7	6.0	6.5	9.2	10.2	19.3
Whites	6.6	3.1	3.2	3.8	5.9	9.5
Latino/White Ratio	2.62	1.71	2.31	2.24	1.41	2.16
Black/White Ratio	2.08	1.94	2.03	2.42	1.73	2.03
New England						
Latinos	14.7	6.1	5.3	5.7	8.1	14.5
Blacks	14.7	6.7	5.5	9.3	10.4	13.8
Whites	6.5	3.2	3.0	3.6	5.5	8.3
Latino/White Ratio	2.26	1.91	1.77	1.58	1.47	1.75
Black/White Ratio	2.26	2.09	1.83	2.58	1.89	1.66
Northeast						
Latinos	13.5	7.5	6.1	7.3	7.9	11.2
Blacks	16.8	9.1	8.1	9.8	9.8	15.6
Whites	8.0	4.0	3.6	3.9	4.9	7.4
Latino/White Ratio	1.69	1.88	1.69	1.87	1.61	1.51
Black/White Ratio	2.10	2.28	2.25	2.51	2.00	2.11
United States						
Latinos	13.7	8.8	8.2	8.0	8.0	8.9
Blacks	19.5	13.0	11.7	11.4	11.3	16.2
Whites	8.4	5.3	4.7	4.5	4.7	6.2
Latino/White Ratio	1.63	1.66	1.74	1.78	1.70	1.44
Black/White Ratio	2.32	2.45	2.49	2.53	2.40	2.61

*With the exception of 1991, rates are annual averages.
†For Boston this figure is for July 1991; for all other areas this figure is for March 1991.
SOURCES: U.S. Department of Labor, Bureau of Labor Statistics (Various years). *Geographic Profile of Employment and Unemployment*, Bulletins 2216, 2305, 2327, 2361, 2381. Washington, DC: Government Printing Office; Unpublished geographic profile data for 1990 and 1991; U.S. Department of Labor, Bureau of Labor Statistics (Various dates). *Employment and Earnings*. Washington, DC: Government Printing Office.

Table 2

Dimensions of Unemployment among Latinos, Blacks, and Whites, in Massachusetts

Dimension	1987	1988	1989	1990
Latinos				
Unemployment rate	5.3	7.4	8.5	8.3
Incidence (%)	15.0	20.9	22.0	22.4
Frequency (spell)	1.75	1.75	1.75	1.75
Duration (weeks)	10.5	10.5	11.8	11.0
Turnover rate (%)	26.3	36.6	38.5	39.2
Blacks				
Unemployment rate	6.0	6.5	9.2	10.2
Incidence (%)	14.9	15.6	19.3	20.3
Frequency (spell)	1.75	1.75	1.75	1.75
Duration (weeks)	12.0	12.4	14.2	14.9
Turnover rate (%)	26.1	27.3	33.8	35.5
Whites				
Unemployment rate	3.1	3.2	3.8	5.9
Incidence (%)	9.3	11.1	12.7	14.4
Frequency (spell)	1.5	1.5	1.5	1.5
Duration (weeks)	11.6	10.0	10.4	14.2
Turnover rate (%)	14.0	16.7	19.1	21.6

SOURCES: Calculated from data in U.S. Department of Labor, Bureau of Labor Statistics. (1989). *Handbook of Labor Statistics*, Bulletin 2340. Washington, DC: Government Printing Office; and U.S. Department of Labor, Bureau of Labor Statistics. (Various years). *Geographic Profile of Employment and Unemployment*. Washington, DC: Government Printing Office.

Table 3

Labor-Force Participation Rates for Latinos, Blacks, and Whites, in Boston,
Massachusetts, New England, the Northeast, and the United States

Race/Ethnicity	1983	1987	1988	1989	1990
Boston					
Latinos	54.8	61.6	60.3	64.3	66.6
Blacks	67.1	60.9	60.8	65.2	60.9
Whites	65.2	68.5	70.0	70.1	71.1
Massachusetts					
Latinos	51.5	56.5	59.2	60.0	62.0
Blacks	67.3	62.1	62.7	64.9	63.9
Whites	66.6	67.5	68.7	69.1	68.9
New England					
Latinos	56.0	63.3	67.0	67.1	67.1
Blacks	66.1	69.2	68.8	70.4	70.9
Whites	66.3	68.5	68.8	69.3	69.6
Northeast					
Latinos	52.5	58.1	58.8	61.0	60.0
Blacks	58.5	60.3	61.7	63.2	62.3
Whites	62.2	64.2	64.4	65.1	65.5
United States					
Latinos	63.8	66.4	67.4	67.6	67.0
Blacks	61.5	63.8	63.8	64.2	63.3
Whites	64.3	65.8	66.2	66.7	66.8

SOURCES: U.S. Department of Labor, Bureau of Labor Statistics. (Various years).
Geographic Profile of Employment and Unemployment, Bulletins 2216, 2305, 2327, 2361,
2381. Washington, DC: Government Printing Office; Unpublished geographic profile data
for 1990 and 1991; U.S. Department of Labor, Bureau of Labor Statistics. (Various dates).
Employment and Earnings. Washington, DC: Government Printing Office.

Table 4

Employment/Population Ratios of Latinos, Blacks, and Whites, in Boston, Massachusetts, New England, the Northeast, and the United States

Race/Ethnicity	1983	1987	1988	1989	1990
Boston					
Latinos	49.5	58.8	56.3	61.3	61.5
Blacks	56.3	58.4	56.9	59.2	54.0
Whites	63.0	66.6	68.0	67.8	67.1
Massachusetts					
Latinos	42.6	53.5	54.8	54.8	56.8
Blacks	58.0	58.3	58.7	58.9	57.4
Whites	62.2	65.4	66.6	66.5	64.8
New England					
Latinos	47.8	59.4	63.4	63.3	61.6
Blacks	56.4	64.5	65.0	63.9	63.5
Whites	61.9	66.3	66.7	66.8	65.8
Northeast					
Latinos	45.5	53.7	55.2	56.6	55.3
Blacks	48.7	54.8	56.7	57.0	56.2
Whites	57.2	61.6	62.1	62.5	62.3
United State					
Latinos	55.1	60.5	61.9	62.2	61.6
Blacks	49.5	55.6	56.3	56.9	56.2
Whites	58.9	62.3	63.1	63.8	63.6

SOURCES: U.S. Department of Labor, Bureau of Labor Statistics. (Various years). *Geographic Profile of Employment and Unemployment*, Bulletins 2216, 2305, 2327, 2361, 2381. Washington, DC: Government Printing Office; Unpublished geographic profile data for 1990 and 1991; U.S. Department of Labor, Bureau of Labor Statistics. (Various dates). *Employment and Earnings*. Washington, DC: Government Printing Office.

Luis M. Falcón
Economic Growth and Increased Inequality: Hispanics in the Boston Labor Market

Introduction

The last two decades of economic activity in the state of Massachusetts present an interesting challenge to students of the Hispanic experience in the United States. Few area economies experienced as much change during the 1970s and 1980s as that of Massachusetts. What has been called the "Massachusetts Miracle" was an unprecedented period where the state's economy was characterized by fast-paced employment growth at rates higher than the national average. Between 1980 and 1987 Massachusetts was close to a full-employment situation, with the state's unemployment rate averaging about 2.4 percent below the national average (Sum, Fogg, and Fogg, 1989). During the same period, average annual wages for workers increased substantially. Per capita income for Massachusetts residents increased from 4.5 percent to 24 percent above the national average between 1979 and 1987 (Sum, Fogg, and Fogg, 1989). Given this context of fast-paced economic growth, near-full employment, and rising incomes, what has happened to the position of disadvantaged groups? It is commonly assumed that economic growth, measured by an increase in income levels and employment, benefits everyone. To paraphrase the question posed by a recent report by the Boston Foundation (1989b), "Were most boats lifted by the rising economic tide of the Massachusetts Miracle?"

A major factor behind the economic growth experienced by the Massachusetts economy was the acceleration of both growth and decline within its industrial sectors. This restructuring process has been long-term and shares some of the characteristics of restructuring at the national level. Over the period of two decades, the industry mix in Massachusetts evolved into a reduced manufacturing employment industry (high-tech and low-tech) coexisting with a burgeoning service industry (Harrison, 1984). In the Boston area, however, the rate of industry growth was not as dramatic as it was at the state level. In fact, many industry sectors that experienced a slight decline at the state level registered marked changes in the Boston area. The manufacturing sector, for example, declined by 9 percent at the state level during the 1965-1987 period, while it lost 50 percent of its jobs at the Suffolk County level.[1] A similar pattern was observed in the wholesale trade sector.

As these changes transformed Boston's job market, the characteristics of the city's employees also changed. Kasarda (1989) has estimated that, between 1970 and 1980, the city of Boston gained over 80,000 jobs where workers had at a minimum some college education. On the other hand, the number of jobs where workers had a high school level education or less declined by about 125,000 jobs. While there is no question that jobs were being created during this period, there seemed to be a growing divide between jobs considered desirable and those less desirable. This type of change in the distribution of jobs can affect the distribution of the employed by failing to create enough jobs in the growing sectors to compensate for those disappearing, by raising the standards required for employment to such a level that it disqualifies some groups at a higher rate than others, and finally, by lowering the benefits derived from employment (i.e., salaries, fringe benefits) to such a level as to encourage high turnover rates or discourage workers from seeking employment altogether.

In many areas of the United States the increase in service-sector employment has softened the impact of the decline in manufacturing employment. However, these two sectors are not equivalent in terms of salaries or benefits. Evidence at the national level (Costrell, 1988) suggests that the gap in earnings between expanding and shrinking industries was substantial, with an average wage of $9.93 in shrinking industries versus $7.70 in those expanding. Mishel and Frankel (1991) show that the gap in average income between shrinking and expanding industries widened to $7,040 during the 1981-1987 period. The gap in benefits between shrinking and expanding industries also widened to $3,365 during the same period. Stagnation in the manufacturing sector and inflation had also taken a toll on incomes. By 1990, average manufacturing sector wages (constant dollars) in Massachusetts were at a level lower than they were in 1983.

Given the characteristics of Boston's restructuring process, its impact has not been uniform across the population. Groups with low education levels, a large proportion of young workers, and workers with a traditional concentration in manufacturing have been disproportionately affected by these trends. At the national level, the percentage of Hispanic workers earning an annual income under the poverty line increased by 10.4 percent between 1979 and 1987 (Mishel and Frankel, 1991).[2] Blacks and whites, on the other hand, experienced increases of 6.7 percent and 5.0 percent respectively. These data suggest that the effects of restructuring are not necessarily applicable only to Hispanics and blacks. However, the demographic and contextual characteristics of Hispanics and blacks make them more susceptible to the impact of aggregate changes in the economy.

A recent article by Osterman (1991) raises the question of the benefits of full employment during the 1980s in the context of Boston's economy. While he argues that full employment benefited groups such as single individuals, apparently some subgroups did not share the economic growth. These subgroups include female-headed families, the low-educated, and children. Poverty rates for these three groups remained high or increased during the Massachusetts Miracle, suggesting that the effects of full employment may be specific to the group and its context. What has happened to the Hispanic labor force in Boston during this period of change, and how have the city's economic shifts related to socioeconomic conditions in general? These are the questions addressed by this chapter. The characteristics of Hispanic workers by the closing of the 1980s will be discussed in the context of the Massachusetts Miracle. Attention will be called to the most pressing problems faced by Hispanics in Boston and to potential policy implications.

Hispanics in Massachusetts

The Hispanic population in Massachusetts has increased at a very rapid pace during the last two decades. In 1970, when the U.S. Census enumerated a total of 66,146 Hispanics in the state, there was not a single city in Massachusetts with an Hispanic population of more than 20,000. By 1980, the Hispanic population in the state had grown to 141,043, for an increase of 113 percent. Between 1980 and 1990, the Hispanic population increased by 103.9 percent to 287,549. By 1990, there were three cities in the state — Boston, Lawrence, and Springfield — with an Hispanic population of at least 25,000. In the 1960s, the original Hispanic population in the state was largely of Puerto Rican origin. This new immigration, however, has diversified the Hispanic population and increased the presence of groups such as Dominicans, Salvadoreans, and Guatemalans (Rivera, 1991). Most of this diversification of the Hispanic population took place during the 1980s. Accordingly, most of the knowledge of the situation of Hispanics in Massachusetts and in Boston today is based on the experience of Puerto Ricans.

There is a vast literature that documents how distinctive the experience of Puerto Ricans is from that of other Hispanic groups. At the national level, Puerto Ricans are more likely to be living in poverty, to have lower rates of labor-force participation, and to have higher rates of female-headed households than other Hispanic groups. National trends suggest that these indicators have worsened during the last two decades (Falcón and Hirschman, 1992; DeFreitas, 1991). In Massachusetts, the pattern is similar to national trends, with indicators suggesting that Puerto Ricans have experienced a decline in socioeconomic status since 1970.

Indicators also suggest that during the period of the Massachusetts Miracle the experience of families within the two largest minority groups in the state of

Massachusetts — blacks and Hispanics — ranged from no change for blacks to a backslide for Hispanics (The Boston Foundation, 1989b). The family median income for blacks was 62 percent of that for whites in 1979. By 1987 it was 61 percent. In contrast, the median income for Hispanics was 49 percent of whites in 1979 and 25 percent in 1987 (Sum, Fogg, and Fogg, 1989). These figures suggest that the situation of Hispanics may have actually deteriorated rather than just not benefiting from the economic expansion. While average family-poverty rates in Massachusetts during the 1979-1988 period hovered around 7 percent to 8 percent, family-poverty rates for Hispanics stood at 50.6 percent in 1988. This was about twice the poverty rate for Hispanics at the national level (26.7 percent) for the same year (U.S. Bureau of the Census, 1989). Sum, Fogg, and Fogg estimated in a 1989 report that the number of Hispanic families living in poverty in Massachusetts increased by 22,400 between 1979 and 1987.

More recent data from the 1990 U.S. Census indicate that Hispanics experienced the largest increase in poverty among all groups in the state. Between 1980 and 1990, the number of people living in poverty among the total state population declined by 2 percent. For the white population in the state the number of poor declined by 16 percent. For blacks and Hispanics, however, the numbers increased by 22 percent and 89 percent respectively (see table 1). Of greater significance are the changes in the number of children living under the poverty level. While for the white population there was a large decline in the number of children living in poverty, blacks and Hispanics experienced a large increase in the number of poor children. This point calls attention to the concentration of Hispanic and black poverty among families with children.

The evidence suggests that the decline in socioeconomic indicators for Hispanics in the state of Massachusetts is a recent phenomenon and one that coincides with the period of the Massachusetts Miracle. In the analysis that follows the situation of Hispanics is offered in contrast to that of blacks and whites in the city of Boston, with emphasis on understanding how the position of Hispanics relates to ongoing changes in the economy, and in particular to the Massachusetts Miracle. In addition, differences among the distinct Hispanic subgroups are highlighted. Following this analysis is discussion of some of the implications of the trends examined and suggestions for policy intervention.

Data from Boston Survey

The data for the analysis part of this chapter are from the "Boston Survey" conducted by the Boston Foundation Persistent Poverty Project between November 1988 and April 1989 (The Boston Foundation, 1989a; 1989b). Its sample is drawn from the population aged 18- to 60-years-old in the city of Boston. Interviews were conducted by two different means: randomly dialed telephone contact and face-to-face interviews with a smaller subsample. The information collected in the survey is extensive. The samples were divided according to poverty status, defined as "above poverty" (those with incomes above 125 percent of the federal poverty standard) and the "near/below poverty" (those whose incomes fell near and below the 125 percent cutoff).[3] The data presented in the tables that follow have been weighted to account for nonresponse and to approximate the actual population distributions of the different racial/ ethnic groups.

Hispanics in Boston

Consistently, Hispanics exhibit lower levels of education than the other two groups in the survey, regardless of poverty status or gender of respondent. Table 2 presents the mean years of education for whites, blacks, and Hispanics. Since education is highly correlated with poverty status, it is not surprising that respondents above the poverty line exhibit higher levels of education than those near and below the poverty line. There is an interesting contrast within poverty categories. Among the groups above the poverty line, almost all exhibited an average of more than 12 years of education, while among those near and below the poverty line only white respondents had an average of more than 12 years of education. This information, taken in the context of the Boston economy, reflects the limitations faced by low-educated groups seeking employment that provides income above the poverty line.

These different educational profiles result in distinctive patterns of activity across racial and poverty lines. The main activity of the respondent during the week prior to the survey is presented in table 3 by poverty status. Hispanics above the poverty line present a similar proportion working to blacks and whites. When pooling together those working with those away from their job but employed (on vacation, leave, etc.), the gap between Hispanics and the other two groups widens somewhat. Together with blacks, Hispanics were more likely to be looking for a job (unemployed) than were whites. The groups near and below poverty present an interesting situation. About half of black and Hispanic respondents whose families lived near and below the poverty line were employed. This information is particularly important in the Hispanic case since this group has a lower educational profile than both blacks and whites.

When the figures for "Main Activity during the Previous Week" are disaggregated by the gender of the respondent (see table 4) the pattern remains consistent. Employment rates among Hispanics males living near and below the poverty line are quite similar to those of their black and white counterparts. Hispanic females, on the other hand, are slightly less likely to work than white and black females. Among the near and below poverty groups the differences are more dramatic. In general, near- and below-poverty blacks and Hispanics are more likely to be working than whites. About 70 percent of black and Hispanic males near and below poverty during the survey were employed. In contrast, only 44.6 percent of white males were working or away from their job. The high levels of disability among the near and below poverty groups (particularly among whites) is noteworthy. Table 5 summarizes the rate of labor-force participation for the different subgroups, excluding those disabled or attending school. The results are changed slightly. Again, above the poverty line there are no major differences between Hispanics and their black and white counterparts in terms of the proportion in the labor force. Hispanics living near and below the poverty line, however, continue to participate in the labor force at a higher rate than whites.

Industry and occupation distributions for Hispanics, whites, and blacks above the poverty line are presented in table 6. Hispanics exhibit a higher level of concentration in the industrial sector than do either blacks or whites. Two sectors — manufacturing and service — account for three-quarters of the Hispanic workers in the city. Hispanics above the poverty line do not remain as concentrated in lower-status occupations, but still predominate in these occupations when compared to whites. Hispanics are half as likely to be in professional jobs and almost three times more likely to be in service jobs than their white counterparts. A calculated index of dissimilarity in occupational distribution between Hispanics and whites indicates that 20 percent of either group would have to change jobs for their distributions to be similar. The corresponding information for the groups living near and below the poverty line can be found in table 7. The manufacturing, retail, and service sectors account for most of the poor Hispanic work force.

Nonpoor Hispanic workers work, on the average, about four hours less than their white counterparts (data not shown). The Hispanic nonpoor are also about 5 percent less likely to work a full week (40 hours or more) than the white nonpoor (74.7 percent versus 69.2 percent). The situation is reversed, however, when those living near and below the poverty line are examined. On the average, the Hispanic poor work about three more hours a week than do their white counterparts. Close to 70 percent of the Hispanic poor were working a full week compared to 52.6 percent and 47.6 percent of the black and white poor, respectively.

The Hispanic population of the city of Boston presents an occupational profile that reflects the changes in the city's economy over the last few years. While still concentrated in manufacturing, Hispanics have moved in large numbers into jobs in the service and retail sectors as manufacturing employment has declined. It can be concluded with some certainty that most Hispanics do not fall into the near- or below-poverty category due to lack of employment. As we have seen, this group presents labor-force-participation rates that are comparable to or higher than their white counterparts. In addition, the working Hispanic poor tend to work longer hours and are more likely to work a full week than their black and white counterparts. These data suggest that Hispanic poverty is rooted not in this group's degree of attachment to the labor market, but in the type of jobs they are able to find within Boston's labor market.

Characteristics of the Different Hispanic Groups in Boston

Is this emerging pattern common among the different Hispanic groups in the city? Tables 8, 9, and 10 present patterns of activity and occupational and industrial distributions for different Hispanic subgroups in Boston according to poverty status. These analyses focus on the three largest components of the Hispanic population in Boston: Puerto Ricans, Dominicans, and Central and South Americans.[4] Among the Hispanic groups living above the poverty line, the Central and South American group has the highest proportion working, followed by Puerto Ricans and Dominicans. Among the Hispanics living near and below poverty the differences are clearer. Central and South Americans exhibit a very high proportion employed. At the other extreme, 52.4 percent of Dominicans and only 24.9 percent of the Puerto Rican respondents were working at the time of the survey. It is also important to note the high proportion of this group who indicated they were disabled at the time of the survey — 18.7 percent of the Puerto Ricans and 11.6 percent of the Dominicans. Separate analyses of the data by gender categories were also done (results not shown). Among the poor for both males and females the percent working was much smaller for Puerto Ricans than for any other group. Among nonpoor Hispanics, Puerto Rican males and females were working at rates comparable to those of other Hispanic groups.

All three groups present a large concentration in the service sector, a pattern that is in agreement with economic trends. The data on Hispanics living near and below poverty are shown in table 10. The job distribution of this group is characterized by concentration not only in manufacturing and service sectors, but also in retail. All three groups have large proportions employed as clerical, operational, and service workers. This could potentially imply a concentration of part-time workers among the poor.

This contrast among Hispanic groups in Boston suggests that poor Puerto Ricans may be the most disadvantaged of all three groups since they have the smallest proportion actively employed and their poor population is more likely to be composed of female-headed families (data not shown). The employment situation of Dominicans is only slightly better than that of Puerto Ricans; and if we consider that within the Dominican group, some of those lacking employment may not have access to some types of public assistance due to lack of documentation, this group may be worse off. In general, the Hispanic poor and nonpoor are concentrated in the economic sectors experiencing growth within Boston's economy. However, a significant proportion of Hispanics, particularly Dominicans, remain in the manufacturing sector. Employment in the retail sector in particular seems to correlate highly with living near and below the poverty line.

Discussion

When compared to Hispanics living above the poverty line, Hispanics living near and below poverty are more likely to be employed as operatives or as service workers. We also find these two groups differ in the proportion employed in professional jobs, in the rate of participation in the labor force, and in their levels of education. In other aspects, however, Hispanics living above the poverty line look more like Hispanics living near and below poverty than they do their white or black counterparts. For example, tables 11 and 12 offer data revealing the form of payment the respondent receives (i.e., salaried or by the hour) and the size of the respondent's work place. Nonpoor Hispanics are less likely to receive payment on a fixed-salary basis than their black or white counterparts. More than half (63.2 percent) of all Hispanics living above the poverty line are paid by the hour, compared to 42.0 percent of whites and 56.7 percent of blacks. And regardless of poverty status, Hispanics are also more likely to be employed in a smaller work place — that is a work place of 25 workers or less — and are less likely to work in places of 100 or more workers.

These differences between Hispanic workers and other groups raise questions about the methods Hispanic workers use to find employment. In table 13 data are presented on how Hispanic respondents found their current or most recent job. Evidently, more traditional means of seeking employment, including advertisements and placement offices, are seldom used by Hispanics. Rather, this group is more likely to rely on friendships, acquaintances, or relatives to find a job. This job-seeking strategy is very different from that employed by blacks or whites, and its emphasis on social networks characterizes Hispanics living above, near, and below the poverty line.

Reliance on social networks as a job-seeking strategy is not surprising given the proportion of immigrants making up the Hispanic population. Factors like poor English-speaking ability or even discrimination may influence this different pattern among Hispanics. Inability to use or lack of access to more standard means of job seeking may force Hispanics to rely on their social network. This issue deserves further exploration given its importance to the economic survival of this population. Social networks composed of individuals with a high probability of living in poverty and of employment in low-status jobs are unlikely to have access to information on more dependable and desirable employment. For example, when respondents were asked if they had friends or relatives who worked at places they would like to work, only about one-third of Hispanics responded in the affirmative (data not shown). There is literature that documents how the use of these social networks to seek employment works to the advantage of the employer by allowing employers to control workers because of ethnic ties and to have access to a labor force that can be easily discharged or hired based on economic fluctuations (Grasmuck, 1984; Pessar, 1984). In addition, reliance on this social network contributes to the concentration of immigrants in ethnically segmented markets with occupations that offer few possibilities of advancement.

The rapid growth of the Hispanic population in Massachusetts and Boston during the last two decades raises questions as to the impact of this inflow on the decline in socioeconomic status of Massachusetts Hispanics as a group. The expansion of the Hispanic population becomes important when comparing data to black and white populations not affected by an immigrant component. Is it possible that the decline in socioeconomic status for Hispanics is due partly to the characteristics of this group's latest arrivals? If recent Hispanic arrivals are more likely to have skills or characteristics (e.g., lower education levels, single parenthood) associated with poverty, the deterioration in social position for Hispanics could result from migration selectivity. The "Boston Survey" asked respondents how many continuous years they had lived in Boston. Interestingly, these data show a similar proportion of recent arrivals among those near and below poverty and those above poverty. Almost two out of every five Hispanics had come to Boston within two years of the survey. More than half had lived in Boston for ten years or less and only a small proportion had lived in Boston all their lives. Nonpoor Hispanics who had lived in Boston less than one year were slightly less likely to be working than those residing in Boston for longer periods.

The length of residence in Boston was examined in relation to participation in the labor force. In general, recent arrivals showed a higher rate of participation than those residing in Boston for a longer period of time. This pattern was the same for the near and below poverty group and those above poverty. Labor-force participation declined with length of residence and the decline was larger for those near and below poverty. Respondents above the poverty line who had been in Boston for less than two years had a rate of participation of 99 percent, while those with more than 15 years of residence had a rate of 93 percent. Among those living near and below poverty, those who had lived in Boston for less than two years had a rate of participation of 83 percent, while those in Boston more than 15 years had a 45 percent rate of participation.

Length of residence in Boston was also examined in relation to having received government assistance (AFDC, Food Stamps, Medicaid). The proportion having received some assistance increased as length of residence increased.

Recent arrivals among the near and below poverty and among those above poverty were thus less likely to have received any kind of assistance than were long-term residents of Boston. This preliminary analysis does not suggest that recent arrivals to Boston contribute negatively to the prevalence of characteristics associated with poverty. More refined analysis that takes into account related factors such as age, education, and gender is needed to be conclusive.

Conclusions

A recent book by the National Research Council on Inner-City Poverty in the United States concludes the following: "In a persistently slack economy, workers with the fewest marketable skills and least education are the least likely to be employed. A lower unemployment rate would reduce the number of people in poverty." The analyses presented above suggest that this statement is not applicable to the situation of Hispanics in Massachusetts. Rather, a robust economy was the context within which Hispanics experienced their most dramatic increase in poverty rates, despite rates of labor-force participation almost as high as other groups.

The interface between the characteristics of Hispanic workers and the changing Massachusetts economy has led to the entrenchment of Hispanic workers into a limited set of occupations and industrial sectors. Many of these workers have entered these sectors by default, as the only areas where they can invest their limited marketable skills. Hispanics are more likely to be employed in smaller firms than blacks or whites. Hispanics are also more likely to be paid by the hour than their white or black counterparts. The issue of job-search strategies for Hispanics becomes important in light of findings that indicate a narrower set of job-search options being used by Hispanics compared to the other two groups. It is difficult to determine to what extent the use of informal networks to seek employment may be working to the disadvantage or limitation of Hispanic workers. Without the use of informal networks, some of these workers may lack the means of entry into the labor market. It is evident, however, that Hispanic workers seem to end up in work settings that are different from those of blacks and whites regardless of poverty status. Assisting Hispanics with job-search strategies so that they may expand their available options is clearly an area that is open to policy intervention and should be considered a priority.

High poverty rates among Hispanics are a direct result of the coincidence of a series of factors including a high proportion of female-headed households, a younger population, and lower educational attainment. The high poverty rate for this group is also a function of economic changes in Massachusetts that have disproportionately affected the employment options available to Hispanic families. In times of fast-paced economic growth, Hispanics have been increasingly marginalized by an economy that benefits the educated. An overall rise in the standard of living for the area has also affected the ability of the type of jobs held by Hispanics to provide decent living conditions. At the same time, the expansion of the service economy — with its polarized income structure — and the concomitant shrinking of manufacturing jobs has released a significant number of workers from the active labor force, while it has sent large numbers of Hispanics workers into low-paying jobs that cannot support living above the poverty line.

High poverty rates among Hispanics do not seem to be due only to the structural mismatch between job characteristics and Hispanic workers. Hispanics — with the exception of female heads-of-household — are able to find employment in the Boston economy. In fact, of nonworking Hispanic respondents asked for reasons for not being employed, only 2 percent to 3 percent reported lack of jobs (data not shown). The issue rather, is the nature of the jobs available to Hispanics; jobs that are likely to offer low pay, few fringe benefits, and limited mobility. The end result is that most Hispanic families, despite having working heads-of-household, spend most of their existence hovering around the poverty line.

The similarities found between the labor-market characteristics of Hispanics living above and those living near and below the poverty line suggest that there may be factors other than place of employment and job characteristics separating these groups along the poverty divide. Demographic differences between these two groups may also play a large role in Hispanic poverty. The poor Hispanic population, for instance, is largely composed of females. Of all poor Hispanic respondents in the "Boston Survey," 67.5 percent were female while only 46.8 percent of the Hispanic nonpoor were female. A predominance of females and/ or female-headed households among Hispanics living near and below the poverty line, and the predominance of male-headed households and/or single males among those living above the poverty line, underscores the interaction between income and household characteristics in determining poverty status. These differences between the poor and nonpoor need to be considered when determining strategies to address Hispanic poverty. It is a poverty primarily of women and, of course, children.

A significant number of Hispanic workers would fare poorly in almost any major metropolitan labor market in the United States. This is particularly the case with young, uneducated, and inexperienced workers. There is also a core of women whose condition — single mothers with young children — further limits the chances of them entering the labor market unless support services are provided to balance out the negative aspects of employment. Some of this author's research on Puerto Rican women in New York City (Falcón, Gurak and Powers, 1990) has shown that there is a core of women in this community who have never held a paying job and who are very unlikely to enter the labor force givcn thcir charactcristics and thosc of thc labor markct. In Boston, about 22 percent of poor Hispanic respondents had never held a paying job. In addition, the portion of the poor Hispanic population with high levels of disability and health problems are also unlikely to be able to engage in active labor.

With lower levels of labor-force participation than any other group, Hispanic females living under the poverty line deserve special consideration. As these analyses in this chapter did not control for age, marital status, and presence of children among Hispanic women, we cannot conclude to what extent these factors influence their absence from the labor force. However, results of the "Boston Survey" suggest that a very large number of the Hispanics living near and below the poverty line were families headed by females (data not shown). Almost 70 percent of the nonworking Hispanic poor indicated that they would like to be working. Of these, 63 percent gave taking care of a child as the primary reason for not being employed. Among poor blacks and whites less than 41 percent listed this reason for not working. Further identification of limitations faced by Hispanic female heads-of-household seeking entry into the labor force should be a high priority.

A final issue of critical importance to this discussion is determining the extent to which more recent arrivals to the Hispanic community experience poverty in relation to earlier arrivals. As a whole this issue of migration selectivity should be explored carefully not only because of its potential contribution to a rapid increase in poverty, but also because of its potential to elucidate areas for public-policy intervention focused on facilitating the settlement process for this population.

In conclusion, the economic growth period of the 1970s and 1980s did not benefit all sectors of the Massachusetts population. Hispanics, in particular, have suffered increases in poverty rates as a direct result of changes in job structure. Low average education levels and poor access to employment information appear to be key explanations for Hispanic poverty during this period, and female heads-of-households and recent immigrants deserve the greatest concern.

Notes

1. The city of Boston is the largest part of Suffolk County.
2. The individual poverty line of 1979 and 1987 was $3,400 and $5,500 respectively.
3. The Boston Foundation, and many city and state agencies, use 125 percent of the federal poverty standard to reflect the high cost of living in Boston.
4. The small sample size for Dominicans above the poverty line (24) precludes any conclusive statements about their characteristics.

References

Costrell, R. (1988). The Effect of Technical Progress on Productivity, Wages, and the Distribution of Employment: Theory and Postwar Experience in the U.S. In R. M. Cyert and D.C. Mowery (Eds.), *The Impact of Technological Change on Employment and Economic Growth.* Washington, DC: National Academy of Sciences.

DeFreitas, G. (1991). *Inequality at Work.* New York: Oxford.

Falcón, L. M. and Hirschman, C. (1992, February). Trends in Labor Market Position for Puerto Ricans on the Mainland: 1970-1987. *Hispanic Journal of Behavioral Sciences, 14*(1).

Falcón, L. M., Gurak, D. T. and Powers, M. G. (1990). Labor Force Participation of Puerto Rican Women in Greater New York City. *Sociology and Social Research, 74*(2).

Grasmuck, S. (1984). Immigration, Ethnic Stratification, and Native Working Class Discipline: Comparison of Documented and Undocumented Dominicans. *International Migration Review, 18.*

Harrison, B. (1984). Regional Restructuring and Good Business Climates: The Economic Transformation of New England Since WWII. In L. Sawers and W. K. Tabb (Eds.), *Sunbelt/Snowbelt.* New York: Oxford University Press.

Kasarda, J. D. (1989, January). Urban Industrial Transition and the Underclass. *The Annals of the American Academy of Political and Social Science, 501, 26-47.*

Mishel, L. and Frankel, D. M. (1991). *The State of Working America.* New York: M. E. Sharpe.

Osterman, P. (1991). Gains from Growth? The Impact of Full Employment on Poverty in Boston. In C. Jencks and P. E. Peterson (Eds.), *The Urban Underclass,* pp. 122-134. Washington, DC: The Brookings Institute.

Pessar, P. (1984). The Linkage between the Household and Workplace: Dominican Women in the U.S. *International Migration Review, 18.*

Rivera, R. (1991). *Latinos in Massachusetts and the 1990 Census: Growth and Geographical Distribution.* Working Paper Series. Boston: University of Massachusetts, Mauricio Gastón Institute for Latino Community Development and Public Policy.

Sum, A., Fogg, N. and Fogg, N. (1989). *Income and Employment Problems of Families in Boston's Low Income Neighborhoods: The Persistence of Family Poverty Amidst Increasing Affluence in Boston and Massachusetts.* Boston: Northeastern University, Center for Labor Market Studies.

The Boston Foundation. (1989a). *Boston Survey Final Field Report, Survey and Codebooks.* Boston: Author.

The Boston Foundation. (1989b). *In the Midst of Plenty: A Profile of Boston and Its Poor.* Boston: Author.

U.S. Bureau of the Census. (1989). *The Hispanic Population in the United States: March 1989.* Current Population Reports, Series P-20, No. 444. Washington, DC: U.S. Government Printing Office.

Table 1

Percentage of Change in the Number of Poor, by Race/Ethnicity, for Massachusetts between 1980 and 1990

Category	Total	Whites	Blacks	Hispanics
Total population	-2%	-16%	22%	89%
Under age 18	-9%	-28%	15%	29%

SOURCE: Adapted from *The Boston Globe,* Thursday June 11, 1992.

Table 2

Mean Years of Education of Respondents by Poverty Status and Gender, City of Boston, 1988-89

Category	Whites	Blacks	Hispanics
All respondents			
Nonpoor families	14.4	13.1	12.0
Near and below poverty-line families	12.6	11.2	9.5
Male respondents			
Nonpoor families	14.3	12.9	11.6
Near and below poverty-line families	12.5	11.1	9.2
Female respondents			
Nonpoor families	14.6	13.3	12.4
Near and below poverty-line families	12.6	11.2	9.6
N=	941	549	624

SOURCE: The Boston Foundation. (1989a). *Boston Survey Final Field Report, Survey and Codebooks.* Boston: Author.

Table 3

Main Activity of Respondents during the Previous Week, by Poverty Status and Race/Ethnicity, City of Boston, 1988-89 (percent)

Activity	Whites	Blacks	Hispanics
Above Poverty			
Working	80.2	82.8	80.1
Away from job	9.6	6.8	4.7
Looking	2.5	4.3	5.2
Disabled	1.9	0.3	2.0
Keeping house	5.2	2.4	5.2
School	0.3	3.5	2.8
Retired	0.2	0.0	0.0
Other	0.1	0.0	1.0
N=	644	177	251
Near and Below Poverty			
Working	25.4	51.7	51.4
Away from job	1.4	3.2	3.2
Looking for job	8.4	8.6	5.2
Disabled	14.9	11.0	11.2
Keeping house	25.6	18.2	25.0
School	23.3	7.3	4.0
Retired	0.5	0.0	0.0
Other	0.3	0.0	1.0
N=	297	372	373

SOURCE: The Boston Foundation. (1989a). *Boston Survey Final Field Report, Survey and Codebooks.* Boston: Author.

Table 4

Main Activity of Respondents during the Previous Week by Gender, Poverty
Status, and Race/Ethnicity, City of Boston, 1988-89

Activity	Males			Females		
	Whites	Blacks	Hispanics	Whites	Blacks	Hispanics
Above Poverty						
Working	82.8%	82.6%	80.7%	77.8%	82.3%	79.1%
Away from job	8.8	9.8	7.1	10.3	4.2	2.2
Looking	3.5	6.0	6.4	1.5	2.8	4.0
Disabled	3.9	0.6	2.3	10.1	4.7	1.7
Keeping house	0.6	0.9	1.4	0.0	6.1	9.3
School	0.4	0.0	2.1	0.0	0.0	3.6
n =	313	79	127	330	96	121
Near and Below Poverty						
Working	42.5%	71.0%	69.8%	20.5%	44.2%	36.7%
Away from job	2.1	0.5	4.4	1.2	4.2	2.4
Looking	25.0	9.5	10.6	3.6	8.3	1.3
Disabled	23.6	10.5	11.6	12.5	11.1	11.3
Keeping house	3.8	6.1	1.5	31.9	23.0	43.4
School	2.0	2.6	2.2	29.4	9.1	4.9
n =	87	79	90	210	293	278

SOURCES: The Boston Foundation. (1989a). *Boston Survey Final Field Report, Survey
and Codebooks.* Boston: **Author.**

Table 5

*Percentage of Respondents in Labor Force by Poverty Status, Gender, and Race/
Ethnicity, City of Boston, 1988-89*

Category	Whites	Blacks	Hispanics
All respondents			
Nonpoor families	94.7%	97.6%	94.5%
Near and below poverty-			
line families	57.9	77.7	70.5
Male respondents			
Nonpoor families	100.0	100.0	98.5
Near and below poverty-			
line families	94.5	93.0	98.3
Female respondents			
Nonpoor families	89.9	95.0	90.0
Near and below poverty-			
line families	44.4	71.2	48.2
n =	827	460	515

SOURCE: The Boston Foundation. (1989a). *Boston Survey Final Field Report, Survey and
Codebooks*. Boston: Author.

Table 6

Industry and Occupation Distribution of Employed Respondents Who Are above
Poverty by Race/Ethnicity, City of Boston, 1988-89 (percent)

Distribution	Whites	Blacks	Hispanics
Industry			
Extractive	0.3	0.0	0.0
Construction	7.3	3.0	1.0
Manufacturing	8.6	8.6	14.2
Transportation	10.1	8.6	5.0
Wholesale trade	0.5	0.6	0.4
Retail trade	11.0	10.4	12.6
Fire	10.0	18.3	7.3
Service	52.0	50.1	59.5
Occupation			
Professional	30.5	15.2	15.3
Semiprofessional/technical	3.1	2.8	4.4
Managerial	13.6	10.9	11.8
Clerical	20.8	29.0	17.6
Sales	8.0	2.7	2.6
Crafts	8.9	3.4	6.5
Operational	2.8	11.7	13.0
Service	10.4	23.2	27.2
Labor	1.8	1.1	1.7
Farm labor	0.0	0.0	0.0
n =	622	171	235

SOURCE: The Boston Foundation. (1989a). *Boston Survey Final Field Report, Survey and
Codebooks.* Boston: Author.

Table 7

Industry and Occupation Distributions of Employed Respondents Who Are near and below Poverty by Race/Ethnicity, City of Boston, 1988-89 (percent)

Distribution	Whites	Blacks	Hispanics
Industry			
Extractive	0.0	0.1	0.0
Construction	8.1	0.8	1.2
Manufacturing	4.6	12.0	15.3
Transportation	7.0	2.0	1.4
Wholesale trade	1.8	0.7	2.3
Retail trade	34.0	9.8	31.3
Fire	2.9	5.4	14.9
Service	41.5	69.1	33.7
Occupation			
Professional	6.8	5.6	3.7
Semiprofessional/technical	0.9	7.0	0.9
Managerial	0.9	0.4	0.3
Clerical	36.9	17.3	35.8
Sales	3.9	0.9	0.3
Crafts	9.7	4.3	2.8
Operational	3.4	15.2	16.7
Service	34.6	46.3	31.3
Labor	3.0	2.4	8.1
Farm labor	0.0	0.3	0.0
n =	235	327	264

SOURCE: The Boston Foundation. (1989a). *Boston Survey Final Field Report, Survey and Codebooks*. Boston: Author.

Table 8

Main Activity of Respondents during the Previous Week by Hispanic Group and
Poverty Status, City of Boston, 1988-89 (percent)

Activity	Puerto Rico	Dominican Republic	Central/ South American
Above Poverty			
Working	77.7	76.6	83.3
Away from job	5.9	3.3	3.8
Looking	4.2	8.4	5.4
Disabled	3.7	1.6	0.4
Keeping house	7.7	6.8	2.4
School	0.8	3.3	4.8
n =	113	26	112
Near and Below Poverty			
Working	24.9	52.4	81.5
Away from job	5.2	0.0	2.0
Looking	7.5	4.2	3.0
Disabled	18.7	11.6	2.2
Keeping house	40.6	26.6	6.5
School	3.0	5.1	4.8
n =	219	73	76

SOURCE: The Boston Foundation. (1989a). *Boston Survey Final Field Report, Survey and Codebooks*. Boston: Author.

Table 9

Industry and Occupational Distributions of Employed Respondents Who Are above Poverty by Hispanic Groups, City of Boston, 1988-89 (percent)

Activity	Puerto Rico	Dominican Republic	Central/ South American
Industry			
Extractive	0.0	0.0	0.0
Construction	0.9	0.0	1.3
Manufacturing	12.1	17.0	15.6
Transportation	4.9	0.0	6.1
Wholesale trade	0.9	0.0	0.0
Retail trade	10.1	12.8	14.9
Fire	6.3	8.5	8.1
Service	64.7	61.7	54.0
Occupation			
Professional	17.3	4.3	15.6
Semiprofessional/technical	4.7	0.0	5.0
Managerial	12.5	21.3	9.1
Clerical	17.9	4.2	20.1
Sales	1.0	0.0	4.7
Crafts	8.5	0.0	6.0
Operational	15.4	21.3	8.9
Service	20.0	48.9	29.6
Labor	2.8	0.0	0.9
Farm labor	0.0	0.0	0.0
n =	104	24	107

SOURCE: The Boston Foundation. (1989a). *Boston Survey Final Field Report, Survey and Codebooks*. Boston: Author.

Table 10

Industry and Occupational Distributions of Employed Respondents Who Are near and below Poverty by Hispanic Groups, City of Boston, 1988-89 (percent)

Activity	Puerto Rico	Dominican Republic	Central/ South American
Industry			
Extractive	0.0	0.0	0.0
Construction	1.0	0.0	1.5
Manufacturing	28.7	10.7	8.6
Transportation	4.8	0.0	0.3
Wholesale trade	9.3	0.0	0.0
Retail trade	14.0	14.0	43.3
Fire	6.2	0.0	22.6
Service	36.0	75.4	23.8
Occupation			
Professional	8.0	4.3	1.9
Semiprofessional/technical	2.4	0.0	0.5
Managerial	1.0	0.0	0.0
Clerical	20.7	9.4	49.8
Sales	0.0	2.0	0.0
Crafts	6.0	6.0	0.8
Operational	33.0	8.2	9.6
Service	24.9	70.0	25.3
Labor	3.9	0.0	12.1
Farm labor	0.0	0.0	0.0
n =	136	58	66

SOURCE: The Boston Foundation. (1989a). *Boston Survey Final Field Report, Survey and Codebooks*. Boston: Author.

Table 11

Percentage of Respondents Who Are Salaried, Hourly, or Other by Race/ Ethnicity, City of Boston, 1988-89

Response	Above Poverty			Near and Below Poverty		
	Whites	Blacks	Hispanics	Whites	Blacks	Hispanics
Salaried	48.3	36.8	24.0	20.4	15.4	13.6
Hourly	42.0	56.7	63.2	69.7	73.2	81. 5
Other	9.7	6.5	12.8	10.0	11.5	5. 0

SOURCE: The Boston Foundation. (1989a). *Boston Survey Final Field Report, Survey and Codebooks*. Boston: Author.

Table 12

Percentage of Workers by Size of Work Place, Poverty Status, and Race/
Ethnicity, City of Boston, 1988-89

Response	Above Poverty			Near and Below Poverty		
	Whites	Blacks	Hispanics	Whites	Blacks	Hispanics
10 or fewer	23.4	24.5	30.7	31.6	38.8	42.9
11 to 25	16.9	20.2	16.3	26.0	17.3	15.3
26 to 50	13.3	9.3	13.8	9.9	11.3	20.7
51 to 100	9.7	8.0	11.6	10.5	6.0	7.1
101 to 500	19.8	21.0	17.0	13.0	18.1	12.6
More than 500	16.9	17.1	10.7	9.0	8.5	1.3

SOURCE: The Boston Foundation. (1989a). *Boston Survey Final Field Report, Survey and Codebooks*. Boston: Author.

Table 13

How Respondents Found Out about Their Current/Last Job by Poverty Status, and Race/Ethnicity, City of Boston, 1988-89 (percent)

Response	Above Poverty			Near and Below Poverty		
	Whites	Blacks	Hispanics	Whites	Blacks	Hispanics
Advertise-ment	21.8	20.5	12.9	28.4	16.4	4.4
Public employ. serv.	3.9	1.7	3.5	2.0	1.4	2.5
Job training program	0.7	1.3	2.9	1.7	1.7	0.4
Walked in from street	10.0	12.5	5.3	13.6	9.4	12.5
School place. office	7.0	8.2	6.6	8.2	3.3	12. 6
Private employ. ag.	4.3	10.0	5.8	1.4	2.5	0.9
Friend/acqu-aint./relative	40.0	39.8	55.9	42.6	63.3	65.0
Prev. working at place	5.6	2.8	3.0	5.0	1.5	0.7
Self-employed	6.0	3.3	4.1	1.6	0.4	1.0

SOURCE: The Boston Foundation. (1989a). *Boston Survey Final Field Report, Survey and Codebooks*. Boston: Author.

Ramón Borges-Méndez
The Use of Latino Immigrant Labor in Massachusetts Manufacturing: Evidence from Lowell, Lawrence, and Holyoke

Introduction

Latino immigrants in Massachusetts manufacturing have been a main source of tractable labor in secondary, unskilled, low-paying jobs at the bottom of the occupational ladder.[1] However, evolving changes in the structure, labor processes, and human-resource management practices of large corporations and smaller firms are transforming this rather uniform pattern. These changes, which have been induced by the strategies and practices of managers and firms coping with the economic volatility and overall decline that has characterized manufacturing in Massachusetts over the last few years, are diversifying the use of Latino labor within the sector. This chapter uses evidence from the manufacturing sectors of Lowell, Lawrence, and Holyoke to demonstrate how Latinos, while largely a source of tractable labor to the sector, have seen their employment opportunities dramatically changed by competitive and firm-based dynamics.[2] These cities were selected because of the relatively large concentration of Latinos in their population, the relatively large number of Latinos employed by their manufacturing firms, and their contrasting trajectory of local economic redevelopment. During the 1960-1990 period, the economic restructuring of the state's industrial base induced contrasting outcomes of economic redevelopment in these cities.

Between the 1840s and 1920s, Western European, Southern European, Eastern European, and French-Canadian immigrants were an important source of unskilled, cheap, flexible, and tractable labor in the development and restructuring[3] of Massachusetts' industries (such as textiles, shoes, paper, and leather). This influx of immigrants decreased drastically between the mid-1920s and the early 1970s due to a combination of restrictionist immigration policies and the successive waves of deindustrialization that repeatedly weakened the state's manufacturing base after the 1920s. A relatively small number of immigrants came to Massachusetts during this period (Blewett, 1990; Cole, 1963; Cumbler, 1990; Gitelman, 1974; Goldberg, 1989; Hartford, 1990; Keyssar, 1986; Mitchell, 1988; Tager and Ifkovic, 1985).

During the early 1970s, immigration began to increase once again, mainly from Latin America (Puerto Rico, Dominican Republic). The wave of Latino immigration was encouraged in part by the need of basic manufacturers (textiles, shoes, paper, leather, and some menial assembly operations) to find sources of cheap labor to slow their decline and to assure their limited survival through drastic restructuring (Glaessel-Brown, 1990; Piore, 1973). After World War II, the decline of the region's manufacturing set the stage for a period of drastic economic restructuring during which basic manufacturing continued its decline accompanied by high-tech reindustrialization, the modernization of some basic manufacturing, and a strong expansion of the service industries (Harrison, 1984; Harrison and Kluver, 1989). In certain subregions of the state, the use of Latinos in the sector became a "match" for the decline, survival, and restructuring of manufacturing. How have Latinos fared from this matching, and what kind of employment opportunities has this industrial change offered Latinos?

The number of manufacturing jobs remained relatively stable in Lowell due to high-tech reindustrialization. During the last 20 years, Lowell's manufacturing has redeveloped and restructured around the creation and maturation of a corporate core composed of high-tech, Fortune 500, multinational corporations whose origins in the region date back to the 1950s and 1960s. Many of these corporations, often headquartered in Massachusetts and New England, have several plant divisions in the area, employing about 400 workers per plant, and use a vast net of subcontractors to purchase components, materials, and services.

Increasingly during 1980s, these corporations combated market volatility and heavy competition through the globalization of markets, rapid product and service diversification, technological innovation and modernization, the outsourcing of many production and service functions (vertical disintegration), and the mixing of various human-resource strategies. Managers of these corporations emphasized a general tendency to replace conventional mass production technology and production-line methods of organization with programmable/flexible machinery to facilitate customization in design and production and "just-in-time" systems for the faster and easier handling of production materials. At the same time they implemented drastic changes in human-resource-management practices. In general, human-resource-management practices tend to emphasize a culture of job stability, independence, and long-term job development in certain skilled positions and occupational categories covered by union contracts, while encouraging an "employment-at-will" atmosphere for nonunion, unskilled and semiskilled, low-paying positions. Such an atmosphere seeks to encourage personnel flexibility through the employment of a footloose labor force that can be easily hired, fired, or redeployed to meet labor- and product-market volatility.

By contrast, during the same period the restructuring of Lawrence and Holyoke's manufacturing left the manufacturing sector practically unchanged due to the relative lack of industrial redevelopment. Manufacturing in these two cities largely remains a labor-intensive sector affected by continuous decline composed mainly of small and midsize firms employing between 75 and 500 employees. Most firms in Lawrence and Holyoke are owned by local (often family-based) private interests or are plant divisions of some relatively small corporations with limited operations in the Northeast, Puerto Rico, and other regions in the United States. They produce both final and intermediate durable and nondurable goods (textiles and fabrics, shoes, computer components, food and kindred products, toys, paper and paper-related products) for consumer markets, other basic manufacturers, and some high-tech industries. In Holyoke, paper production and converting and paper-related industries that produce office and school supplies still dominate the city's manufacturing activity.

Surviving labor-intensive firms in both cities met the volatility of the period (and have sought to reduce costs) by increasing the use of cheaper and more tractable sources of labor and by investing little or no capital in technological modernization. This trend has intensified even further in the context of the current decline of the sector. These firms have not retooled within the last 10 to 15 years, have done "piecemeal" modernization that has created a small number of unskilled and semiskilled jobs, or have cut payroll in very specific production departments of the firms.

But between Lowell's large high-tech corporations and Lawrence and Holyoke's labor-intensive firms, a third group of small and midsize manufacturing firms have managed to survive. These firms have become stable and profitable enterprises through a combination substantial technological modernization and human-resource experimentation. Within this group of firms exist both old and new, labor-intensive and modernizing enterprises. These firms are either locally-owned, private firms or branches of relatively small, privately-owned, regional/national corporations. On average, each employs between 100 and 300 people per plant and grosses about $50 million or less in annual sales. They produce a combination of nondurable and durable manufacturing goods (textiles and fabrics, plastics and adhesives, printed paper goods and office stationary). In Lowell, some of these firms often serve as subcontractors to larger high-tech corporations.

Some of Lowell's labor-intensive firms, unlike those in Lawrence and Holyoke, have transformed their human-resource practices to encourage job and skill development while engaging in relatively minimal technological innovation. As in more traditional labor-intensive firms in Lawrence and Holyoke, these labor-intensive firms in Lowell continue to use old technologies and conventional assembly-line techniques of production. However, against conventional wisdom, they are saving on labor costs by discouraging high labor-turnover rates, the fragmentation of labor tasks, the creation of unskilled jobs, and the hiring of a footloose labor force. More specifically, these firms are strengthening job development and stability in the lower and middle categories of the occupational ladder. They have achieved this by expanding the internal and extra-firm educational opportunities available to workers and increasing workers' independence and responsibilities in the work place. Also, in Lowell and Holyoke a share of small, modernizing firms have engaged in both substantial technological innovation and human-resource development. In these firms, the employment of new technologies and methods of production such as "just-in-time" systems, flexible, computer-aided machinery, and teamwork have been accompanied by the development of the basic and critical-thinking skills of workers at the bottom and middle of the occupational ladder. The use of those new technologies demands better numeric, organizational, and expression skills as workers are often required to time the ordering of working materials, self-schedule production runs, adapt machinery for customized orders, perform on-the-spot quality control, and file periodic performance reports. Intensive in-house (and extra-firm) training and basic skills (reading, writing, and math), English-as-second language (ESL), general educational development (GED), and college education courses paid by the firm are a common feature of the employment relationship.

The experience of industrial change in the manufacturing of these small cities suggest three distinct patterns in the use of Latino immigrants, each associated with significantly different labor-market outcomes in terms of occupational concentration, wages, opportunity to handle new technologies, training and advancement opportunities, and the command of higher job responsibilities and independence. First, Latinos are marginally used in large, high-tech corporations to staff jobs downgraded by the technological and organizational modernization of production. Basically, very few Latinos entered high-tech manufacturing throughout the period of reindustrialization, and those employed are concentrated in low-level, low-skilled, low-paying occupational categories with little opportunity for training, advancement, and job development. Second, Latinos are heavily used in labor-intensive, small and midsize manufacturing firms to staff unskilled and semiskilled jobs that pay low wages and offer little prospect for wage increases, training, advancement, and job development. Third, Latinos are moderately used by some labor-intensive firms and by modernizing small and midsize manufacturing firms to staff jobs within their entire occupational structure. In this third situation Latinos command relatively better wages than in the first two and confronted relatively better prospects for training, advancement, and job development. The first and third situation predominate in Lowell; the second pattern is prevalent in Lawrence; and in Holyoke the second and third situations are more apparent.

In the first part of this chapter, some of the general changes taking place in the structure, labor processes, and human-resource practices of the manufacturing sector are discussed, and their implications for the use of immigrant labor are drawn. In the second part, the factors affecting the use of Latino labor in the manufacturing of the cities of Lowell, Lawrence, and Holyoke are analyzed in greater depth. The summary offers some conclusions and relevant policy implications of this research.

The Changing Face of Manufacturing and The Use of Immigrant Labor

Between the late 1940s and late 1960s, the American industrial structure appeared divided into a core sector of capital-intensive, monopolistic corporations and a peripheral sector of labor-intensive, smaller and flexible firms. In these two sectors jobs were qualitatively different, and the presumed open competitiveness of the labor market was severely curtailed. This industrial and labor-market dualism resulted from a combination of the differences in the technological development of firms, the strategies used by corporations and managers to avoid class solidarity among workers, the institutionalization of labor-market regulation, and the sociohistorical conditions that governed the insertion of certain racial/ethnic groups into the social division of labor (Berger and Piore, 1980; Blauner, 1972; Doeringer and Piore, 1971; Edwards, Gordon, and Reich, 1982).

Since the early 1970s, however, the globalization of the American economy, falling profit rates, technological changes, the incremental erosion of the dominant economic position of the country, and significant shifts in the demographic composition of domestic labor supplies have all combined to modify the strategies adopted by both core corporations and peripheral firms in overcoming market volatility and economic change (Bluestone and Harrison, 1982; Sabel and Piore, 1984). In manufacturing in particular, these newer corporate strategies and employment practices have partially changed the morphology of post-World War II industrial dualism. For instance, corporations and firms in the core sector have adopted economic strategies and employment practices often reserved for peripheral firms, and vice-versa; employment security in some core firms is no longer encouraged at certain levels of the occupational ladder while peripheral firms are encouraging job development and employment stability (Doeringer, et al., 1991). In this context, the use of immigrant labor seems less characterized by the strong industrial dualism of the immediate post-World War II era and more by the particular characteristics and the prerogatives of the restructuring of both core corporations and peripheral firms (Piore, 1986). Immigrant labor remains largely employed in the peripheral sector yet increasingly plays a strategic role in a broad range of corporations and firms facing diverse conditions of growth, decline, and adaptation.

Structurally, corporations have became less vertically integrated and more geographically mobile, sometimes dismantling large parts of their United States operations in old industrial areas and moving them to other "green" areas in the United States or abroad. This restructuring has contributed to depressing regional and local labor markets that had depended heavily on manufacturing and that historically have shown high concentrations of immigrants, and it has degraded job opportunities at the bottom of the occupational ladder (Bluestone and Harrison, 1982; Noyelle and Stanback, 1983; Sabel and Piore, 1984; Scott and Storper, 1986; Sassen, 1988, 1991; Waldinger and Bailey, 1991). Vertical disintegration and technological modernization has reduced potential employment opportunities for immigrants in core firms while increasing their use in peripheral subcontracting firms and independent producers that supply larger firms. For example, immigrant (Mexican) female labor in the southwest of the United States, traditionally concentrated in basic manufacturing and agriculture, is being used by electronic firms that are subcontractors to major electric appliance and computer hardware corporations (Fernandez-Kelly, 1983). In New York City, decaying garment-manufacturing sectors have revived due to the entrepreneurial activity of immigrants (Asian and Latino), hiring other immigrants and subcontracting for large clothing and apparel producers (Waldinger, 1986). In sum, deindustrialization, corporate vertical disintegration, and capital mobility seem to be creating contrasting and diverse trends in the use immigrant labor within the manufacturing sector due to the restructuring of the relationship between core and peripheral firms.

Equally important in the transformation of post-World War II industrial dualism has been the shift away from the technical and organizational principles of mass production in both the primary and secondary sectors.[4] The growing use of computerized, more efficient, flexible technologies seems to be integrating work tasks — dramatically transforming the way work is organized in factories, the internal labor markets, and the skills demanded from workers. In both primary and secondary firms, more occupational flexibility and knowledge-based skills are being demanded from workers, and production-line forms of organizing work are being phased-out. These are being replaced by concepts such as teamwork and job rotation as a way to cope with market volatility without reducing or affecting productivity (Kelley, 1990; Kochan, Katz, and Mckersie, 1986; Sabel and Piore, 1984).

It is difficult to establish how industrial changes have affected the use of immigrant labor because little research has been done in this area, and the recency of the transformation has yet to produce definite patterns. However, the available evidence indicates that immigrant workers are being used as a cheap supply of transitional labor in the process of deploying and "breaking-down" new, capital-intensive technologies, as a way to break the resilience of unionized domestic workers and forcing them to accept the occupational changes caused by modernization, or as a source of cheap, flexible labor that permits manufacturers to combine "piecemeal" modernization and old assembly methods without skill and wage improvements (Morales, 1983; Papademetriou and Bach, 1989).

Finally, human-resource-development and management practices have experienced a major change, and several human-resource-development models are proliferating and intermixing in different industrial sectors and within the manufacturing sector in particular (Doeringer, et al., 1991; Kochan, Katz, and McKersie, 1986; Osterman, 1988). The industrial-relations model, once dominant in major manufacturing industries such as the auto and steel industries, has collapsed due to the institutional rigidity that grew out of many years of confrontation between labor and management and efforts by firms and corporations to restructure occupational categories, technology, and work outside the legal and customary framework provided by the system of industrial relations (Hecksher, 1988; Katz and Keefe, 1991; Kochan, Katz, and McKersie, 1986). This model of human-resource-management practices, established in American industry during the 1940s and heavily influenced by the trade union movement, was characterized by narrow job classifications and rigid ladders of mobility where seniority played a central role in job assignments and layoffs and where managers preserved their prerogatives over command and control functions in the work place. By contrast, the employment-at-will and the full-employment models, once prevalent in labor-intensive, competitive manufacturing and in large, nonunion corporations respectively, have come to influence human-resource-management practices in a broad range of both core and peripheral manufacturing firms. The employment-at-will model is mainly characterized by little commitment on the part of the firm to human-resource development, by the encouragement of high turnover, and the employment of a footloose labor force. The full-employment model, to the contrary, emphasizes human-resource development through work-place training, encourages work-place stability and the creation of an employment culture that fosters occupational flexibility, fosters worker's self-management, and encourages less rigid work rules (Doeringer, et al., 1991).

Some of the on-going changes in human-resource-management practices could enhance the ability of immigrant workers to improve their training and educational opportunities. This could particularly be the case in small and midsize modernizing firms located in areas with a high concentration of immigrants where features of the industrial relations and full-employment models are being combined to create the organizational flexibility required to cope with periods of economic volatility. In these firms, the human-resource-management environment may contribute to changing the stereotypical images that have reinforced the long-term seclusion of immigrant workers to low-skilled, low-paying occupational categories.[5]

The strategies and practices devised by corporations and firms to cope with the economic volatility and change of the last decade are transforming the morphology of post-World War II industrial dualism. In this context, the analysis of the conditions that have traditionally regulated the use of immigrant labor needs to be reassessed in view of what corporations and firms are doing to cope with change. Most importantly, however, it is the need on the part of firms and corporations to continue finding and creating sources of tractable labor suitable to meet their specific strategic objectives that is governing the use of immigrant labor in manufacturing, whether these needs are to slowdown decline, facilitate an exit from the market, or create the technological and organizational flexibility required to adapt to rapid change.

The Marginal Use of Latinos in Lowell's High-Tech Manufacturing

Between the early 1970s and late 1980s, very few Latinos seem to have been employed in Lowell's high-tech, corporate core, and most of those employed seem to have been concentrated in low-skilled, low-wage occupations. Latinos were largely employed in nondurable manufacturing. By the early 1990s, right before the current recession fully unfolded, the Latinos employed in the corporations that were interviewed comprised no more than 3 percent of the total labor force of any of the particular plants. They were concentrated in low-skilled, low-wage occupational categories such as material handlers, unskilled operatives, and general help and commanded wages no higher than $6.50 per hour. These jobs offer few opportunities for mobility, general training, and development.

The marginal use of Latino immigrants in Lowell's high-tech core may have developed due to a combination of forces, some related to the dynamics of restructuring of the sector and others to the technological strategies and human-resource practices pursued by corporations while adapting to market changes and volatility. First, the formation of — and to a certain extent the consolidation of — the city's high-tech, corporate core took place during the 1970s when there were very few Latinos living in the city and when the decline in traditional manufacturing had left many skilled and unskilled native workers unemployed. Thus, the tidal wave of job creation in high-tech industries literally bypassed Latinos, and to some degree corporations seem to prefer hiring able, "passive," native workers affected by the local deindustrialization or workers that were exiting traditional manufacturing jobs seeking greater stability elsewhere in the sector. One informant familiar with the employment of Latino workers in high-tech industries stressed that good jobs in the sector were difficult to access because training and apprenticeship programs were heavily guarded by Anglo-dominated (craft) unions that directly connected their membership in declining industries to opening jobs in high-tech. It seems that the few Latino workers (mostly Puerto Rican) that gained access to high-tech manufacturing during the

1970s did so through several federally-funded employment and training programs that created a limited amount of subsidized employment slots among defense contractors in the area.

When Latinos grew in number in the city and began penetrating the high-tech, corporate core during the 1980s, the maturation of this core induced an incremental reduction in the labor demand for certain occupations, particularly entry-level, low-skilled jobs and semiskilled jobs and intermediate occupations in assembly work. This further increased the competition for the few remaining positions at the bottom of the occupational ladder. For one computer manufacturer, corporate strategies of survival and adaptation such as outsourcing and the streamlining of internal labor markets reduced (or totally phased-out) the number of unskilled and semiskilled, entry-level and intermediate job opportunities that would have been available to Latinos and to other workers. Many of these jobs were downgraded and shifted to a peripheral segment of subcontractors in the city or to other geographic areas in the United States and the Third World.

While the modernization and automation of production processes in the corporate core has upgraded the quality of some jobs, it has downgraded others — mainly those jobs at the bottom of the occupational ladder likely to be occupied by Latinos. For instance, the new jobs created in a fully-automated facility making specialty materials and components do not require anything more than handling materials and performing various monitoring and quality-control tasks requiring little skill or for that matter education (although language skills are considered extremely important due to the potentially hazardous conditions of production). Sophisticated technicians and production engineers fundamentally control the entire operation, and entry-level, unskilled and semiskilled workers mainly follow strict and rigorous instructions regarding the handling of materials, the reading of precision instruments, and the charting and reporting of very specific aspects of the production environment. While the jobs available to Latinos have changed in form, they have remained virtually the same in terms of quality.

The jobs held by Latinos at the bottom of the occupational ladder have been artificially subdivided into a progression of multiple occupational categories of unskilled and semiskilled work with relatively long job-tenure requirements that reflect few significant improvements in job quality. This creates occupational and wage stagnation and fosters rapid turnover. This practice is used to preserve a footloose and expendable labor force at the bottom of the occupational ladder to facilitate adjustment during market swings or downturns. The period of time that a worker must wait between the point of job entry and the time that significant pay raises, job mobility, and job quality improvement accrue is long and creates a disincentive to stay on the job. For instance, at one of the corporations interviewed, it may take a worker a period of 18 months or more to move up three unskilled occupational categories (depending on the availability of positions above the ladder) and reach a semiskilled job that pays $45 more a week than the base, entry-level, unskilled $260 weekly wage.

The training and educational opportunities available to Latinos at the bottom of the occupational ladder in the corporate core are minimal and difficult to benefit from. Corporations interviewed occasionally offer reduced tuition reimbursement plans for GED and basic skills education at institutions in the area (community colleges). This basically remedial training translates into little improvement in job mobility at the bottom of the occupational ladder. It should also be noted that many Latino workers only find employment working night or early morning shifts that do not allow them to take advantage of the few educational opportunities available to them.

Finally, the incremental dismantling of federally-funded employment and training programs throughout the 1980s has been an equally important factor in the marginal use of Latinos by high-tech industries. This shift has weakened or eliminated already loose recruitment contacts between these corporations and Latino or other community organizations. Without the institutional framework provided by these programs, corporations often downsized their recruitment efforts aimed at particular types of workers, and community organizations lost their ability to offer outreach, job counseling, job training, and placement services.

In Lowell's high-tech, corporate core the marginal use of Latino immigrant labor is the result of a process of corporate restructuring and maturation in which the abundance of cheap and tractable labor has become relatively unimportant to improving profitability, at least when weighted against other corporate needs such as market diversification and rapid technological innovation. The need for cheap and tractable labor has been reduced or phased out through modernization and vertical disintegration, and the remaining entry-level positions are isolated as positions that can be easily downsized or eliminated. Thus, opportunities for Latinos in this segment of the manufacturing sector continue to diminish.

The Heavy Use of Latinos in Labor-Intensive Manufacturing in Lawrence and Holyoke

Between the early 1970s and late 1980s, Latinos became the main source of labor to labor-intensive firms in these cities. In both Lawrence and Holyoke, Latinos represented between 30 percent and 80 percent of the total labor force of the firms interviewed during the early 1990s. These workers are concentrated in entry-level, unskilled or semiskilled positions with little or no opportunities for training, advancement, or job development. (In fact, some of these firms are slated to be closed in the near future.) In some specific cases where Latinos represented an overwhelmingly large proportion of the firm's labor force (60-80 percent), they are marginally represented in skilled and supervisory positions, yet not enough to offset their overrepresentation at the bottom of the occupational ladder. Hourly wages in these firms range from $4.50 to $6.00, often with piece-rate bonuses, and some these firms have remedial language and basic literacy courses taught on their premises.

Several factors explain the heavy use of Latino immigrant labor by Lawrence and Holyoke's labor-intensive manufacturing firms, and the poor labor-market outcomes of Latin workers in these cities. Since the early 1970s the simultaneous decline of the sector and the heavy growth of the Latino population in Lawrence and Holyoke provided firms with the necessary cheap labor to "ride" the decline (which often ended in plant closings). This source of cheap labor also permitted firms to continue operating without any major investments in technology, job training, and development. The "matching" of Latinos and labor-intensive manufacturing happened in the context of a strong period of deindustrialization and decline that constrained Latinos' job opportunities. In one of the firms interviewed, Latinos grew to 80 percent of the firm's labor force during the time the firm was being readied for shutdown.

The dynamics of technological development in labor-intensive firms also limited or further eliminated the development of good opportunities for Latinos. On the one hand, the lack of technological innovation limited the ability of Latinos to develop new skills or limited their ability to interact with new methods of production; on the other hand, where some reduced technological innovation took place, it reduced the number of jobs or downgraded the skill content of jobs available. For instance, at one clothing manufacturer the automation of coloring, pressing, and cutting operations through computer-aided, flexible machinery — while it has improved quality control by reducing waste and minimizing errors — has reduced the number and the quality of jobs. Since automation, coloring no longer requires an "experienced eye" running the operation, pressing can be done by even less skilled workers than before, and cutting no longer requires cutters who were considered semiskilled or even skilled workers.

Given that unskilled and semiskilled jobs predominate in these firms (with the exception of a few mechanical and electrical jobs), human-resource practices have never focused on the training and development of workers. Most training happens informally on the job and is related to very specific aspects of the production process. Because of this, the skills developed often are not transferable to other employment situations. Also, learning a skill in these technologically outdated firms can involve handling machines or processes that are obsolete. In a carton printing shop, for example, some Latino workers were learning to operate printing machines that were not only about 20 years old but were extremely dangerous due to their poor mechanical condition.

These firms, intending to assure a steady supply of cheap, tractable labor, have devised formal and informal labor-recruitment practices that in time have created a "captive" and "controlled" Latino labor force with little prospect of developing other employment options, particularly in the context of declining manufacturing. Many of these firms have established formal contacts with Latino and non-Latino community groups and organizations through their local private industry councils (PICs) to maintain a steady flow or pool of workers. These arrangements, although they often solve Latinos' immediate, short-term problem of obtaining employment in high-unemployment areas, lack a long-term perspective in terms of job development and retraining. This lack of a long-term perspective can be attributed to limited resources and performance-based standards that accompany government employment and training programs that solely emphasize the quantity and not the quality of placements. Also, in some of these firms personal and informal networks of recruitment are institutionalized to the extent that a firm may only recruit new workers recommended by current employees. Sometimes an employee that recruits a new worker that stays on the job for a specific amount of time is compensated with a fee or prize. While these arrangements often work to the advantage of Latinos who need to preserve employment niches in a declining sector or who need quick employment placement upon arriving in the United States, they also regularly operate to control the employment outlook of Latinos and self-perpetuate poor employment situations. With this arrangement, employment happens within a tacitly coercive atmosphere in which supervising and control functions are transferred from managers onto workers, as workers are made indirectly responsible for the behavior and performance of the newly-hired. The peer group this creates, frequently from the same ethnic and racial group, feels pressured not only to keep attracting workers when needed, but to avoid any "bad performance" of their group in order to preserve their collective standing with managers and the firm — even when working conditions are appalling. This situation was particularly patent at one carton box manufacturer that recruited only Latinos recommended by Latino employees.

Finally, Latino representation in unions is an important factor in consolidating the insertion of Latinos into some labor-intensive firms, particularly in Lawrence. Although most jobs in these firms are unskilled and semiskilled, unions are fighting hard to improve or preserve them. In Lawrence, more than in the other cities considered here, Latinos participating in unions often play leadership roles and are actively involved in labor struggles and initiatives such as the Merrimack Valley Project, a labor-community coalition that seeks to preserve manufacturing jobs in the greater-Lawrence area.

The survival of labor-intensive firms in Lawrence and Holyoke, in contrast to Lowell's high-tech, corporate core, is intricately linked to the heavy use of Latino labor, particularly during the last 10 years of decline. Given the characteristics of these labor-intensive firms and the scope of their activities, their ability to survive largely depends on preserving a market edge through employing cheap, abundant, tractable (and often undocumented) labor. The concentration of Latinos in these manufacturing establishments in part reflects the fact that Lawrence and Holyoke have a heavy concentration of Latinos in their population. But more importantly, it seems that this match is the result of a dual dynamic in which these labor-intensive firms have actively sought Latinos, while Latinos have increasingly moved into this area seeking to survive in a shrinking manufacturing sector.

The Moderate Use of Latinos in Labor-Intensive Firms in Lowell and in Modernizing Firms in Holyoke and Lowell

In some of Lowell's labor-intensive firms and in modernizing firms in Lowell and Holyoke, Latinos were found to be represented in a broader range of occupations and to have better wage, mobility, and job development opportunities than in the two previous groups of corporations and firms discussed. Latinos represented between 10 percent and 40 percent of the workers employed by each firm interviewed for this section. They held not only unskilled and semiskilled entry-level positions but also midlevel technical, mechanical, and supervisory positions commanding wages that range from $6.50 to $9.00 per hour for entry-level positions and up to $15.00 per hour for other positions. Relatively better labor-market outcomes for Latinos in these firms are the result of a combination of factors related to the technological and human-resource strategies these firms adopted in their restructuring.

Both the labor-intensive and the modernizing firms encourage training and job development at all levels of the occupational ladder, which has resulted in better employment prospects for Latinos. In a labor-intensive firm in Lowell, for instance, while Latinos have reduced opportunities to interact with new technologies, they are offered generous tuition reimbursement plans that can be used at a range of educational settings for either ESL, basic skills, GED training or other college-level education, and vocational training. After the training, workers are encouraged through meetings with plant and human-resource managers to develop their own ideas and plans as to how their newly-acquired skills can be put to use in the work place. Similar arrangements exist in other modernizing firms in both Lowell and Holyoke.

In modernizing, small and midsize firms, the use of new technologies and of new production processes (flexible, computer-aided machinery, "just-in-time" systems, quality-control circles, better management groups) demands greater worker independence and self-management, which in turn requires an improvement in the numerical, language, and communication/interaction skills of workers (and managers). Latino workers in this new environment are expected to plan, schedule, and record production activities, which requires more personal interaction among workers and between managers and workers, more calculation and estimation of the materials and labor to be used in production runs, and greater knowledge of the entire production process (since job rotation is commonly used). Firms in areas with a high concentration of Latinos such as Holyoke could easily jeopardize their economic viability by deciding not to train and facilitate the adjustment of workers to the new production environment. Thus, these firms have decided to fully integrate Latinos into their modernizing efforts. Two firms located in Holyoke illustrate the point.

A synthetic textile firm replaced the water-jet looms conventional to the industry with high-speed, computer-aided, air-jet looms that permit rapid shifts between different product lines, making customization easier without major calibration and tuning. Loom operators, mechanics, and supervisors — among them some Latinos — were sent to Belgium, where the looms are manufactured, to be trained to use and maintain the new technology. Trained workers then developed workshops to train other workers on the new aspects of production. A textile producer in Lowell illustrates a similar dynamic. Illustrating a second scenario, a stationary firm hired a full-time educational consultant to asses the educational needs of those in their labor force who do not speak English, Latinos included, and to develop an integrated ESL, GED, and basic skills, work-based curriculum that facilitates the adjustment of the workers and the firm to the new "just-in-time" inventory systems, quality-control circles, and teamwork production arrangements. The effectiveness of new methods was being seriously affected by problems of miscommunication and lack of work-place coordination.

In both the labor-intensive and modernizing firms examined by this study the presence of Latino supervisors contributed greatly to the betterment of the occupational situation of Latino employees:

Latino supervisors contributed by dispelling stereotypical notions about the performance and productivity of Latino workers, commonly cast as "shiftless," "problematic," or "insubordinate." To break the self-perpetuating cycles of discrimination and prejudice that accompany social stereotypes, Latino supervisors created opportunities for Latino workers by assigning special tasks and projects through which workers could demonstrate their reliability and commitment to their employment relationship with the firms.

Latino supervisors also contributed to designing work rules and mechanisms of communication sensitive to the cultural and social problems that affect Latino immigrant workers. For instance, Latino workers occasionally needed to take extended leaves of absence (beyond what they are normally entitled) in order to attend family problems in Puerto Rico or in other countries. Because of either poor communication with Anglo supervisors or because Latino workers lacked knowledge of the firm's extended leave rules, absences identified as poor working behavior and generally resulted in dismissal. Latino supervisors, aware of this problem, not only made it easier for Latino workers to communicate their problems, but also helped to design rules of extended leave of absence that resulted in the preservation of employment.

In the context of a rapidly changing technological environment, Latino supervisors were able to convey instructions and changes without creating unnecessary friction between Latino workers and non-Latino workers, and between Latino workers and higher management.

Latino supervisors were key in fostering mentoring and apprenticeship relationships that benefited Latino workers in lower-level positions. In certain firms where teamwork and craftwork were an integral part of the production process, like paper laminating firms in Holyoke, apprentice-ship opportunities were critical to improving skills and increasing occupa-tional mobility.

Another factor affecting the use of Latinos in modernizing firms is the technological innovation that requires occupational reclassification and results in the relaxation of occupational categories. This process has apparently improved the opportunities for occupational mobility for Latinos. However, in some cases, this has not happened without creating conflicts with some older, white, male craft workers, particularly in unionized firms.

At two nonunion textile manufacturers, one in Holyoke and one in Lowell, the relaxation of occupational categories was relatively swift and opened the access of Latinos to more occupationally meaningful positions since the transition between positions was not regulated by union-protective clauses or apprentice-ship ladders controlled by the craft. The access of Latinos to these positions has not been perceived as undermining the power of craft unions. On the other hand, in two firms in Holyoke that produce paper-related goods, the relaxation of occupational categories and the penetration of Latinos into certain craft-guarded apprenticeship categories was met with union resistance. A combination of technological, union, and racial dynamics created segmentation and conflict between Latino apprentices and white craft workers. Some Latinos were union members, but they did not participate much in unions affairs because senior, white males in top craft positions maintained close control. Most Latinos were young, nonunion members in entry-level, semiskilled, apprentice positions created by the technological innovation. In both of these cases, employers seemed committed to improving the occupational situation of Latinos by offering a broad array of educational and training opportunities that promised to improve the access of Latinos to more skilled positions. In this context, Latino workers have come to represent the future of the firm while white craft workers have become remnants of the old technology and occupational categories.

Finally, the better employment situation of Latinos in modernizing firms can be attributed to the careful selection of the best Latino workers available through specific arrangements between community-based organizations that offer employment and training and recruitment programs organized by local businesses. This is particularly evident in Holyoke. Substantial Latino recruitment for Holyoke's modernizing firms is done by the Holyoke Employment Partnership, a program of the Greater Holyoke Chamber of Commerce. The program started in 1987, and in 1988 it was expanded with seed monies from a community-development block grant and organizational help from the local private industry council. It is a relatively small operation with a full-time Latino coordinator working out of an office at the Chamber of Commerce. In 1988-89, the program placed 123 individuals in full-time, private sector, mainly manufacturing jobs in Holyoke. In 1989-90, the program placed 151 individuals with a greater emphasis on clerical jobs. During the first two years of the program's operation, about 70 percent of the placements were Latino workers from Holyoke.

In summary, some labor-intensive firms in Lowell and modernizing firms in both Lowell and Holyoke tend to rely more on Latino labor for their entire operation. It is possible to perceive that, to some extent, many of these firms have assumed Latinos as one of their main supplies of labor, thus making at least nominal commitments to improving their relative position within the firm. Latinos have tended to be more evenly spread across the different occupations in production at these firms, and they are also significantly represented in some skilled and supervisory positions. Against conventional wisdom, better employment outcomes for Latinos in labor-intensive firms seem to be the result of strategies aimed at saving labor costs through improving the quality of workers' skills, encouraging job development and stability, and using Latino supervisors. Although Latinos have fewer opportunities to experience working with new technologies, they are offered educational incentives to develop and improve their job situation, potentially expanding their future employment outlook. In modernizing firms, better employment outcomes are the result of not only making educational and training opportunities available and the presence of Latino supervisors, but also of the opportunities created by modernization and accompanying job development. The use of Latino labor in these firms, while answering the need to preserve profitability by creating a flexible labor supply and cushioning the costs of deploying relatively sophisticated new work-place technologies, has in some other ways opened new opportunities for a limited number of Latino workers.

Conclusion and Policy Implications

During the last decade in Massachusetts, much attention was devoted to praising the macroeconomic benefits of industrial redevelopment, while little attention was given to the microeconomic and firm-based dynamics that affect the employment situation of individuals and groups. The 1980s industrial redevelopment of Massachusetts did indeed benefit a good portion of the working population of the state, but it fell short of improving the relative employment situation of Latinos (Cotton, 1991; Falcon, 1991; Osterman, 1988). Latinos became even poorer during the decade, making the state's Latinos the poorest in the nation (Melendez, 1992). At the macroeconomic level we are able to identify some of the factors that contributed to the deepening poverty status of Latinos. However, the microeconomic and firm-based causes of this weakening economic position has yet to be fully understood. This research tries to show some of the firm-based dynamics that contribute to the weak positioning of Latinos, as well as those dynamics that contribute to improving their position.

The decline and restructuring of Massachusetts manufacturing during the post-World War II era has created contrasting patterns of redevelopment in the various subregions of the state, contributing to the creation of a broad mosaic of declining basic manufacturing firms, growing high-tech firms and corporations in an almost permanent state of change, and slowly restructuring basic manufacturing firms seeking to survive through various forms of technological, organizational, and human-resource redevelopment. This restructured mosaic has not only diversified the use of Latinos within the manufacturing sector, particularly at the local level, but has also forced Latinos to face a broad array of constraints and opportunities that need to be documented and better understood.

In the manufacturing firms of Lowell, Lawrence, and Holyoke, Latinos remain largely concentrated in unskilled, low-paying jobs in peripheral firms. However, their opportunities are improving in some of Lowell's small and midsize, labor-intensive firms that are seeking to enhance their competitive survival through human-resource development and encouragement of job stability. In these firms, while little technological redevelopment has taken place, the emphasis on improving the quality of the work force has benefited the employment outlook for Latinos. In some of Lowell's and Holyoke's modernizing firms, the employment situation of Latinos has also improved but mainly as a result of both substantial technological and human-resource development. It is important to note that the number of jobs in these small firms is limited and often offers little room for expansion. Both types of firms have integrated Latinos in ways that contrast traditional employment and human-resource-development practices used for immigrants in small and midsize firms in the peripheral sector.

Conversely, in Lowell's high-tech, corporate core, Latinos are marginally represented, and those employed seem increasingly unable to benefit from the modernization and the relatively improved employment opportunities that presumably exist in this segment of the manufacturing sector. The same seems true for the labor-market opportunities Latinos encounter in most of Lawrence's and Holyoke's labor-intensive firms, where they are a main supply of labor. Employment opportunities in labor-intensive firms offer few prospects for growth and development, and limited opportunities are further compounded by the even more drastic tendencies of job decline and elimination that continue affecting this type of manufacturing in these two cities.

To improve the current and future labor-market opportunities of Latinos in manufacturing, employment and training programs must combine a number ingredients that attend to the specificity and variability of local labor markets, firms, and corporations. For instance, employment and training programs need to incorporate issues related to the changing world of work that go beyond simple and quick "computer-literacy" courses. They need to develop new competencies that relate to the ways corporations and firms are adapting to a new competitive environment and seeking improvements in productivity. This can be done by addressing some of the new production and management concepts currently employed in modernizing firms. In general, firms seem to be looking for greater flexibility in the skills and the knowledge-base of workers because they associate greater flexibility with improvements in productivity. These programs must also be combined with broader policies that contribute to preserving manufacturing in areas affected by rapid decline and that encourage workers' participation in the formulation of firm-based reactions to the problem of decline.

Notes

1. Tractable labor are workers who for a broad variety of reasons (citizenship, sexual and racial/ethnic prejudice, laws, custom, extended unemployment) are unprotected by unions, the state, and other institutions, and who tend to be employed in jobs unwanted by native populations and union workers. They are generally perceived to be more "passive, docile and unorganized," "ideal" for easing drastic work-place changes and easily hired and fired depending on the interests of employers.

2. I made a total of 21 in-depth interviews with personnel and human-resource managers, public policymakers, and other informants. Sixteen of these interviews were with human-resource managers at various types of firms: two were at high-tech corporations in Lowell; eight were at small and midsize, labor-intensive, manufacturing firms in Lawrence and Holyoke; six were at small and midsize, labor-intensive, modernizing firms in Lowell and Holyoke. The names of firms were chosen randomly from the *1989 Directory of Massachusetts Manufacturers*. Their names have remained anonymous as a condition of the research. Of the remaining interviews, two were with local policymakers, one at the Private Industry Council of the city of Lawrence and the other at Holyoke

Chamber of Commerce. The other three interviews were with individuals who offered a historical perspective on the labor-market insertion of Latinos in Lowell, Lawrence, and Holyoke.

3. The term "restructuring" is conventionally used in business and economics to refer to the financial and structural reorganization of corporations aimed at restoring profitability through means such as merging, recapitalization, and integration. More recently, the term has been recast to capture the economic, political, and social practices that since the 1960s countries, firms and corporations have devised in coping with macro- and microeconomic volatility: drastic technological and work-place redesign; geographic relocalization of industrial clusters; corporate negotiating compacts; deindustrialization; and linkage development planning, among others. In this work, the term is generally used to denote a combination of these processes.

4. Mass production is defined in two dimensions. First, it is defined as a form of producing goods in which a combination of technological and organizational (managerial) practices create the possibility of increasing the speed and volume of the flow of materials, and therefore of output, by replacing manual operations with machines arranged to integrate and synchronize (coordinate) productive activities within a single industrial establishment (Chandler, 1977). Increases in speed and volume permit economies of scale that lower production costs and increase output per worker, per machine. Secondly, it is defined as a set of institutional (social and political) arrangements that reproduce and legitimize the predominance of this form of production over other forms of organizing production (Sabel and Piore, 1984).

5. The industrial relations model by itself often hindered the occupational mobility of immigrant labor (women and other racial/ethnic minorities), particularly in white, male-controlled, union shops, or the model simply never proliferated in secondary manufacturing where immigrant labor was concentrated and where the employment-at-will model generally ruled. The full-employment model took shape largely in employment and occupational settings with little or no immigrant workers so that it has barely impacted the insertion and use of immigrant labor.

References

Berger, S., and Piore M. J. (1980). *Dualism and Discontinuity in Industrial Societies.* Cambridge, England: Cambridge University Press.

Blauner, R. (1972). *Racial Oppression in America.* New York: Harper & Row.

Blewett, M. (Ed.). (1990). *The Last Generation: Work and Life in the Textile Mills of Lowell, Mass., 1910-60.* Amherst, MA: University of Massachusetts Press.

Bluestone, B., and Harrison, B. (1982). *The Deindustrialization of America.* New York: Basic Books, Inc.

Chandler, A. D., Jr. (1997). *The Visible Hand: The Managerial Revolution in American Business.* Cambridge, MA: Harvard University Press.

Cole, D. B. (1963). *Immigrant City: Lawrence, Massachusetts, 1845-1921.* Chapel Hill, NC: University of North Carolina Press.

Cotton, J. (1993). A Comparative Analysis of the Labor Market Outcomes of Latinos, Blacks, and Whites in Boston, Massachusetts, and New England, 1983 to 1991. In E. Meléndez and M. Uriarte (Eds.), *Latinos, Poverty, and Public Policy: A Case Study of Massachusetts*. Boston: University of Massachusetts, Mauricio Gastón Institute for Latino Community Development and Public Policy.

Cumbler, J. (1990). Immigration, Ethnicity and the American Working-Class Community: Fall River, 1850-1900. In R. Asher and C. Stephenson (Eds.), *Labor Divided: Race and Ethnicity in United States Labor Struggles, 1835-1960*. Albany, NY: State University of New York Press.

Doeringer, P. B., Christensen, K., Flynn, P. M., Hall, D. T., Katz, H. C., Keefe, J. H., Ruhm, C. J., Sum, A. M., and Useem, M. (1991). *Turbulence in the American Workplace*. New York: Oxford University Press.

Doeringer, P. B., and Piore, M. J. (1971). *Internal Labor Markets and Manpower Analysis*. Lexington, MA: Heath, Co.

Edwards, R., Gordon, D. M., and Reich, R. (1982). *Segmented Work, Divided Workers: The Historical Transformation of Work in the U.S.* New York: Cambridge University Press.

Falcón, L. (1993). Economic Growth and Increased Inequity: Hispanics in the Boston Labor Market. In E. Meléndez and M. Uriarte (Eds.), *Latinos, Poverty, and Public Policy: A Case Study of Massachusetts*. Boston: University of Massachusetts, Mauricio Gastón Institute for Latino Community Development and Public Policy.

Fernandez-Kelly, M. P. (1983). Mexican Border Industrialization, Female Labor Force Participation, and Migration. In J. Nash and M. P. Fernandez-Kelly (Eds.), *Women, Men and the International Division of Labor*. Albany, NY: State University of New York Press.

Gitelman, H. (1974). *Workingmen of Waltham: Mobility in American Urban Industrial Development, 1850-1890*. Baltimore, MD: Johns Hopkins University Press.

Glaessel-Brown, E. E. (1990). *Immigration Policy and Colombian Textile Workers in New England*. Immigration Policy and Research Working Paper 4. Washington, DC: U.S. Department of Labor, Bureau of International Labor Affairs.

Goldberg, D. (1989). *A Tale of Three Cities: Labor Organization and Protest in Paterson, Passaic and Lawrence, 1916-1921*. New Brunswick, NJ: Rutgers University Press.

Harrison, B. (1984). Regional Restructuring and Good Business Climates: The Economic Transformation of New England Since W.W.II. In L. Sawers and W. K. Tabb (Eds.), *Sunbelt/Snowbelt*. New York: Oxford University Press Inc.

Harrison, B., and Kluver, J. (1989). Re-assessing the Massachusetts Miracle. L. Rodwin and H. Sazanami (Eds.), *Deindustrialization and Regional Economic Transformation*. Boston, MA: Unwin and Hyman.

Hartford, W. F. (1990). *Working People of Holyoke: Class and Ethnicity in a Massachusetts Mill Town, 1850-1960*. New Brunswick, NJ: Rutgers University Press.

Hecksher, C. (1988). *The New Unionism*. New York: Basic Books.

Katz, H. C. and Keefe, J. H. (1991). Industrial Restructuring and Human Resource Preparedness. In P. B. Doeringer, et al., (Eds.), *Turbulence in the American Workplace*. New York: Oxford University Press.

Kelley, M. R. (1990, April). New Process Technology, Job Design and Work Organization: A Contingency Model. *American Sociological Review, 55*(2), 191-208.

Keyssar, A. (1986). *Out of Work: The First Century of Unemployment in Massachusetts*. Cambridge, England: Cambridge University Press.

Kochan, T. A., Katz, H. C., and McKersie, R. B. (1986). *The Transformation of American Industrial Relations*. New York: Basic Books.

124 Ramón Borges-Méndez

Meléndez, E. (1993). Latino Poverty and Economic Development in Massachusetts. In E. Meléndez and M. Uriarte (Eds.), *Latinos, Poverty, and Public Policy: A Case Study of Massachusetts*. Boston: University of Massachusetts, Mauricio Gastón Institute for Latino Community Development and Public Policy.

Mitchell, B. C. (1988). *The Paddy Camps: The Irish of Lowell, 1821-61*. Chicago: University of Illinois Press.

Morales, R. (1983). Transitional Labor; Undocumented Workers in the Los Angeles Automobile Industry. *International Migration Review, 17*, 570-596.

Noyelle, T., and Stanback, T. M. (1983). *The Economic Transformation of American Cities*. Totowa, NJ: Rowman and Allenheld.

Osterman, P. (1988). *Employment Futures*. New York: Oxford University Press.

Papademetriou, D. G., and Bach, R. L. (1989). *The Effects of Immigration on the U.S. Economy and Labor Market*. U.S. Department of Labor, Immigration Policy and Research Report 15. Washington, DC: Government Printing Office.

Piore, M. J. (1973, May). *The Role of Immigration in Industrial Growth: A Case Study of the Origins and Character of Puerto Rican Migration to Boston*. Working Paper Number 112a. Cambridge, MA: Massachusetts Institute of Technology, Department of Economics.

Piore, M. J. (1986, May). The Shifting Grounds for Immigration. *Annals, APSS, 48*, 23-33.

Sabel, C., and Piore, M. (1984). *The Second Industrial Divide*. Boston, MA: Basic Books.

Sassen, S. (1988). *The Mobility of Labor and Capital*. Cambridge, England: Cambridge University Press.

Sassen, S. (1991). *The Global City: New York, Tokyo and London*. Princeton, NJ: Princeton University Press.

Scott, A. J., and Storper M. (Eds.). (1986). *Production, Work and Territory: The Geographical Anatomy of Industrial Capitalism*. Boston, MA: Allen and Unwin.

Tager, J., and Ifkovic, J. W. (Eds.). (1985). *Massachusetts in the Guilded Age*. Amherst, MA: University of Massachusetts Press.

Waldinger, R., and Bailey, T. (1991). The Changing Ethnic/Racial Division of Labor. In *The Dual City: Restructuring New York*. New York: Russell Sage Foundation.

Waldinger, R. (1986). *Through the Eye of the Needle: Immigrants and Enterprise in New York's Garment Trades*. New York: New York University Press.

Part III
Public Policy and
Community Strategies

Miren Uriarte
Latinas and the Massachusetts Employment and Training Choices Program

In 1983 the Massachusetts Department of Public Welfare began the five-year implementation of its Employment and Training (ET) Choices program. The program began as a demonstration under the provisions of the federal Work Incentive (WIN) Program, which required all states to develop programs where adult recipients of General Relief and Aid for Families with Dependent Children (AFDC) were also involved in work.

At the time of its development ET Choices represented some important departures from the traditional ways that work-welfare programs were implemented across the country. Foremost among these was its concept of choice. Unlike other states that often required participants to be involved in work activities in order to qualify for benefits, ET Choices was based on the assumption that AFDC clients wanted to work and that, given the right kinds of supports and opportunities, they would do so without coercion. AFDC recipients in Massachusetts were required to register for ET (so that the state could qualify for WIN reimbursements) but actual participation in employment and training was not forced upon them.

The time of the implementation of the ET Choices program coincided with a period of rapid economic growth and full employment in Massachusetts. With "Opportunity for All" as a slogan, ET was boasted as the means through which the state's prosperity would filter down to the poor.

The actual design of the program attempted to integrate choice on the part of clients, concrete assessment and evaluation mechanisms, and an array of services meant to meet, in a flexible manner, a variety of client needs. According to the program design, benefit workers were to register all new clients and all clients being redetermined to be eligible for AFDC in ET. Those clients who wished to participate in the program were then referred to the ET worker. Clients who did not participate after registration were regularly sent correspondence explaining the program and encouraging them to join. Colorful posters and newsletters, and at times even videos of ET participants, were regularly available to AFDC clients in the waiting rooms of welfare offices.

Once a client agreed to participate, the ET worker conducted an appraisal and employment plan. This appraisal might include basic assessment of client plans

for employment, discussion of choices of programs and of employment strategies (if the client was ready for work), and assessment of the need for support
services. From appraisal, clients moved to the core of available employment,
training, and educational programs. These programs ranged from intensive
assessment of skills and educational training needs to a wide array of educational
skills-training options to supported work and direct job-placement services.

The implementation of the ET Choices program coincided with the rapid
expansion of the Latino population in Massachusetts. During the 1980s the
Latino population of Massachusetts grew by 70 percent; by 1990 Latinos had
become the largest minority group in the state (Rivera, 1991). Latinos, however,
appear to have benefited very little from the state's economic growth during the
1980s. By mid-decade Latino poverty was becoming strongly reflected in the
state's AFDC caseload. Between 1983 and 1987 the number of Latinos receiving
AFDC increased by 32 percent, while the number of white and black families on
AFDC decreased by 11 percent during the same period. By October 1987
Latinos accounted for 22 percent of the AFDC caseload in Massachusetts
(Atkins, 1987, p. 8). In Holyoke and Lawrence Latinos accounted for over 60
percent of the AFDC caseloads. In Boston 24 percent of all AFDC cases were
Latino families.[1]

In this chapter I analyze how the ET Choices program addressed the
challenges posed by this rapidly growing and desperately poor population.
Studies assessing Latino involvement with programs funded under the Comprehensive Employment and Training Act (CETA) and, later, the Job Training
Partnership Act (JTPA), revealed that the challenge was great. Participation of
Latinos in both CETA and JTPA programs has been documented as being among
the lowest of all groups. A 1980 study by the Mexican American Legal Defense
and Education Fund (MALDEF) found that most of the 30 CETA programs
across the United States failed to meet their participation and employment goals
for Latinos (Estrada, 1980). Analyses of Latino participation in JTPA have
considered structural aspects of the programs — decentralization, reliance on
private-sector partnerships that exclude Latino community organizations, eligi-
bility requirements, etc. — that have hampered Latino participation in JTPA.[2]
Throughout the literature, problems of access are cited as the most salient factor
in Latino participation in employment and training programs.

This study of Latino participation in the Massachusetts ET Choices program,
conducted in collaboration with the Massachusetts Department of Public Welfare (DPW), focuses on the experiences of 300 Latinos in Boston who began their
participation in ET in the summer and fall of 1987. The study follows
participants up until the spring of 1990. I have combined both statistical and
qualitative methods in data gathering and analysis. In addition, 30 in-depth
interviews were conducted with a self-selected group of participants from the

sample. I also conducted interviews with directors and program managers of seven ET contractors with large Latino caseloads (over 50 percent). The main goal of this study was to ascertain both individual and program factors that affected the participation and outcomes of Latinas in the program. For the most part Latina participation in ET Choices was fairly high. Community-based organization (CBO) contractors were instrumental in the recruitment and provision of support services that made substantive Latina participation in the program possible. In fact, CBOs provided services to the hard-to-serve population and succeeded in helping them overcome language barriers, family responsibilities, lack of work experience, and other factors preventing labor-force participation. Both the motivation of Latinas to better their employment possibilities and their desire to become independent were also important when joining and successfully completing training programs.

A key finding of the study, however, was that upon completion of the ET program Latinas had a substantially lower job-placement rate when compared to other participants. The study also revealed that more than 70 percent of Latina job-finders remained below the federal poverty standard. The job-placement rate for Latinas was only 28 percent, while for all other participants it was 44 percent. Most Latinas who found jobs earned between $6.00 $6.50 an hour, which is about the same rate teenagers earned in fast-food restaurants in 1987. While the low wages of Latinas resulted in part from the skills and educational characteristics that they brought to the program, the study's findings suggest that low-wage outcomes for Latinas also resulted largely from their high participation in those programs that lead to very low-wage jobs.

Participation of Latinas in ET Choices

Earlier evaluations of ET revealed that Latinas participate in the program at rates that closely approximate their representation in the AFDC caseload (Ammott and Kluver, 1986). This study corroborates the high participation rates of Latinas: of the Latinas who registered (enrolled) in ET between July and October of 1987, 48 percent went on to participate in a program. The overall program participation rates for Latinas in ET were lower than those found among the overall ET population (66 percent), but well above the program-participation rates prevalent among AFDC recipients nationwide, which hovers around 40 percent.[3]

Participation rates, as they are generally measured, represent the rate at which people join a program, not necessarily the rate at which they actually participate in it. For example, in a primary evaluation of the Massachusetts ET Choices demonstration, participation is defined as "having done something beyond simply attending initial orientation and assessment" (Urban Institute, 1990, p. v). "Having done something" may mean in some cases having taken English-as-a-second-language (ESL) classes for a week or skills training for a day; whereas in other cases it may mean having taken a full year of college courses or over 300 days of ESL. Clearly, such scenarios represent substantial differences in the quality of participation.

To correct for the problems inherent in using participation rates as an index of program participation, I estimated the rate of substantive program participation. Substantive program-participation rates assess whether an individual was enrolled in the program for a sufficient amount of time for actual benefits to accrue. As expected, when the more stringent criteria for participation were applied, the rates of program participation decreased substantially. Nevertheless participation rates for Latinos remained fairly high at 41 percent of the total AFDC participants.

Given the relatively high participation rates of Latinas, the question becomes: What factors explain program participation? When assessing the success or impact of a program, policymakers are particularly concerned with distinguishing between the influence of individual characteristics and the influence of program structure. To test for how both individual and program factors are associated with substantive program participation among Latinas, I used proportional reduction of error. Of the individual factors tested — age, level of educational attainment, primary language, work experience, having dependents, number of dependents, and length of last welfare spell — only the number of dependents was weakly associated with program participation. Program-related variables, on the other hand, had a much stronger association with program participation among Latinas. Method of registration and whether or not the individual had gone through an appraisal process had a particularly strong association with the participation of Latinas in ET.

The importance of program variables in the participation outcomes of Latinas led to an examination of both the registration and appraisal processes as critical junctures determining Latina participation in ET Choices. Data from the DPW, as well as data from both client and provider interviews, showed that there were two general ways Latinas entered ET. Some were registered and enrolled by their DPW social worker, while others were enrolled in ET after beginning participation in a training or educational program in an agency with a contract for ET services. Backdoor registration, as this latter path is commonly called, indicates the extent to which clients are being recruited to the program from outside the DPW — that is, by agencies providing employment and training services.

The data indicate that agencies providing employment and training services play a large role in the recruitment of Latina participants in the ET program. While only 8 percent of those who registered in the program did so through the backdoor, a full 78 percent of the registrants who actually went on to become participants had registered through the backdoor. Substantial differences also emerged between the backdoor and regular registrants in terms of attrition after the registration/enrollment process. Among backdoor registrants 29 percent did not go on to start a program component, while 55 percent of regular registrants ended their participation at this point. The association between registration and program participation (r=-.378, p=.05) was the strongest factor affecting participation. Of the backdoor registrants, 70 percent went on to participate substantively in ET programs, while 30 percent of the regular registrants did so. This strong association between method of registration and substantive participation (r=.295, p*=.001) indicates that ET contractors not only recruit Latinas to the program, but that they actively promote substantive participation.

The types of contracts through which community-based agencies provided employment and training services to the Latina participants followed for this study potentiated both the recruitment and retention of Latinas in the program. Most agencies operated under a contract that allowed them to secure payment for 70 percent of the contract value upon meeting recruitment goals and maintaining clients through to the termination of program activities. (The final 30 percent of the contract value was paid if 70 percent of participants achieved positive termination.) Interviews with ET contractors serving Latinas confirmed that contractors were highly successful in achieving their recruitment and retention goals because of effective outreach programs that usually resulted in waiting lists for the programs. However, other factors also played a key role, including the high level of motivation among the clients and the degree of sophistication the agencies have achieved in providing a range of support services, including followup, for their ET clients.

One important finding of the study is that the differences found in the rates of participation were not due to differences in the profiles of the clients served by DPW on the one hand and those served by community-based contractors on the other. Private contractors are commonly perceived as "creaming" the best and most job-ready applicants, which would result in higher rates of participation. Backdoor registrants, however, generally fit the profile of the more hard-to-serve clients: They were older and generally had more children, they tended to be Spanish speakers, and they often had longer welfare spells than those reached by the DPW. In terms of education and work experience, the groups were comparable.

Interviews with clients exposed some of the barriers that the welfare department presented in the process of recruitment and orientation to the program. Language. for instance, was a major barrier between Latina clients and DPW social workers. Women spoke about the fact that they could not understand the worker's directions and explanations; yet even when told of the language problem workers seldom made efforts to alleviate it by using a translator. "He kept talking as if I understood even though I told him I couldn't," one client said, adding: "He would not get an interpreter." Another client recalled: "She said that I understood enough, but I didn't." These instances reflect the dilemma of the individual who knows enough English to "get by" but not enough to clearly understand the complexities of a program such as ET. Although it is evident that communication is a critical part of the role of the case manager, it appears that in many cases communication could not take place adequately because of language.

An important factor affecting the participation of Latinas in ET appears to be the high level of motivation of the women, as revealed by interviews with the women themselves and as confirmed by program operators. Many Latinas said that they participated in ET in order to better their employment possibilities. Most women spoke eloquently about their uncomfortableness with welfare and their desire to obtain a job that allowed them to support their families independently. Most of the women interviewed had worked or were working at the time they participated in ET; many had worked on and off for most of their adult life. Many needed the support of welfare, either because their current jobs did not provide them with enough income to support their families (their salaries still made them eligible for AFDC) or because they had recently lost a job. Many were not working because their children were young.

Most women asserted that a "good job" — a job that would allow for economic independence — was their goal in participating in the training program. They identified a low educational level, the lack of job skills, and — especially among non-English speakers — the lack of English proficiency as important barriers to obtaining a good job. "Learning English" or "improving my English" were commonly cited motivations for participation. For the women who had worked or were working, "developing myself" through education was also credited as an important motivation when joining a program. For these women learning a concrete skill that would lead to a different and better job was often an important reason for joining ET.

Latinas interviewed also had other reasons for joining training programs. Education and learning English, aside from the fact of whether it would lead to a job, were also cited as important. Many women spoke of the need to educate themselves better for the sake of their children; they also spoke of a desire to learn English in order to become more independent and more assertive about their needs. For many of the women the ET programs provided the means to break through a profound isolation imposed by language barriers, newness to Boston, and the responsibility of caring for a large family with young children. The programs offered through ET were seen as opportunities to reach the goals that were important to them.

In sum the rate of participation of Latinas in the ET Choices program was high both because of the decentralized way the program operated and the motivation of the women to participate. In many ways need met opportunity very propitiously: Latinas were looking for ways to "better" themselves and the state, by allowing contractors to recruit clients to ET Choices, gained from the recruitment capacity of community-based programs. The structure of the program promoted participation in other ways as well. The contracting process served to reinforce the strength of community-based programs by providing a sizable piece of the contract value for recruiting clients and maintaining them through program completion. Success in client retention was also a matter of the ability of community-based programs to provide a variety of support services and to achieve a brisk followup.

Outcomes of Latinas in ET Choices

Despite good participation rates, the outcomes — job placements and wages — for Latinas in ET Choices programs were not satisfactory. While 44 percent of all participants in ET are placed in a job (Urban Institute, 1990, p. 45), the placement rate for Latinas in this study was only 28 percent. The median hourly wage for Latino job-finders was $6.25, the equivalent of a salary of $13,000 per year. At that wage more than 70 percent of the Latino job-finders remained below the federal poverty standard.

JOB PLACEMENT

In order to ascertain the relative importance of factors affecting job placement, I used two tests for variables representing the individual characteristics of the participants and program-oriented variables. The findings indicate that, with the exception of previous work experience, demographic variables — often mentioned as the critical factor in job placement for Latinos and other program participants — had no association on their own to the job-placement experience of Latinas. Language and education, the presence, number, and ages of children, and the length of an individual's last welfare spell had no bearing on the rate of job placement.

By contrast the actual programs in which Latinas participated while in the ET Choices program had a strong bearing on the placement of Latinas in jobs. The seven participation paths of Latinas in the ET Choices program are summarized in table 1. They include paths where the women participated only in remedial education programs or ESL, as well as paths that combined education, skills training, and job placement.

Participants in educational components — which represent the paths most frequently chosen among Latinas — had very low job placements. Those in skills-training paths and in paths that combined some sort of skills training and job placement had higher rates of job placement, although very few Latinas participated in skills-enhancement programs. No other program characteristics — including registration, going through the appraisal and assessment process, or having substantive participation — were associated with successful job placement.

WAGES

Wages are perhaps a better indicator than job placement of the success of employment and training programs in providing the potential for an independent subsistence. Overall the median wages attained by Latina job-finders were uniformly low. For most Latinas getting a job through ET did not represent a "route out of poverty"; for more than 70 percent of them, in fact, the wages they received for their work in ET jobs failed to bring them up to the federal poverty standard.[4]

Although there were some differences in the wages attained by individuals with different characteristics, my general findings conform to those of other studies. Only work experience and previous wages were statistically associated to the wages attained in ET jobs. Participants under 18 earned the lowest median wage of all age groups, $4.75 an hour; 85 percent of the participants in this age bracket earned a wage that did not allow them to rise above the poverty level. Those who had completed 9 to 11 grades of schooling had the lowest wages, even lower than those with less than an eighth-grade education. Wages also tended to be lower for Spanish speakers than for English speakers as well as for those with shorter welfare spells when compared with those whose last spell was longer. In both cases the differences were slight. As was the case in job placement, education and language — both of which one might have expected to impact on wages — were not found to be factors in the wages obtained by Latinas in ET.

The study's findings also indicate that the program activities in which Latinas participated were a factor in the wages they received from their participation, although overall the wages for Latinas were low regardless of the component in which they participated. The difference between the mean wage of high earners and that of low earners was $1.51. The findings suggest that the low-wage outcomes for Latinas result from high participation in those programs that lead to very low-wage jobs (Basic Education, ESL and Job Placement). Programs that enhance the labor-market skills of participants and therefore lead to higher paying jobs — such as skills training, supported work, etc. — are not as readily accessible to Latinas.

PARTICIPATION IN SPECIFIC PROGRAM PATHS

Since participation in specific programs was determined to have such an impact on job placement and, to some extent, on the wages of Latinas, we undertook further analysis of program participation data. We also conducted interviews with participants and program operators to ascertain the ways in which Latinas made their way into specific programs.

Analysis of the data indicates that the actual content of participation — the specific programs in which the women participated — was related to both individual and program factors. On the one hand, as table 2 shows, it is evident that the demographic characteristics of participants in each of the specific programs vary considerably. For example, an older woman with low educational attainment and with work experience is likely to participate in a job-placement path. Latinas with the same educational profile but without work experience are more often than not in Adult Basic Education (ABE) and English-as-a-second-language (ESL) programs. The younger, more educated Latinas with work experience generally comprise the participants of the skills-training programs and combined skills training and education programs. As educational level reaches high school, the participation in skills-training programs and programs that combine skills training with other programs increases. In sum, the combined paths tend to include younger, more educated women with some work experience; that is, women who are more likely to get a "good job." The skills-training and job-placement tracks, on the other hand, seem to be populated by "job-ready" women, but not necessarily those who will attain good wages. ESL and Adult Basic Education programs, the most popular paths, generally include women who are less job-ready due to educational deficiencies and a relative lack of work experience.

Program factors also had a role in determining the actual path of the participants. Method of registration, for instance, was associated with participation in some paths, but not in others. It was often the case that participants in Adult Basic Education and ESL had registered through a contractor (backdoor registration). These are also the programs more prevalent at the community level. Participation in the job-placement path, on the other hand, was associated with having registered through the DPW (regular registration).

Program operators often referred to the "ideological divide" that differentiated the approach of the community agencies from that of the DPW. Most community-based programs emphasized education — and took the opportunity offered by ET to seek funds for educational programs — because they felt this would be most beneficial to the women in the long run. The welfare department, by contrast, prioritized job placement because for them it was primary in defining a successful outcome.

Interviews with program contractors revealed other ways in which program characteristics affect the funneling of participants to some programs and not others. First, from the perspective of program operators, demographic characteristics became important because contracting practices base some of the financial reward for the contractor on the performance of their clients (Duran, 1991). A good assessment of the type of client who will be successful in the program was not only a programmatic decision but a financial one. As noted earlier, under the performance-based contract system, the final 30 percent of the contract value was paid to contracts only when at least 70 percent of their ET participants achieved positive terminations. Contractors were also held to strict outcome standards; for example, a positive termination from a skills-training program was not only a job, but a job at a certain rate of pay. Outcome standards for educational programs were somewhat more lenient. Educational programs could count enrollment in a higher level of the program (Beginning ESL to Intermediate ESL), moving participants from one type of educational program to another (from an ESL program to an ABE program) or from an educational program to a skills training program (from ABE to skills training).

Since performance-based contracts leave little margin between revenue and actual costs, they also leave little margin for error on the part of program operators. Contractors report that program operators tend to have standards for entry into the program in order to mitigate the risk of enrolling people who will not complete the program positively (Duran, 1991). Skills training contractors, who are held to the strictest of standards for assessing "positive terminations," reported making "creaming" intake decisions more often than did education contractors (Duran, 1991). Admissions standards for entry into skills-training programs can include, for example, a particular level of education and the requirement that participants speak only English during the time in training. In the case of Latinos who are perceived to be harder to serve, less job-ready and less capable of terminating successfully, the rules of performance-based contracting result in some contractors refusing to take what they perceive to be a risk in enrolling Latinas in their programs.

Performance-based contracting has another unintended consequence: It encourages single program participation, especially with educational programs. Again, contractors gain when they can positively terminate a client by moving her into another program; they gain even more if the client remains in a program offered by the agency. Most community-based agencies are specialists rather than generalists; they specialize in skills training or education, very few specialize in both. The movement of clients from an educational to a skills-training program, then, often requires a referral outside the agency and the risk of loosing a participant who has proven herself to be serious in her participation.

In addition, say contractors, the small margin between revenues and actual costs that results from performance-based contracts has prevented agencies from developing the necessary range of services needed by the population they serve. Contractors who have experience with Latino clients have argued that simultaneous delivery of programs would make the most sense and, in fact, some experimentation in integrating ESL and ABE has taken place (Duran, 1991). But investing in the development of integrated skills training and education is a costly step because it often requires expertise not available within a singular agency, given that agencies usually specialize in one type of service or another.

The implications of a pattern of reliance on sequential use of single programs rather than participation in combined or integrated programs are important in a population with such great educational and skills deficiencies. Importantly, it is also a pattern that differs markedly from that reported by the Urban Institute for all ET participants. In looking at all ET participants, the Urban Institute found that the percentage of ET workers participating in a combination of programs was consistently higher across all programs than participation in each program singly (Urban Institute, 1990, Pp. 37-38). Combined participation is also important because there is evidence that those who participate in programs that integrate, for example, skills training and education, are more effective with populations demographically similar to that of Latino participants (Burghardt and Gordon, 1990). The important point here is that Latino participation in ET is quite different both from that reported for ET participants as a whole and from participation patterns that have been shown to be effective with Latinos in other areas of the country.

Finally, as is evident from the data, Latinos are largely dependent on community-level programs to make their way to ET and to participate substantively in the programs. They are also dependent on the range of services offered in these agencies. According to contractors, the lack of broad availability at the community level of skills-training programs, supported work programs and programs that combine and integrate different types of educational and skills training has an impact on Latino participation in these areas. Conversely, ESL programs are plentiful at the community level, and the percentage of participation in these programs among Latinos is very high (Duran, 1991).

Conclusion

Most studies of employment and training programs focus on the characteristics of individuals as the most important factor in the participation in and outcomes of the program. This study of Latinas in Massachusetts shows that program structure is more important than the characteristics of participants for assessing participation in the program as well as job placement. Only when high earners are differentiated from those who attain lower wages in ET jobs do individual characteristics gain more prominence, and even then the association is not very strong.

The structure of the ET Choices program potentiated the participation of Latinas primarily because it relied very heavily on community-based contractors for the recruitment and retention of participants in programs. This finding coincides with the recommendations of several studies of Latinos and JTPA programs that were based on provider interviews. In this case, client participation data, as well as participant interviews, provide evidence that programs at the community level in fact promote the participation of Latinos in employment and training programs.

This study also reveals that the contract structure of the program and its uneven distribution of types of services between the more established programs and those at the community level led to uneven participation on the part of Latinas. Most Latinas participated in educational programs because those were the programs most often offered at the community level by recruiting contractors; those were also, however, the programs that had the lowest success rates in job placements and the lowest wages. Latinas had little access to skills-training programs offered by JTPA contractors, the Bay State Skills Corporation, or others who had the lion's share of the skills-training programs funded by the DPW. As we have seen, skills-training programs have higher job-placement rates.

The contract structure also potentiated the tracking of Latinos into the educational programs and away from the skills-training programs. There is evidence that the background of individual participants is not a direct factor in this tracking, but rather that such tracking can be linked to the constraints placed on skills-training contractors to meet performance standards that they perceive are hard to achieve with a group that has the profile one finds among Latinos. Thus the individual background of the participants in interaction with the contracting process provides the context for the tracking of Latinos into those programs that have the worst job-placement and wage outcomes.

The same process tends to encourage Latino participation in single programs rather than in combined or integrated programs, which have proven more successful in both job-placement and wage-level attainment in similar populations. The current contracting process discourages contractors from making referrals to other types of programs that may not be found in their agencies and, even more importantly, it discourages the development of more effective, integrated program strategies in their own agencies.

Most Latinos who were placed in jobs obtained placements by participating in the employment-service program, without the benefit of improvement in skills. This led to the funneling of most Latina job-finders into low-wage jobs. In 1987 and 1988, it was not hard to get a job in Boston and the employment service found jobs for Latinos. The problem is that the jobs they found where low-wage jobs, among the lowest attained by Latinos in the program. Although this may have led to better job-placement outcomes, it is doubtful that it led to a better life for the women. In fact, in the absence of other social and financial support mechanisms, many of the women who achieved such placements returned to welfare. Thus, in many ways, reliance on the employment-service program to achieve job outcomes among Latinos represents a "revolving door" rather than an adequate and humane alternative to welfare.

Wage outcomes for Latinas in ET poses the thorniest question for policymakers. Do employment and training programs provide job-finders with the kinds of jobs that will allow women with children to risk leaving welfare support? The findings of this study indicate that in the case of Latinas the answer is clearly no. This study suggests that neither the individual characteristics of participants nor the program they participate in have even a moderate impact on the wages Latinas attain after participation in the program. In Massachusetts, even at a time of full employment and buoyant economic conditions, what faced Latino women who were placed in jobs were jobs with low pay — jobs that were too risky for them to take or to keep.

The current assumption is that employment and training programs are a "route out of poverty" for those who participate in them and that, therefore, such programs provide an alternative to expenditures in entitlement programs. Such a position fails to take into account forces in the labor market that keep people out of good jobs. The danger is that this perspective also leads to unreasonable program goals and, ultimately, to unrealistic expectations of participants. In time, as these goals and expectations are not met, such a perspective may also lead to increasingly punitive practices. In the case of employment and training programs the danger is that public sentiment will begin to blame participants for not obtaining good jobs at good wages, which could coerce women first into participating in programs that make little difference in their life situations and then into taking jobs that are too economically risky for them and their families. Finally, misguided public pressure could actually result in the removal of the few economic supports that these women now have.

Notes

1. The percentage of Latino families on AFDC varied significantly amongst Boston's five field offices: Roxbury Crossing, 48 percent; Church Street, 35 percent; Bowdoin Park, 30 percent; Grove Hall, 14 percent; Roslindale, 10 percent; and South Boston, 0.5 percent.

2. See Meléndez, E., (1988), The Impact of New York City E and T Programs on Latinos/as, New York: Institute for Puerto Rican Policy; and National Commission on Employment Policy, (1990), Training Hispanics: Implications for the Job Training Partnership Act, Report No. 17, Washington, DC: Author.

3. Nationally, overall rates of participation — defined as a person is assigned to a program — are about 40 percent. See Urban Institute, (1990), Evaluation of the Massachusetts Employment and Training (ET) Choices Program, Washington, DC: Author, p. v.

4. In determining the relationship of wages to the poverty standard, the number of dependents was taken into account.

References

Ammott, T., and Kluver, J. (1990). ET: A Model for the Nation? In The Urban Institute, *Evaluation of the Massachusetts Employment and Training (ET) Choices Program.* Washington, DC: The Urban Institute.

Atkins, C. M. (1987, October 14). AFDC Caseload Trends, memorandum from Atkins, Commissioner, Department of Public Welfare to Philip W. Johnston, Secretary, Executive Office of Human Services.

Burghardt, J., and Gordon, A. (1990). *The Minority Female Single Parent Demonstration, More Jobs and Higher Pay: How an Integrated Program Compares with Traditional Programs.* New York: The Rockefeller Foundation.

Duran, J. (1991, September). Summary of Interviews with Latino Community Based Agencies Contracted to Provide Services through ET Choices between 1986-1988. Unpublished.

Estrada, C. et al. (1980, July). *CETA: Services to Hispanics and Women.* San Francisco: Mexican American Legal Defense and Education Fund, Inc.

Rivera, R. (1991). *Massachusetts Latinos in the 1990 Census: Growth and Geographic Distribution.* Publication No. 91-01. Boston: University of Massachusetts at Boston, Mauricio Gastón Institute for Latino Community Development and Public Policy.

Urban Institute. (1990). *Evaluation of the Massachusetts Employment and Training (ET) Choices Program.* Washington, DC: Author.

Table 1

Paths of Substantive Participation by Latinos

Path	Percent of Substantive Participants	Job Placement Rate (%)	Median Wage
ESL: Participation only in ESL programs	26.73	10.34	$6.00
Basic education: Participation in Adult Basic Education and G.E.D.	17.97	7.69	$5.25
College education: Participation in educational activities at a college or university	7.37	25.00	$7.48
Job Placement: Participation in job placement and job development only	20.28	63.64	$6.00
Skills Training: Participation in JTPA and other skills training programs	14.74	43.75	$6.83
Combined skills training and education: Participation in a combination of skills training and education programs	7.83	33.33	$6.25
Combined skills training, education path and job placement path: Participation in a combination of education, skills training, and job development/job placement programs	5.99	53.85	$6.50

Table 2

Percentage of Participants by Selected Demographic Characteristics and by Participation Path

Characteristics	No Sub	ESL	Basic Ed	College Ed	Job Place	Skills Train	Comb Skills/ Ed	Comb Skills/ Ed/IDP
Age								
19 to 25	23.29	20.69	25.64	43.75	11.36	25.17	40.00	15.38
26 to 35	47.95	44.83	43.59	50.00	43.18	45.52	40.00	61.54
Over 36	24.66	34.48	25.64	6.25	43.18	26.90	20.00	23.08
Language								
English	52.05	48.28	53.85	68.75	44.19	62.50	66.67	53.85
Number of Dependents								
Has 0 to 1 deps	36.99	25.86	30.77	37.50	45.45	53.13	20.00	30.77
Has 2 deps	32.88	29.31	33.33	25.00	20.45	21.87	46.67	30.77
> 3 deps	30.14	44.83	35.90	37.50	34.09	25.00	33.33	38.46
Age of Dependents								
W/ deps < = 5 yrs	57.53	50.00	61.54	87.50	45.45	71.87	86.67	46.15
W/ deps > = 6 yrs	64.38	72.41	66.67	43.75	70.45	43.75	46.67	61.54
Duration of Unemployment								
Last spell = 6 mos	54.79	31.03	40.24	25.00	43.18	37.50	26.67	30.77
Last spell > 2 yrs	33.16	46.16	37.50	34.48	22.73	18.75	53.34	30.77
Level of Education								
Less than 8th grade	26.42	25.00	25.00	8.33	31.82	17.39	0.00	16.67
9 to 11	45.28	47.50	41.94	8.33	40.91	39.13	40.00	8.33
HS or GED	22.64	15.00	12.90	16.67	22.73	26.09	40.00	58.33
College	5.66	12.50	6.45	66.67	4.55	17.39	20.00	16.67
Work Experience								
Never worked	32.08	42.50	54.84	41.67	18.18	39.13	30.00	16.67

Peggy J. Levitt
The Social Aspects of Small-Business Development: The Case of Puerto Rican and Dominican Entrepreneurs in Boston

The view that small-business development can effectively reduce poverty and promote community development in minority communities emerged from the War on Poverty in the 1960s (Bendick and Egan, 1989). Since Richard Nixon's call for "Black Capitalism," federal, state, and local governments have encouraged minority, small-business development through initiatives such as managerial training and subsidized loan programs, procurement set-asides for minority-owned firms, public-private partnerships between business and government, and urban enterprise zones.

Minority, small-business-development programs have received mixed reviews. Proponents argue that small firms effectively decrease poverty, create jobs, and stabilize neighborhoods. Critics claim that small businesses generally fail or create little new employment. They add that policymakers often mistakenly assume that small-business development alone can effectively alleviate poverty when a combination of social and economic interventions is what is really needed.

It is not my purpose to enter into the debate on the economic benefits of small-business-development strategies. Rather, my research on Dominican and Puerto Rican business owners in Boston suggests that the terms of this discussion are too simplistic. To evaluate Latino business performance accurately, social factors must also be taken into account. By not taking into consideration the way in which Latino small-business owners use ethnic resources, or their traditions, values, skills, and ethnic characteristics (Light and Bonacich, 1988; Waldinger, Aldrich, and Ward, 1990), policymakers fail to understand a critical element that makes business ownership possible and molds business performance and growth. The use of strictly economic criteria also underestimates the importance of the crucial role these businesses play in Latino community formation and development.[1]

Methodology

This chapter reports on 34 in-depth interviews with 26 Puerto Rican and

Dominican business owners (11 Puerto Rican and 15 Dominican) and 8 Latino community leaders (including social-service-agency directors, city-government officials, community activists, and long-time residents) conducted between January and July of 1991.[2] I identified the respondents using an informal, snowball sampling strategy: a leader from each of the five most important Latino neighborhoods in Boston introduced me to a group of business owners who, in turn, suggested other potential respondents.[3] Some respondents provided me with names of prior business owners and community leaders who I also tried to contact, with limited success. Though business owners from each community were interviewed, the sample is not representative of all Latino businesses in Boston.

Each interview, which lasted on average one and one-half hours, covered a range of questions about the history of the business, its clients, financing, labor, merchandise, owner's background, and Latino community development in Boston. I also encouraged respondents to discuss other topics if they were so inclined. Approximately 65 percent of the interviews were conducted in Spanish; approximately 50 percent were taped.

Despite the presence of sizable Cuban and Central and South American communities in Boston, this study focused on Puerto Ricans and Dominicans for three reasons:

1. Puerto Ricans are the largest longest-standing Latino group in the city; Dominicans are the second largest group, numbering approximately 10,000 in 1991 (Staff, 1991).

2. Findings from an earlier study of poverty in Boston found that Latinos enjoyed fewer gains than blacks and whites during the 1980s "Massachusetts Miracle." Puerto Ricans and Dominicans appeared to do even worse than other Latinos, though the sample size for these groups was too small to be conclusive (Osterman, 1990).

3. To date, few Central or South Americans have created businesses. This may be because the Central and South American communities are smaller and arrived later or because they include more illegal aliens and political refugees who want to return home as soon as circumstances allow.

Table 1 summarizes the kinds of businesses included in this study. The businesses opened between three months and 22 years ago; 16 of the businesses started within the last five years (average length of operation was 7.76 years). They employed a mean of 1.8 full-time employees (ranging from 0 to 15 employees). Only one of the businesses manufactured items for other retailers. Three store owners produced small lots of garments they themselves sold.

The Case for and against Small-Business Development

Small-business-development proponents argue that small firms stimulate national and regional economic growth, increase economic equality for women and minorities, and decrease poverty in low-income urban and rural areas. They are also said to:

Create more jobs than other sectors relative to their share of total employment (Birch, 1987);

Generate more of the innovations and inventions introduced in certain employment sectors because they can identify and respond to specialized markets and consumer tastes better and more quickly than their larger counterparts (U.S. Small Business Administration, 1986);

Behave countercyclically, creating more jobs during economic downturns, and thereby mitigating the effects of economic recessions (Kirchoff and Phillips, 1987);[4]

Create more stable, long-term sources of employment because they are less likely to move out of the communities where they are located; and

Hire more minorities than other firms, thereby providing jobs, training, and experience to immigrants who often bring little formal education and limited English proficiency to the labor market.

While critics of small-business development generally agree that small firms create jobs, they claim that most positions pay low wages, involve few benefits, and offer few opportunities for advancement. In addition, since small firms allegedly have high failure rates, they are not a permanent solution to unemployment.[5] Finally, critics claim that small-business development cannot alleviate poverty unless it is combined with labor-market and human-capital development strategies.

My research suggests that both critics and proponents of small-business strategies overlook a crucial aspect of Latino businesses. Policymakers lack a complete understanding of Latino businesses because they do not take the social relationships and norms upon which these businesses rest nor the ways in which these relations influence business growth and performance into account. They also fail to see that Latino businesses are equally important for their social as well as economic role in community life. The remainder of this chapter addresses these neglected issues.

An Overview of Latino Small Businesses

Puerto Ricans and Dominicans exhibit lower rates of self-employment than other foreign-born groups in the United States. In 1980, the average business-participation rate for Puerto Ricans and Dominicans was 1.1 percent and 1.5 percent respectively, compared to the national average of 4.9 percent among the 50 largest foreign-born ancestry groups (Fratoe and Meeks, 1985).[6] Based on a 1987 sample of all the minority-owned businesses in the United States, only 2 percent of all Latinos and 0.7 percent of all Puerto Ricans owned their own businesses, compared to slightly more than 6 percent of the population at large (Waldinger, Aldrich, and Ward, 1990).

Self-employment among Latinos in Massachusetts appears to be consistent with these trends. Between 1969 and 1982, less than 1 percent of the Latino population owned their own business (U.S. Bureau of the Census, 1969, 1972, 1979, 1977). Table 2 shows a racial/ethnic breakdown of Boston's self-employed population in 1985 (7 percent of all residents) and the proportion that are self-employed among each racial/ethnic group.

Interview findings from this study also support the view that there has been little small-business development in the Latino community. Taking an historic perspective, one Boston city government official remembered:

There was never a great deal of business. Folks didn't come with those kinds of skills. They were migrant workers. Their concept was of marginal survival. They didn't really know how to run a business. They were working people who saw an opportunity and created a visual replica of what they saw back home ... and there was only so much business the community could support.[7]

Other interview respondents proposed several possible explanations for these trends. First, the original wave of Latino migrants, who arrived in Boston in the 1960s, were primarily farm workers from rural Puerto Rico. They had neither the language, education, nor capital with which to start small businesses (Piore, 1973). A 1989 survey reported that average education levels among Latinos in Boston remain low: 52 percent of Puerto Ricans and 59 percent of Dominicans had not graduated from high school (Osterman, 1990). On the other hand, business owners tended to be more educated than their nonentrepreneurial counterparts: two-thirds of the Dominicans and one-third of the Puerto Ricans in this study reported some university training.

Second, the next wave of Puerto Rican migrants, which began in the 1970s, consisted primarily of middle-class professionals and semiprofessionals. Though they had the necessary skills, they generally chose social service, city govern-ment, or teaching jobs over business ownership. Third, some respondents recalled more business activity between 1975 and 1985 but suggest that many owners had sold their stores during the Massachusetts real-estate boom and moved away to other areas.

It is difficult to predict the extent to which Dominicans will pursue small-business ownership since they are a relatively new group. An informal survey of business ownership indicates that Dominicans are currently overrepresented in the small-business sector relative to their group size.

Other factors, such as the regional economy, bank policies, government programs, and race relations also influence the number of businesses that are created and how well they do. For example, most Latinos arrived in Boston after the state's industrial sector was already in decline. As a result, newly-arriving immigrants faced a shrinking labor market and heightened competition for small-business ownership opportunities. Latinos were pushed out of the white, small-business sector and pulled into the emerging ethnic market where their poor English skills and lack of familiarity with white culture posed less of an obstacle. The Latino community, however, could support only a limited number of stores because of its small size and low mean income ($11,864 in 1980) (U.S. Census, 1980).

Lack of capital and poor access to resources also mitigated against small-business development. Because Latino entrepreneurs were so highly concentrated in the retail sector, they had few opportunities to establish the types of coethnic networks of wholesalers and distributors that have created successful immigrant enclave economies in other parts of the country (Portes, 1987). Furthermore, business owners seemed to have little contact with the formal banking system. One third of the business owners in the sample wanted to borrow money from banks but were either sure their loan request would be turned down or were in fact refused. Though one cannot reconstruct what actually occurred in each of these cases, discriminatory lending practices were common during this period (Massachusetts Commission against Discrimination, 1991). Finally, only four business owners had ever taken part in a government small-business-development program. They either did not know such programs existed, were confused about how to sign up, or distrusted the services being offered.

How then, armed with few resources and in the face of a difficult and volatile market, have Latinos been able to start and sustain small businesses? The answer is that ethnic resources, or the conventions, standards, and practices that community members share, allow business owners to compensate for the skills, capital, and prior business experience they lack. Ethnic resources ease the burden of economic downturns. They streamline what is often a confusing bureaucratic system. They generate information and capital. For most of the business owners in this study, ethnic resources gave rise to the elements that made business ownership possible.

In turn, Latino business owners anchor their community by imbuing it with a sense of identity and by acting as social service providers, bankers, trainers, information dispensers, and advice givers. Their social role is as valuable as their economic one. That Latino entrepreneurs rely so heavily on ethnic resources, however, is not without cost. At the same time that ethnic resources facilitate business development, they can also constrain business performance and growth.

Social Characteristics of Latino Businesses

In many ways, the social and economic life of the five Latino neighborhoods covered in this study resembles an urban village (Gans, 1962) or what one might imagine life to be like in a small rural town. Most people know one another. In fact, many of the Dominicans living in Jamaica Plain come from the same Dominican city, Bani, while a number of those in Dorchester come from the city of Santiago. Business owners and their customers form part of the same integrated social and economic network. What are normally thought of as market relationships are much more informal and personalized. What might be termed social interactions also have economic consequences.

The social networks, customs, and values that Latino community members share are the source of much of the labor, capital, clients, skills, and information that business owners use and cannot get elsewhere. For example, most of the entrepreneurs in this study went into businesses requiring minimal start-up funds, ranging from $3,000 to $15,000. While they pursued a variety of strategies to raise start-up capital (e.g., personal savings, pension funds, credit-card debt, or selling merchandise door-to-door), over two-thirds of the business owners received loans from family members and friends. They also rely on members of their social network to furnish influxes of cash during slow periods or when investment opportunities arise. In some cases, the individuals who loan money are close relatives. In others, they are distant acquaintances who make loans because the borrower is a coethnic. In one case, Dominican businessmen in New York loaned a video-store owner money simply because his family had a good reputation in their hometown.

These moneylenders constitute a quick, easily accessible, informal banking system. Business owners generally borrow small amounts from a number of individuals. It is not uncommon to borrow from one individual to pay back another. In general, no formal papers are exchanged — the borrowers' standing in the community and the assumption that they want to maintain their status serves as collateral. The interest charged, if any, is calculated according to the needs of the lender and the borrower. In other words, money lending is often a social service rather than an investment strategy.

Ethnic social networks play an important role in helping business owners identify opportunities and make decisions about business locations. Eight of the nine business owners in the study who purchased already existing businesses bought them from other Latinos. Those who started their own businesses often found out about vacant storefronts from coethnics. Many business owners chose a particular location because it was close to friends and family members. For example, a clothing store owner and an immigrant-services-firm owner, both from Bani, chose to open their stores in a building owned by two other "Banilejos," despite its location off the main thoroughfare in a high-crime neighborhood. They viewed this arrangement as mutually beneficial to both parties — landlords exchanged lower rents and a streamlined leasing process for the greater likelihood that their rent would be paid because their tenants felt a sense of obligation toward them.

Social networks also generate much of the labor power used by these businesses. Family members or friends work in approximately two-thirds of the businesses in the study; about one-half are paid while the others receive small gifts or training as compensation. Business owners claim that hiring family members improves business performance because: (1) it lowers costs; (2) they have more trust in family members, particularly with respect to money; (3) they can depend on family members to change hours or work extended shifts at short notice; and (4) they can establish more egalitarian relationships with their employees, which makes them more comfortable with their role as boss and heightens productivity.

Coethnics provide critical technical assistance and skills training largely free of charge. Most store owners reportedly learned their technical and managerial skills through on-the-job training in Latino-owned stores or through friends and family members who helped them informally as they went along. For example, one botanica owner learned her business by helping its former owner with accounting and purchasing. He was so anxious to sell his business to someone that he knew, he offered it to her for $3,000 and continued to help her manage the store until she could do so on her own.

Most of the businesses in this study serve an overwhelmingly Latino clientele. Eighty percent reported that between 60 percent to 99 percent of their customers are Latino. Business owners know the majority of their clients personally, from community life in Boston or in their country of origin. Store owners depend upon their social ties and reputation in the community to attract and keep their clients. They view their success as strongly tied to their reputation for serving their customers and to how well they are said to contribute to the collective good.

In sum, ethnic resources generate much of the capital, labor, and expertise that drive these businesses. They allow a small group of potential entrepreneurs to overcome barriers to entry raised by the training and resources they lack and to create viable small businesses. These same resources, however, may inherently limit business performance. In approximately two-thirds of the businesses in this study, it appeared there was a threshold beyond which social ties and shared values impeded further growth.

For example, since most businesses do not work with banks or establish lines of credit with suppliers, their ability to expand, take risks, or withstand slow periods is largely circumscribed by the size and liquidity of the community's coffers. Since community members also furnish most of the technical assistance and management training that business owners use, few new ideas, techniques, or information about outside business opportunities seem to infiltrate the community. Furthermore, most businesses continue to sell ethnic products to a largely Latino clientele — still a bounded market with limited economic power. Finally, for fear of alienating or offending their customers, business owners must continue to grant credit, bargain about prices, or employ family members, even in instances where the economic costs of such practices outweigh their benefits.

An evaluation of Latino businesses based on economic-efficiency criteria alone might conclude that small-business-development programs will do little to alleviate poverty. The Latino community can only support a small number of businesses that are, at best, only moderately successful. Such a view, however, misses the critical role that these businesses play in Latino community formation, stabilization, and perpetuation.

In the late 1960s, when Latinos first came to Boston and had little sense of themselves as a community, small businesses declared the emergence of a Latino neighborhood by their very presence. Today, this identity-creation function is superseded by an identity-affirmation function. The visual and auditory cues that customers perceive when they enter Latino stores make them feel that they are in Puerto Rico. Customers sense they are members of a group that belongs — a fact attested to by the presence of the stores themselves.

Particularly in the early days of the Puerto Rican community, but still today, small businesses double as impromptu social centers where people come to exchange news, gossip, or simply pass time together. This practice continues traditions from Puerto Rico, where the bodega is often the village gathering place. In Boston, the barbershop is full, not because everyone is getting a haircut, but because people socialize in commercial spaces rather than in their homes. This even happens in large stores:

> That customer is here every morning. He is here all day. That is typical of a Puerto Rican store ... the employees even like to come and talk to us on their days off. The store is like another room in their house.

Customers often come to stores just to greet the store owners, even if they do not need anything.

People who come frequently, it is like a social visit. Sometimes people come and they say, oh, I came only to say hello. They tell their problems and ask advice. They ask for help and emotional support.

Store owners generally feel it is their job to help their customers and that it contributes to their success. "It is the role of the business person to give back a little of what they have received from the community." A botanica owner described her job as part social worker. A large grocery store owner described himself as an important figure in the community because he supplies families with quality food. The fact that he has never been robbed, even though his store is in a high-crime area, is proof to him that others believe he is fulfilling his responsibility to the community.

Prior ethnographic research documented the role of the Puerto Rican business owner as community leader. In New York, business owners routinely founded neighborhood clubs and organizations, dispensed advice, and actively participated in neighborhood activities (Sanchez-Karroll, 1983). In Boston, business owners also frequently contribute or loan money:

If anybody dies in this community, the first place they come is over here. It is like in Puerto Rico, they come over here, we pick out a big can, we make a collection. We start first with all our employees and sometimes we collect up to $500 for any burial in the community for anybody that dies. If you go to any American store, you can't tell them to do that. They won't do that. This store is like a community institution.

We are always making contributions to the poor, to the city of Boston, to funerals. It is a pleasure to me. I even go to the funerals. Sometimes those I give to are not my customers and I say you are asking me but you never buy from me, but then I say, someday that could happen to me. I see how much they appreciate it.

These contributions also help country-of-origin communities. At the time of this study, Dominican store owners were collecting money to build an aqueduct in Boca Canasta, a small town near Bani.

The role of the store owner as moneylender is especially important because there are few, if any, bank branches in Latino neighborhoods. Store owners represent a rapid, no-questions-asked source of funds for people who probably do not qualify for bank loans, though business owners often charge higher than average interest rates. Many store owners also act as surrogate banks by cashing checks.

Store owners are an important source of advice and information:

When they need any ideas or they have any questions they call Casa Noel.

Is Alfredo around? Is Alfredo around? In many cases I go to their house. Whether it is a customer or not. I don't care if it is a Hispanic person. If he or she needs help, I try to help them. Most of them need counseling. What to do, how to do it. Sometimes they need a few hundred dollars and if you have it to lend them, you do. Sometimes they pay you, sometimes they don't. I get involved in stuff like that because like I said when I came here I had nobody, and I know what struggling is.

Store owners also create a social safety net by ensuring that there is a basic supply of goods available locally and by easing access to them (Tendler, 1983). First, ethnic businesses sell products to those who lack the money or the means to travel to large chains or malls. Second, "a customer who has little has to spend little." Latino businesses ease the terms of exchange by allowing people to buy small quantities, such as a single piece of cake or half a loaf of bread, and by granting people credit. Also, store owners often allow people to take their purchases even if they are a few dollars short:

The other thing I do, say you finish buying. You buy five or six items and I add it up, and it happens sometimes, it is a dollar short or two dollars short. You take it and next time you remember to bring it. I have the person feel comfortable which the Anglo doesn't do. You go to a market and if five cents are missing from a gallon of milk, you have to take it back.

Finally, anecdotal accounts suggest that many entrepreneurs who can afford to move choose to continue working and, in many cases, living in the Latino community. Particularly successful business owners either move into larger stores in the same area, open a second store, or as in the case of a record store owner, enter into related businesses that also serve Latinos, such as promoting Latino musical events or running the Latino dance night at a Boston nightclub.

Staying in the neighborhood is both a choice and an externally imposed constraint. A second shop that a record store owner opened in a more integrated neighborhood failed because he continued to sell mostly Latino music. Most store owners, however, agreed with this community activist's assessment: "The idea is not to move out of the ghetto but to make the ghetto better." In contrast to other minority communities, whose members move out as they achieve middle-class status, Latino small-business owners may be more likely to remain in the barrio, thereby contributing to greater economic and social stability.

To evaluate Latino businesses, then, based solely on their economic performance is to ignore the critical contribution they make to the well-being of their community. Latino business owners consider it their responsibility to be the provider of last resort when people need food or money, thereby providing crucial social insurance. They help community members find jobs, housing, and health care. They are role models and teachers. The community conducts its social life and affirms its identity within the walls of their stores. Particularly important is their practice of selling things on credit, in small quantities, and at the local level so that a continued supply of goods to the very poor is ensured.

Conclusions and Policy Implications[8]

Findings from this study are consistent with the argument that ethnic resources furnish the missing elements that many Latino entrepreneurs need to go into business. Shared social bonds, values, networks, and entrepreneurial styles generate most of the resources these businesses depend upon. Ethnic resources enable a limited group of Latino entrepreneurs to create and sustain highly functional, small-scale businesses that are fairly successful in the self-contained ethnic market in which they operate. Their experience lends credence to the view that nonassimilation may be a more effective means to economic mobility than assimilationist strategies (Portes, 1987).

Regardless of their economic record, this study shows that Latino small businesses play a critical role in integrating and providing for the Latino community. For their social role alone, these businesses merit support. There are a number of ways that policymakers and planners can strengthen the Latino small-business sector:

Locate small loans with long-term repayment periods. Some business owners clearly expressed interest in bank loans; others might do so if the loan application and repayment process was simplified. Easing access to capital would provide those business owners who want to expand and are currently constrained by cash flow problems with the means to do so. Other business owners may want loans for targeted, one-time projects such as physical plant repairs or technical assistance in marketing or management.

Lower costs through centralized distribution system. Since most Latino small-business owners in Boston are in the retail business, they are unable to organize the supply, production, and distribution networks that have lowered costs in other ethnic enclaves. Government officials and community-development practitioners might try to configure such a system artificially by organizing groups of stores to purchase merchandise in bulk or collectively transport products.

Organize professional or trade associations. In a similar vein, there is currently no formal channel through which Latino business owners can organize cooperative activities or lobby for their own interests. City-government officials might want to promote the organization of such a group.

Provide help translating skills into employment. It is not a lack of skills that prevents many individuals from starting their own business; it is knowing how to use those skills in the U.S. market. For example, many Puerto Ricans have carpentry skills because people often build their own homes or do their own home improvements in Puerto Rico. To be able to use these skills in Boston requires proper licensing, understanding building codes, and knowing how to market oneself. City-government and community-development agencies could help many individuals by offering short classes that would socialize people into the culture of particular trades in the United States. They could also ease access to licensing.

Diversify the commercial base. There are a number of small businesses found in other ethnic enclaves throughout the United States that have not taken root in Boston. These include trucking, landscaping, construction, plumbing, and electrical companies; small-scale manufacturing; and food production. Most of these businesses are production-oriented and are located in low-capital, low economy-of-scale industries that may have potential in the Boston market. By encouraging the diversification of the commercial base, policymakers could increase the range of opportunities available to Latinos for small-business ownership.

Future research should look more closely at the differences between Latino groups. A larger, more longitudinal study might reveal differences in the business strategies used by national and religious subgroups. A more comparative approach that included native-born ethnics and nonethnics would help to clarify the extent to which ethnic entrepreneurship as described here is also practiced by business owners in small towns and other urban villages. A clearer understanding of why some business owners are able to overcome the constraining effect of social resources more than others would also be useful. Finally, we need to take a closer look at the role of the informal sector in Latino business development.

I want to close by adding my voice to those critics of small-business development who argue that entrepreneurship alone is not enough. Policymakers and practitioners should work to strengthen and support the viable small-business sector that Latinos have created, largely with their own resources. However, this does not relieve them of their responsibility to pursue parallel antipoverty strategies such as improving education and creating better jobs.

Notes

1. For the purpose of this study, I use Stinchcombe's definition of the petite bourgeois labor market: wholesale trade, retail trade, taxicab services, real estate, detective and protective services, personal services, sports, entertainment and recreation (Stinchcombe, 1979). The study does not include professionals, such as doctors and lawyers, who are also self-employed.

2. The current study is part of a larger research effort on entrepreneurship among six immigrant groups in Boston being conducted by the Institute for the Study of Economic Culture at Boston University under the direction of Dr. Marilyn Halter. This research is partially funded by the Mauricio Gastón Institute for Latino Community Development and Public Policy at the University of Massachusetts in Boston.

3. These neighborhoods include the South End; Centre Street in Jamaica Plain; Egleston Square in Jamaica Plain; Bowdoin/Geneva Avenue in Dorchester; and Dudley Street in Roxbury.

4. Kirchoff and Phillips caution against generalizing from their findings because they base their argument on only two recession-expansion cycles.

5. Small-business failure rates are widely cited as 80 percent to 90 percent, although there is a great deal of debate on these figures.

6. Business-participation rate = (number of self-employed/total persons in the group) X 100.

7. Unless otherwise specified, all quoted material is taken from the study's interviews as described in the section on methodology.

8. I am grateful to Dr. Edwin Meléndez for our discussions about these points.

References

Bendick, M., and Egan, M. L. (1989, June 14). *Linking Business Development and Community Development: Lessons from Four Cities.* Unpublished paper prepared for presentation at the Community Development Research Center, New School for Social Research, New York.

Birch, D. (1987, September). The Rise and Fall of Everybody. *Inc Magazine.*

Fratoe, F. A., and Meeks, R. L. (1985). *Business Participation Rates of the 50 Largest U.S. Ancestry Groups: Preliminary Report.* U.S. Department of Commerce, Minority Business Development Agency. Washington, DC: Government Printing Office.

Gans, H. (1962). *The Urban Villagers.* Glencoe, IL: The Free Press.

Kirchoff, B., and Phillips, B. (1987, April). *Examining Entrepreneurship's Role in Economic Growth.* Paper presented at Seventh Annual Babson Entrepreneurship Research Conference, Boston.

Light, I., and Bonacich, E. (1988). *Immigrant Entrepreneurs.* Berkeley, CA: University of California Press.

Massachusetts Commission against Discrimination. (1991, March). *Public Hearings on M/WBEs: Report, Findings and Recommendations.* Boston, MA: Author.

Osterman, P. (1990). *In the Midst of Plenty: A Profile of Boston and Its Poor.* Boston, MA: The Boston Foundation.

Piore, M. J. (1973). *The Role of Immigration in Industrial Growth: A Case Study of the Origins and Character of Puerto Rican Migration to Boston.* Working Paper No. 112A. Cambridge, MA: Massachusetts Institute of Technology, Department of Economics.

Portes, A. (1987). The Social Origins of the Cuban Enclave Economy in Miami. *Sociological Perspectives, 30.*

Sanchez-Korrol, V. (1983). *From Colonia to Community.* Westport, CT: Greenwood Press.

Staff. (1991, April 4). Census Data Show Boston's Changing Face. *The Boston Globe.*

Stinchcombe, A. L. (1979). Social Mobility in Industrial Labor Markets. *Acta Sociologica, 22.*

Tendler, J. (1983, March). mbe, A. L. (1979). Social Mobility in Industrial Labor Markets. *Acta Sociologica, 22.*

Tendlernal Development Evaluation Special Study No. 12. Washington, DC: Government Printing Office.

U.S. Bureau of the Census. (1970, 1980, 1990). *Census of Population.* Washington, DC: Government Printing Office.

U.S. Bureau of the Census. (1969, 1972, 1977, 1979, 1982). *Survey of Minority-Owned Business Enterprises.* Washington, DC: Government Printing Office.

U.S. Small Business Administration. (1986, July). *Issue Alert No. 8: Innovation in Small Firms.* Office of Advocacy. Washington, DC: Government Printing Office.

Waldinger, R., Aldrich, H. E., and Ward, R. (1990). *Ethnic Entrepreneurs.* Newbury Park, CA: Sage Publications.

Table 1

Types of Businesses in the Study

Retail		Service	
Type	Number	Type	Number
Video	1	Radio station	1
Video/clothing	1	Immigrant services*	1
Furniture	1	Catering	2
Small grocery	3	Tailor	1
Large grocery	2	Barbershop	1
Clothing	4	Restaurant	1
Botanica†	2		
Gift shop	1		
Record store	1		
Bridal shop	1		
Plastic slipcover	2		

*Prepares immigration papers, insurance, and income taxes
†Sells religious articles and medicinal herbs

Table 2

Self-Employment among Boston Residents* by Racial/Ethnic Breakdown, for 1985

	Whites	Blacks	Asians	Latinos/Others
Percentage of all self-employed	79	14	2	5
Percentage of racial/ethnic group self-employed	9	5	—	6

*7% of all residents
SOURCE: Boston Redevelopment Authority. (1987, June). *Results of the 1985 Household Survey, Volume III: Labor Force.* Boston, MA: Author.

Nanette Robicheau
The Uphams' Corner Model: Comprehensive Commercial Revitalization in Multiethnic, Low-Income, Inner-City Communities

Introduction and Methodology

In Massachusetts, Latino business ownership is concentrated in the retail sector, most notably in the form of small grocery stores known as "bodegas" and clothing stores that cater to Latino tastes. The majority of Latino-owned stores are located in low-income, multiethnic, inner-city neighborhoods, interspersed among businesses owned by Anglos and other ethnic entrepreneurs. Frequently, these inner-city neighborhood shopping districts face a number of obstacles to business development, including low-income levels and high unemployment in the community; lack of an anchor tenant such as a major supermarket or department store to attract large numbers of shoppers to the area; declining physical conditions of buildings and infrastructure; inadequate municipal services; crime; lack of convenient parking; and a lack of business skills and access to financing among local merchants.

Furthermore, business development in the inner city is often constrained by ethnic and racial diversity among both residents and merchants. Ethnic diversity among residents makes it more difficult for local merchants to develop a strong customer base, while ethnic diversity among merchants makes it more difficult for business owners to develop a common agenda and leadership to effectively advocate for the interests of the business district in the larger institutional environment.

In this chapter, it is argued that in order to overcome these obstacles, commercial revitalization and business development must be seen in a broad context that includes other elements of economic and community development. In a multiethnic, low-income community, commercial revitalization should be viewed as a community-development goal in its own right, as well as a tool to advance other community-development objectives.

This chapter is based upon research conducted in Uphams' Corner located in Dorchester, Massachusetts, an area within the city of Boston. Uphams' Corner is an ethnically and racially diverse, low-income, inner-city neighborhood, with Latinos comprising approximately 30 percent of the population. Latino-owned businesses constitute the largest group of ethnically-owned businesses in the shopping district, yet they do not make up a majority. In this context, Uphams' Corner is representative of Latino integration in numerous Massachusetts neighborhoods. While this chapter will describe a set of recommendations for a comprehensive commercial-revitalization strategy based upon the unique needs and strengths of the Uphams' Corner community, these recommendations are applicable to many other inner-city neighborhood business districts where Latino merchants are located.

The Uphams' Corner model is a comprehensive commercial-revitalization strategy that integrates the following elements: (1) organizing local actors; (2) improving public safety; (3) developing local businesses and attracting new ones; (4) supporting the development of a multicultural identity; (5) strengthening and supporting local, community-based agencies; (6) linking business development to community development; (7) promoting and marketing the neighborhood business district; and (8) improving physical conditions.

The Uphams' Corner Commercial District

There are currently 91 commercial establishments operating in the Uphams' Corner business district. They represent a mix of retail chain stores, several smaller, locally-owned enterprises, and several shops with a regional draw that help maintain the stability of the commercial district (Mt. Auburn, 1992). At present, there is no supermarket or department store in the area. The retail sector is characterized by small, owner-managed enterprises that offer a severely limited selection of goods and services.

Slightly over half of locally-owned businesses in Uphams' Corner are owned and managed by members of ethnic and racial groups including Latino, Cape Verdean, Pakistani, Chinese, Greek, Korean, Eastern European, and Arabic. Fourteen of these stores are owned by Latinos. Some merchants cater primarily to patrons from their own ethnic group, while most serve all groups.

The high number of Latino and other ethnic entrepreneurs in Uphams' Corner can be explained by a combination of four factors. First, many immigrant and ethnic groups have high rates of entrepreneurship and self-employment in response to barriers to labor-force participation. Second, because many ethnic group members cater to the consumer preferences of their own ethnic group, they locate their shops in neighborhoods where the concentration of coethnics is high. Third, ethnic entrepreneurs frequently locate in inner-city neighborhoods that have been abandoned by traditional retailers because these locations offer low rent and little competition. Finally, there is a high concentration of ethnic merchants in the retail sector because these businesses are relatively easy to start and manage with limited financial resources and business experience (Waldinger, Aldrich, Ward, and Associates, 1990).

According to the 1990 U.S. Census, the population of Uphams' Corner is approximately 31,000, 32 percent black (non-Latino), 26 percent white (non-Latino), 25 percent Latino, 14 percent "other" (believed to be primarily Cape Verdeans), and 3 percent Asian. (The "other" figure underestimates the Cape Verdean population as many classified themselves as black.) Average household income in the area is estimated to be $23,000 and per capita income is estimated to be $7,200. Per capita income in Uphams' Corner is 46 percent of statewide per capita income, estimated to be $15,500 (Mt. Auburn, 1992).

There are four community-based, nonprofit agencies that have successfully operated in this area for many years: the Uphams' Corner Health Center, the Strand Theater, Dorchester Bay Economic Development Corporation, and the Bird Street Youth Center. These agencies serve to stabilize the neighborhood in several important ways. They provide for many health and social service needs of the community, serve as a large source of employment for community residents, attract large numbers of people to the area, advocate for the interests of the community in the larger institutional context, link the area with important government services, and aid in the development of community identity and political empowerment.

Currently, crime poses a major obstacle to revitalizing commercial activity in the business district by contributing to the perception of Uphams' Corner as a hostile place in the minds of both residents and outsiders. Fear of crime is particularly linked to groups of teenagers and drug traffic (Mt. Auburn, 1992).

In addition to crime, many other factors contribute to fragmentation, instability, and a lack of a clear identity in the Uphams' Corner community. Poverty and deteriorating conditions in the area contribute to high residential turnover and disinvestment. Ethnic, racial, linguistic, and cultural diversity can create barriers to communication among those who live and work in Uphams' Corner. And divisions among the several school districts, two police and court districts, several districts for City Council, the State House of Representatives, and the State Senate that represent Uphams' Corner lead to fragmentation and a lack of political power.

In the fall of 1991, the merchants of the Uphams' Corner Board of Trade, Boston's Public Facilities Department, the Dorchester Bay Economic Development Corporation, and several other neighborhood-based agencies joined forces in a collaborative effort to develop and implement a commercial revitalization plan for Uphams' Corner. Research presented in this chapter is based upon a case study of this revitalization effort. The Uphams' Corner model for commercial revitalization is based on previous literature in the field of economic and community development, past studies of Uphams' Corner, and on fieldwork this author conducted at the early stages of the revitalization focusing on development goals local residents and workers think are most important for the community.[1] The next section reviews previous research in this area.

Three Models for Commercial Revitalization in the Inner City

Decline, disinvestment, and neglect have reduced many once-vital, inner-city business districts to a haphazard collection of marginal businesses scattered amongst vacant, boarded-up storefronts. Similar to Uphams' Corner, these neighborhood business districts are characterized by limited availability of goods and services, high crime rates, and few shoppers. The over-arching goal of commercial revitalization and Latino business development in a low-income, multiethnic, inner-city business district is to improve economic, physical, and social conditions in the neighborhood. This goal is accomplished by building upon the strengths of local businesses while working to alleviate factors that have led to decline and disinvestment in both the commercial district and the residential area.

Among the potential economic gains of commercial revitalization are increased access to goods and services, job creation and retention, private investment, new business starts, and an expanding tax base. Physical improvements include rehabilitation of declining properties and refurbishment of storefronts and public spaces. Among the social goals are a renewed sense of pride, improvement in the quality of life in the area, and a brighter hope for the future.

A review of previous research reveals three different economic development models that are applicable in this setting. The first is the Main Street Model for commercial revitalization in older, declining business districts; the second is the Ethnic Enclave Model for business development among ethnic, minority, and immigrant communities; and the third is the Business Development-Community Development Linkage Model for development in economically disadvantaged inner-city communities. Taken alone, none of these strategies is adequate for revitalization efforts in a low-income, multiethnic business district. Elements of each of these models, however, are being used to inform a successful strategy for Uphams' Corner.

The Main Street strategy (National Trust, 1990) for commercial revitalization is a four-point plan based upon the following elements:

1. Organization: a collaborative approach with community and institutional involvement in planning and implementation.

2. Promotion: a strategic approach to marketing in order to improve the image of the commercial district and promote goods and services.

3. Design: rehabilitation of existing buildings around a theme of historical preservation and other physical improvements, such as improved traffic circulation and increased access to parking.

4. Business development: strengthening current businesses and attracting new ones.

While these elements are important to successful revitalization efforts in Uphams' Corner, they fall short of addressing two key concerns: ethnic diversity and low-income levels in the community.

A second model, the Ethnic Enclave Model, refers to a commercial district that is developed by and for a predominant ethnic group and shaped by the consumer preferences and practices of that group (Waldinger et al., 1990). The Ethnic Enclave Model is not focused on revitalization, but rather describes how revitalization can occur as a result of an influx of population and capital into an area by a specific ethnic group. Two of the best documented examples of thriving ethnic enclaves are the Cuban community in the Miami area and the Korean community in Los Angeles. Both of these densely-concentrated ethnic populations have achieved a high degree of political and economic power owing to cohesiveness and recirculation of capital among ethnic group members within the enclave (Light and Bonacich, 1988; Wilson and Portes, 1985). Moreover, a successful ethnic enclave eases social dislocation and helps maintain community cohesion among coethnics through the development and maintenance of community institutions that promote ethnic pride and cultural identity while they strengthen family ties (Light, 1985; Light and Bonacich, 1988; Wilson and Portes, 1985).

A third model, the Business Development-Community Development Linkage Model (Bendick and Egan, 1991), addresses issues of development in economically disadvantaged, inner-city communities and places commercial revitalization in the broader context of poverty alleviation. This model asserts that by linking business development to community development, elements of either strategy enhance the effectiveness of the other. Community development is defined as an effort to improve the overall social and economic quality of life through methods that include renovating housing, refurbishing streets and public buildings, upgrading public services, promoting community identity and pride, providing job training and other social services for community residents, and increasing political power. Business development refers to efforts to assist the founding, survival, growth, and profitability of individual enterprises through such means as managerial training and counseling, subsidized financing, procurement set-asides, and tax incentives (Bendick and Egan, 1991).

According to this model, business development can contribute to community development by expanding employment, improving consumer services, creating business markets, rehabilitating real estate, and fostering community role models and leaders. At the same time, community development can create opportunities for business development by reducing firms' operating costs and expanding markets for outputs (Bendick and Egan, 1991).

By combining selected elements of each of these models, a comprehensive, eight-point strategy for commercial revitalization can be developed for multiethnic, low-income, inner-city communities.

The Uphams' Corner Model

1. ORGANIZE LOCAL ACTORS

The first task for a successful commercial revitalization effort is to bring together the actors who will plan and implement the strategy including merchants, residents, the city government, local community-based agencies, law enforcement officials, and financial institutions. Latinos must work with members of other ethnic groups in order to build effective coalitions, and local actors must work together in order to build confidence that conditions in the district can improve and to encourage cooperative action toward the attainment of community-development goals.

In order to rebuild the area's image, revitalize its economic base, and set a positive direction for its future, community leaders and merchants must work to establish a consensus and goals, bring together diverse groups, and develop a strong Board of Trade that can fill a central management function for the neighborhood business district. An effective Board of Trade can facilitate communication between active and influential individuals and groups in the community, manage districtwide promotion and marketing efforts, advocate for public improvements and investment in the business district, attract resources to the area, represent the interests of the district in the larger institutional environment, and continue revitalization efforts when city involvement in the area is reduced. Currently, Boston's Public Facilities Department funds what they call a neighborhood business manager, a bilingual (Spanish/English), full-time employee who works to strengthen the Board of Trade and promote development in the business district.

According to interviews with area merchants, the need for organization in Uphams' Corner is particularly urgent. The majority of the area's businesses are small enterprises, owned and managed by one individual with few other employees. Local merchants struggle against a host of internal and external constraints to business development, and frequently lack access to the information, financing, and business expertise that could help make their businesses more successful. The difficulty of organizing an effective Board of Trade is compounded by the tremendous ethnic and racial diversity among the merchants of Uphams' Corner. This diversity frequently results in cultural and linguistic barriers that inhibit communication, the development of communal goals, and a coherent vision for what the business district could become. Despite these barriers, instances of demonstrated success brought about by collective effort have helped encourage increased participation in the Board of Trade and are bringing about a renewed sense of hope in the district.

2. IMPROVE PUBLIC SAFETY

Interviews with local actors reveal that one of the major obstacles to business development in Uphams' Corner is the high level of crime in the district and the perception of the area as a hostile environment. In Uphams' Corner the problems of street crime and loitering represent three distinct challenge

First, the level of crime — especially drug trafficking — must be reduced with increased law enforcement, including more surveillance and arrests. Second, perceptions of the area as an unsafe place must be altered. And finally, local young people need increased access to recreational activities that will help them resist the "lure of the streets." Most of the young people "hanging" on street corners are not involved in illegal activity; they simply have no place else to go. Yet their presence intimidates users of the commercial district. Community policing, implemented by the Boston Police Department (BPD) in 1991, emphasizes the importance of joint, cooperative, public safety efforts between police and the residents and businesses they serve. In Uphams' Corner, community policing has meant that two "beat cops" have been assigned to patrol the area, on foot, on a daily basis. It is hoped that these "walk and talk" shifts will encourage familiarity, trust, and increased communication between local citizens and the police in order to reduce the level of criminal activity through both law enforcement and crime prevention.

Currently, the two police officers assigned to the area, along with BPD community affairs officers, have been attending meetings of the Board of Trade on a regular basis. Local merchants are hopeful that the new "beat cops" will have a positive impact on the area. One local merchant interviewed noted, "We need the security of the cop on the street at all times, one that we would be able to pass info onto. There's a need for trust. We have to get the kids off the street. It only takes one good cop to do this. If we call 911, we get 20 cruisers when one good cop could have prevented it in the first place."

3. DEVELOP LOCAL BUSINESSES AND ATTRACT NEW ONES

It is important to recognize that in Uphams' Corner, as in any business district, changes in the commercial sector are market driven. Shoppers will patronize the area based upon their perceptions of what the district has to offer with regard to variety of stores, quality of goods and services, convenience, price, and safety. Entrepreneurs will invest in the area based upon their perceptions of market opportunities, ease of doing business, level of profitability, and possibility of long-term business stability and success. Thus, in order to improve conditions in the district, a comprehensive commercial revitalization strategy must include efforts to strengthen current businesses and attract new ones.

The high number of ethnic merchants in Uphams' Corner suggests that one strategy for revitalizing the area could be to develop the area around an ethnic theme. One option is to develop the area as a center of Latino commerce; another is to develop it around a multiethnic theme. In either case, a well-promoted and marketed theme emphasizing the variety of ethnic-based goods, services, and restaurants in the area, the multiethnic cultural and entertainment offerings of the Strand Theater, and the street festivals and other activities that celebrate different cultures could succeed in drawing large numbers of people to the business district. Experience has shown that the task of attracting new businesses to Uphams' Corner can best be achieved through the combined efforts of the neighborhood business manager and the Board of Trade. Recruiting prospective business owners requires a concentrated effort and commitment to the overall success of both the business district and individual merchants. Efforts on the part of the neighborhood business manager, working one-on-one with local entrepreneurs and property owners who have commercial space to lease or sell, could significantly increase prospects for attracting more businesses to the area (National Trust, 1990).

Local merchants and residents agree that one possibility for new business development in Uphams' Corner is the establishment of an ethnically-based food market. A market that sells groceries and household goods in addition to ethnic specialty food items could be very successful in Uphams' Corner and an asset to the entire community, bringing needed goods and services, occupying underutilized space, creating jobs for community residents, and helping to support ethnic diversity in the area.

Another possibility for new development is a "mercado," a large building with many stalls where a variety of items are sold by individual vendors. These booths could include fresh produce, meats, seafood, prepared food, as well as nonfood items such as ethnic handicrafts, plants and flowers, beauty supplies, and books. Services offered in the mercado could include shoe repair, dry cleaning, and an automated bank-teller station (Bickerdike Redevelopment, 1992).

Mercados have been successfully developed and leased by community-development corporations in low-income, inner-city neighborhoods nationwide in areas including Miami, Los Angeles, Pittsburgh, and Chicago. This concept serves as a combination community market and small-business incubator. Rental of stalls, booths, or pushcarts within the market is affordable for small-business owners or those just starting a business. A similar concept is that of an indoor, permanent flea market where locally-produced handicrafts, clothing, secondhand goods, and new merchandise can be sold, bartered, or traded.

In a more individualized approach to business development, local merchants need access to technical and business support focusing on specific operational problems including marketing, finance, accounting, inventory management, purchasing, and personnel supervision. Technical support could be offered through the Neighborhood Business Division of the Public Facilities Department. It is important that business training and counseling be sensitive to the cultural and linguistic backgrounds of the entrepreneurs in the district.

By pursuing an ethnically-based theme, the commercial area of Uphams' Corner could successfully attract more patrons and entrepreneurs to the area, while at the same time supporting other community-development goals like increasing employment and strengthening ethnic identity and community pride in the area.

4. SUPPORT THE DEVELOPMENT OF A MULTICULTURAL COMMUNITY IDENTITY

During the last decade, ethnic diversity has been increasing in Boston and members of many ethnic groups, including Latinos, are becoming increasingly more dispersed in neighborhoods throughout the city. According to the 1990 U.S. Census, new immigrants in Boston have helped push the minority population from 29 percent to 41 percent since 1980. The number of Latinos in the city increased by 72 percent by 1990. The diversity of newcomers, in addition to their scattered residential patterns, makes it difficult to build the political alliances so essential to the advancement of minorities (Rezendez, 1992). Cultural and linguistic barriers to communication, coupled with a lack of understanding and agreement upon common goals, has served to inhibit political empowerment and community and economic development in Uphams' Corner. At the same time, this diverse mix of peoples and cultures invigorates the community.

Uphams' Corner does not quite fit with traditional patterns of racial, ethnic, or immigrant adaptation in American cities. It is not an ethnic enclave, because no one ethnic group predominates. It is not a "melting pot" where recently arriving immigrants are quickly assimilated into mainstream cultural norms and practices. Nor is it an African-American neighborhood. Residents and merchants alike agree that it is a multiethnic community where many different kinds of people live and work together.

Some merchants, residents, community activists, and policymakers see diversity in Uphams' Corner as one of the area's greatest assets, while others see it as a liability. And while some see Uphams' Corner as one of Boston's most successfully integrated communities, where interaction between the members of various ethnic groups is open and dynamic and residents identify themselves as members of a proud, vibrant, multiethnic community, others see Uphams' Corner as a fragmented community, lacking cohesion, a common identity, and a clear vision of where it wants to go.

Still other community members and local policymakers argue that Uphams'

Corner is not really a multiethnic community, but rather a community in transition. They contend that the current diversity results from a demographic transition, an interim period where there is an overlap between one ethnic group leaving the neighborhood and another moving in. These policymakers believe that since the 1960s the demographic composition of Uphams' Corner has been altered by successive waves of newcomers that first included African Americans, later Latinos, and now Cape Verdeans.

However, several members of the Board of Trade as well as many local residents contend that while the rate of residential turnover is high, the basic ethnic mix of roughly four equal parts African American, Latino, white, and Cape Verdean has remained the same for the last 10 to 15 years, making the area a truly multicultural community.

The concept of multiculturalism is a relatively new one and has been described as a form of social relations in which different ethnicities "maintain their identities, but engage in extensive interaction and mutual influence." When multiculturalism occurs, "relations between single minorities and the dominant culture are complemented by organized interaction among minorities" and members of ethnic groups become "able and willing to communicate and cooperate across cultural boundaries" (Heskin and Heffner 1987, p. 526). In the process each group's identity is continually enriched and reconstructed (Heskin 1991, p. 104).

The development of a multicultural community identity in Uphams' Corner extends beyond interethnic tolerance. It means forming effective coalitions between groups in order to advance community-development goals that can benefit the entire community. One of the most important contributions that the current revitalization effort can make is to help build coalitions between members of different ethnic groups and facilitate the development of a multicultural community identity. Furthermore, because the tremendous racial and ethnic diversity in Uphams' Corner is somewhat unique among Boston's neighborhoods, it is an ideal attribute to attract people to the commercial district from all over the city.

5. STRENGTHEN AND SUPPORT LOCAL, COMMUNITY-BASED AGENCIES

One of Uphams' Corner's greatest assets is the dedicated group of professionals and community members who work for and support local, community-based agencies. These institutions are important anchors of both the neighborhood business district and the surrounding residential areas. All have ethnically and racially diverse staffs and boards of directors who emphasize the importance of community building across ethnic and racial groups and offer services that are sensitive to the customs, preferences, and practices of these groups.

The Uphams' Corner Health Center, for example, has been in the community for over 20 years and has grown continuously during this period. The Health Center provides "cradle to grave" health care and currently serves 19,000 community members regardless of their ability to pay. The Center occupies four buildings in Uphams' Corner and is the largest employer in the neighborhood, employing nearly 200 people, 65 percent of whom are neighborhood residents. The staff of the Center reflects the diverse ethnic backgrounds of community residents and boasts combined fluency in seven different languages: English, Spanish, Cape Verdean, Creole, Haitian Creole, Cambodian, Vietnamese, and Laotian.

The Strand Theater, also known as the McCormack Center for the Arts, presents a wide range of performances that appeal both to the various ethnic groups represented in the area and patrons throughout the metropolitan area. The Strand attracts a larger number of people to Uphams' Corner than any of its other institutions. Because of the Theater's emphasis on community-based programming and contact with community residents through local social-service agencies and community institutions, the local audience at the Strand has grown enormously in the last three years. The Strand also sponsors a youth internship program that serves 100 teens per year and rents theater space to local religious and civic groups.

Dorchester Bay Economic Development Corporation (DBEDC) is another key player in the current revitalization effort. During its 12 years of operation in Uphams' Corner, DBEDC has successfully rehabilitated 192 units of affordable housing. Currently the corporation has undertaken a more comprehensive approach to community development in order to address three areas of need in Uphams' Corner: physical development, economic development, and social development. In addition to affordable housing projects, current community-development projects include planning reuse of commercial buildings for office/retail or residential/retail, mixed-use occupancy, building neighborhood coalitions to enhance crime prevention, and planning new social-service programs and neighborhood youth recreational facilities.

The Bird Street Youth Center has also operated in Uphams' Corner for many years and offers recreational facilities and activities as well as social services to area youth and their families. The Youth Center offers programs for parents and young people that focus on contemporary family concerns including drug use, sex education, and violence. The center also offers a youth development program involving peer leadership that helps local teens learn responsibility. A street-worker program is another innovative program offered by the center as part of an effort to reach those teens who do not use the center. Currently, the Youth Center is initiating a summer job-placement program to train 15 local youths for summer employment with Uphams' Corner merchants.

Each of these community-based organizations plays a vital role in helping the community attain economic, physical, and social development goals. By providing health and social services for the community, employment opportunities for local residents, youth development programs, affordable housing, and other community- and economic-development initiatives, these organizations help improve the quality of life for local residents. Without the services of these agencies many basic needs of Uphams' Corner residents would go entirely unmet.

These organizations also play a strong leadership role within the community. They have the capacity and the commitment to advocate for the interests of the community in the larger institutional context and currently form the mainstay of the Board of Trade. Furthermore, because these agencies have embraced diversity in the community, they are in a unique position to help develop and strengthen a vision of a proud, dynamic, multiethnic community identity in Uphams' Corner.

The community-based organizations in Uphams' Corner can help to overcome the level of fragmentation that currently exists in the delivery of services to the area. By working collectively in conjunction with the Board of Trade, local organizations can advocate for improved and more efficient delivery of city, state, and other services such as education, public health, sanitation, public safety, employment placement and training, and youth development.

6. LINK BUSINESS DEVELOPMENT TO COMMUNITY DEVELOPMENT

In order to enhance the possibilities for successful revitalization in the Uphams' Corner commercial district, business development should be linked with community development to attain objectives including stabilizing residential areas, expanding employment, recapturing local spending, strengthening community identity, developing local leadership and political power, and providing increased educational and job training opportunities for community residents (Bendick and Egan, 1991).

The commercial center in Uphams' Corner is inextricably linked to the surrounding residential areas, and vice versa. Thus efforts to rehabilitate buildings and revitalize business activity must be linked with efforts to increase the availability and the quality of affordable housing in the area. A thriving, well-maintained business district makes the local housing stock more desirable, while attractive residential neighborhoods make the business district more appealing. Similarly, improving other conditions in the district such as public safety, sanitation, and traffic circulation can help attract more shoppers and residents to the district and increase the profitability of local businesses. These improvements will also attract new businesses to Uphams' Corner, thus increasing the availability of goods and services for local residents.

Job creation and employment placement and training are urgently needed by local residents who are affected by a high unemployment rate. Commercial revitalization in the business district is likely to increase the number of jobs available to community residents, particularly part-time jobs that are typical in the retail sector. Retail development alone, however, is not likely to create enough new employment opportunities for unemployed community residents. Nevertheless, job creation can be expanded by linking retail development with the promotion of light industry in the neighborhood or with the creation of services that cater to the needs of local businesses such as accounting, tax assistance, insurance, photocopying, printing, and legal services. Additionally, the large amount of underutilized space and the central location of Uphams' Corner combine to make it an ideal setting for an employment-training and placement program that could be developed by the Dorchester Bay Economic Development Corporation or the Uphams' Corner Health Center. An employment training center in Uphams' Corner could offer job training and placement for local residents, utilize currently vacant commercial space, and attract large numbers of potential shoppers to the district.

There is also an urgent need for more youth activities in the area. Local youngsters need access to wholesome recreational activities, job-training and placement services, and other social services in order to help them develop self-confidence and a positive vision of their future. The Bird Street Youth Center, the Uphams' Corner Board of Trade, and the Public Facilities Department's current effort to fund and develop a youth program that will train and place 15 local teenagers in part-time, paid, summer jobs with Uphams' Corner merchants is an excellent example of the way business development can be linked to community development. In addition to providing employment opportunities for local teenagers, this program helps merchants become more involved with the community at large and serve as role models for local young people.

Local merchants can also play important leadership roles in the community, and as role models they can help strengthen community identity and pride and bring stability to the neighborhood. They can also help maintain informal networks of job contacts and sources of information about housing, employment, local services, and community resources. As a symbol of success, minority entrepreneurs are especially important to members of their ethnic groups and are a powerful reminder that "members of my group can make it too." Local merchants also provide opportunities for residents to meet and interact within the neighborhood, thus strengthening the development of community among residents.

Finally, it is important that local business people remain involved in the neighborhood and actively support the attainment of community- and economic-development objectives that can benefit all community members. By remaining involved and active in the community, merchants can help improve the quality of life in the area and can dispel the perception expressed by some residents interviewed that they only take from the community. Interviews with community activists and local residents reveal that some view commercial revitalization and business development as "welfare for the rich." They argue that business development only benefits business people and that there is no economic trickle-down to benefit the community. To dispel these negative perceptions of entrepreneurship and commercial development it is important that local merchants and development agencies make every effort to ensure that local merchants and the Board of Trade act to strengthen local businesses while also making efforts to ensure that the business district and local merchants play a positive role in the life of the community.

7. PROMOTE AND MARKET THE NEIGHBORHOOD BUSINESS DISTRICT

The goal of promotional activities in Uphams' Corner is to improve the image of the commercial district in order to attract shoppers and investors to the area and rekindle community pride. Effective promotion can be achieved through the joint efforts of the Board of Trade, the Strand Theater, and local businesses to sponsor activities, events, and retail sales that will increase activity in the district and revitalize its image as a dynamic area.

The Main Street Model describes five different types of promotional activities that are useful for developing a strategy for Uphams' Corner: project promotion, image promotion, retail sales promotion, special events, and targeted promotions (National Trust, 1990).

Project promotion
During the initial stages of commercial revitalization, promotion of the revitalization project itself should be the main thrust of promotional efforts. Residents, merchants, and other users of the district must be informed that positive changes are taking place.

Image promotion
Image promotion is designed to increase community awareness of the neighborhood business district as a distinct, identifiable area for shopping, business, and cultural and recreational activities. Two of the most distinctive attributes of the Uphams' Corner commercial district are the Strand Theater and the ethnic diversity of residents and merchants. These two elements can be highlighted in a campaign that links the multicultural entertainment and cultural activities of the Strand Theater with the varied and lively atmosphere of the neighborhood shopping district. Linking these two features will help create a unified image of

the shopping district and help to develop a distinct community identity for its members.

Retail sales promotion
Joint merchandising and promotional efforts are also important in reinforcing the image of a unified commercial district. Districtwide retail sales should be coordinated with events at the Strand, holiday activities, and other community events. Cooperation around activities such as sales events, sidewalk sales, late closing hours, and advertising campaigns can help to increase shopping activity in the district.

Special events
The purpose of special events is to provide entertainment with communitywide impact that will draw large numbers of people to the area. Special events help increase shopping activity for local businesses while supporting other commu-nity-development goals by creating opportunities for community members of diverse backgrounds to come together and socialize in the neighborhood business district.

In Uphams' Corner special events could involve a wide variety of community groups including local merchants, the Strand Theater, community-based orga-nizations, the city government, schools, local arts groups, resident associations, youth groups, ethnic associations, religious organizations, and athletic associa-tions. It is important for the community to feel that the neighborhood business district is a vital commercial and cultural community center, available for everyone's use and enjoyment (National Trust, 1990).

Special events could include art shows, street fairs, sidewalk sales, arts and crafts fairs, flea markets, a weekly farmers' market, and bicycle races. Other options include celebration of historical, athletic, seasonal and ethnic cultural events, or theatrical and musical entertainment events at the Strand (National Trust, 1990).

Ethnic festivals such as those celebrated in other neighborhoods of Boston (the Puerto Rican festival in the South End and the Chinese New Year celebration in Chinatown) could be successfully promoted. A festival could feature ethnic-based entertainment, music, refreshments, and handicrafts in addition to games, amusements, and recreational activities. By drawing more patrons to the district and by celebrating ethnic themes and holidays, these events will help increase understanding and awareness of cultural diversity in the Uphams' Corner community.

Targeted promotions
Targeted promotions refer to specialized, ongoing, promotional campaigns like

business recruitment or public relations. Business recruitment can be carried out by the Board of Trade and the Neighborhood Business Manager in coordination with local realtors and property owners. A public relations/media relations campaign is crucial to an ongoing promotional effort. Media coverage of promotions and special events can help create a positive image of the district and influence the way the community and the public perceive the area.

8. IMPROVE PHYSICAL CONDITIONS

A stroll through the Uphams' Corner business district is a study in starkly contrasting visual images. On the one hand, the area is graced by several stately brick buildings attesting both to Uphams' Corners' former economic significance and its future potential. Yet the area is also blighted by a number of vacant and boarded-up properties, poorly maintained storefronts, and litter-filled lots. High vacancy rates in some portions of the district contribute to a feeling of desolation and abandonment.

Physical revitalization of the area will help to achieve both business-development and community-development goals. An attractive business district creates a positive image of the neighborhood, its resources, residents, and merchants. It will help revitalize economic activity within the business district while helping to stabilize adjoining residential areas.

At present there is a large amount of vacant commercial space in the district, located primarily in three large buildings. One development option would be to utilize this space for expansion of community-based agencies in Uphams' Corner or to attract other cultural or social-service institutions that reflect the diversity of the community. Alternatively, the space could be used to house an ethnic food market or a mercado developed by the Dorchester Bay Economic Development Corporation and other local institutions.

Another area of concern for both shoppers and merchants in the district is traffic congestion and the availability of convenient parking. On-street parking is limited and the municipal parking lot is underutilized due to fear of crime. Currently, the Board of Trade is seeking funds to hire an armed municipal police officer to maintain security in the lot and encourage its use.

In addition to efforts to reduce high commercial vacancy rates in the area and increase use of the municipal parking lot, the Board of Trade and the Public Facilities Department are currently involved in an effort to develop design guidelines for the commercial district with the participation of local merchants and community residents. It is important that these design standards reflect the unique characteristics of the neighborhood and its residents in order to strengthen community identity with a physical environment that community members can relate to.

Implications of the Uphams' Corner Model

Uphams' Corner is an important case study because it is a harbinger of a new settlement pattern in American cities. Increasingly, the populations of many urban areas are becoming more ethnically diverse, and as members of different ethnic and minority groups — including Latinos — become increasingly dispersed among city neighborhoods, the development of multiethnic, multicultural communities will occur more frequently. In order to foster economic growth and enhance the quality of life in these communities, members of different ethnic groups will need to develop effective alliances.

This paper argues that in a low-income, multiethnic community, successful commercial revitalization must be seen as part of a larger effort to develop the community economically, physically, and socially. The overarching goal of revitalization efforts in this setting is to improve the quality of life in the neighborhood by building upon the strengths of the community while working to alleviate factors that have led to decline and disinvestment in both the commercial district and residential areas. In order for commercial revitalization to be successful and contribute to both community and business development, the broader context must also include efforts to improve housing, employment, educational and investment opportunities; build coalitions among local actors that bridge ethnic boundaries and strengthen political empowerment; and develop a proud, multicultural community identity by promoting improvements and activities involving neighborhood residents from diverse cultural and ethnic backgrounds.

Note

1. The author conducted 25 interviews with local merchants and residents, the staff of agencies working in the area, and economic-development professionals in the fall of 1991 and the spring of 1992. Surveys were administered to 108 shoppers and 29 merchants in the Uphams' Corner business district by Mt. Auburn Associates early in 1992.

References

Bendick, M., Jr., and Egan, M. L. (1991). *Business Development in the Inner-City: Enterprise with Community Links.* Paper prepared for the Community Development Research Center of the New School for Social Research, New York.

Bickerdike Redevelopment Corporation. (1992). *Mercado Public Marketplace.* Chicago, IL: Promotional Materials for Bickerdike Redevelopment Corporation.

Heskin, A. D., and Hefner, R. A. (1987). Learning About Bilingual, Multicultural Organizing. *The Journal of Applied Behavioral Science.*

Heskin, A. D. (1991). *The Struggle for Community.* Boulder, CO: Westview Press.

Light, I. (1985). Immigrant And Ethnic Enterprise in North America. In N. Yetman (Ed.), *Majority and Minority: The Dynamics of Race and Ethnicity in American Life.* Boston, MA: Allyn and Bacon.

Light, I., and Bonacich, E. (1988). *Immigrant Entrepreneurs.* Berkeley, CA: University of California Press.

Mt. Auburn Associates. (1992, March). *Revitalization Strategy for Uphams' Corner Commercial District.* Report prepared for the City of Boston Public Facilities Department, Boston, MA.

Rezendez, M. (1992, April 14). The Changing Face of the City: Immigrants Give Diversity, Display New Hope. *The Boston Globe.*

Robicheau, N. (1990). *Bringing Back Urban Vitality.* Washington, DC: National Trust for Historic Preservation.

Waldinger, R., Aldrich, H., and Robin Ward and Associates. (1990). *Ethnic Entrepreneurs: Immigrant Business in Industrial Societies.* Newbury Park, CA: Sage Publications, Inc.

Wilson, K. L., and Portes, A. (1985). Immigrant Enclaves: An Analysis of the Labor Market Experiences of Cubans in Miami. In N. Yetman (Ed.), *Majority and Minority: The Dynamics of Race and Ethnicity in American Life.* Boston, MA: Allyn and Bacon.

Michael E. Stone
Latino Shelter Poverty and Housing Strategies

As Latinos have become an increasingly large proportion of the population of the greater Boston region, housing has emerged as one of the most difficult issues they confront. While Latino households experience a whole host of housing problems, ultimately most are manifestations of either affordability or discrimination or both.

This chapter examines the housing affordability situation of Latinos in metropolitan Boston through the lens of a concept called "shelter poverty" — a measure that is more realistic than the traditional percent-of-income concepts. The shelter-poverty standard is a sliding scale of affordability that reflects the interaction among incomes, housing costs, and the costs of nonshelter necessities.

The principal source of data for the analysis is the American Housing Survey (AHS) for 1985 (U.S. Bureau of the Census, 1988, 1989), which was the most recently detailed compilation of housing data for the Boston region at the time this study was being carried out. While the AHS data permit an overview of the housing situation of Latino homeowners as well as renters, the small proportion of metropolitan Boston Latinos who are homeowners does not permit determination of shelter poverty among such homeowners.

Sixty percent of Latino renters in metropolitan Boston are shelter poor versus 40 percent of all renters in the region. Latino shelter poverty is most severe among two- and three-person households, who are mostly single-parent families; and among five or more person households, who are mostly married-couple families. The incidence of shelter poverty is almost the same as the incidence of Latino households exceeding the 25 percent-of-income standard and somewhat higher than the incidence on the 30 percent-of-income standard. The distribution is quite different, however, as shelter poverty is more strongly concentrated among low-income households of all sizes and large moderate-income households. Nearly 60 percent of Latino renters nationally are also shelter poor. However, those who are shelter poor in the Boston area are considerably poorer than their counterparts nationally. The scope and depth of shelter poverty among Latinos will require that the problem be confronted from both the income and the housing side of the issues. In order to have a significant and lasting impact, housing strategies will need to redress the patterns and consequences of discrimination in the housing market affirmatively and also challenge the prevailing mechanisms of housing production, ownership, and financing.

The Housing Market Context

Over the past two decades research on housing affordability and discrimination has gradually begun to recognize and incorporate the situation of Latinos. Studies based on data through 1980 have revealed that even prior to the last decade Latinos experienced substantial housing deprivation in relation to whites in terms of location, homeownership, degree of overcrowding, physical adequacy, and relative cost (Krivo, 1982; Lopez, 1986). In relation to blacks, Latino renters had as high an incidence of affordability problems, although Latino homeowners had a somewhat lower incidence (Stone, 1993, Chapter 5). In terms of residential segregation, Latinos were found to experience considerably more segregation than Asians, but considerably less than blacks. Nonetheless, the observed degree of segregation of Latinos has not been explainable simply in terms of economic factors, i.e., income and housing cost differentials; social factors and institutional practices have been implicated as well (Darden, 1986; Massey and Denton, 1987, 1989; Woolbright and Hartmann, 1987). Furthermore, Latino segregation was found to be relatively higher in some metropolitan areas experiencing substantial Latino immigration and population growth (Massey and Denton, 1987).

The housing experience of Latinos during the 1980s has yet to be fully analyzed, but there is no evidence of relative improvement and some indications of relative deterioration toward even closer convergence with the situation of African Americans. A very recent, large-scale, national study of housing discrimination conducted for the U.S. Department of Housing and Urban Development has revealed that in searching for rental housing, Latinos experience an overall incidence of discrimination only slightly below that of blacks, while in the sales market Latinos face virtually the same rate of discrimination as blacks (Turner, Struyk, and Yinger, 1991). The affordability situation of Latino renters remains comparable to that of black renters (Lazere and Leonard, 1989; Stone, 1993, Chapter 5), and physical conditions are only slightly better for Latino renters (Dolbeare and Canales, 1988). The affordability situation of Latino homeowners remains slightly better than that of black homeowners, but there has been some convergence since the mid-1980s (Stone, 1993, Chapter 5).

Until detailed census tract data from the 1990 U.S. Census have been analyzed, we cannot ascertain whether residential segregation of Latinos increased during the 1980s and whether there has been convergence toward the "hypersegregation" of African Americans (to use Massey and Denton's term). However, the findings from the 1970-1980 decade that show some relationship between Latino segregation and high rates of immigration and population growth are certainly suggestive of what is likely to have been taking place. Indeed, these earlier patterns would seem to be consistent with anecdotal and visual indications of a high degree of residential segregation associated with the substantial growth of the Latino population in Massachusetts.

The rapid expansion of the Latino population in the state during the 1980s occurred, of course, within the context of rapid economic growth but with increasing income polarization on the one hand and enormous speculative increases in the cost of housing on the other. From 1979 to 1989 the median gross rent in metropolitan Boston increased 30 percent faster than the overall rate of inflation; the median price of a single-family house rose 87 percent more than overall price increases (Joint Center for Housing Studies, 1990, Table A-10). The level and increases in rents and house prices have been among the highest in the country for most of the past decade. In 1989 median gross rent in the Boston Consolidated Metropolitan Statistical Area was $612 a month (U.S. Bureau of the Census, 1991, Table 2-13). Yet even these figures fail to reflect fully the market conditions faced by low-income households, as tens of thousands of lower-rent, unsubsidized apartments in the Boston area have been lost since the 1970s due to gentrification in some areas and arson and abandonment in others.

During this same period federal support for subsidized housing was substantially reduced. From the peak in fiscal year 1978 to the trough in fiscal year 1987, net new budget authority for federal housing assistance declined by nearly 85 percent in inflation-adjusted dollars (Congressional Budget Office, 1988, 42) before leveling off and turning up slightly over the past several years. In addition, beginning in the late 1980s hundreds of thousands of existing federally subsidized units under various programs started to reach the point where use restrictions and/or subsidy contracts would expire, with only limited protections and resources for preserving this housing for lower-income households (Clay, 1987; Achtenberg, 1989, 1990; Low-Income Housing Information Service, 1991).

The one major offsetting factor in Massachusetts during the 1980s was the growth of state government support for housing. Expansion of rental assistance programs, support for community-based as well as for-profit mixed-income housing, and the creation of programs to assist middle-income, first-time homebuyers were all part of a fairly extensive public agenda. Lower-income Latinos were among the major beneficiaries of the rental assistance programs. Nonetheless, these state endeavors could not even come close to compensating for the forces at work in the private market and the reduction of federal housing support. Furthermore, at the close of the 1980s growing fiscal problems and political shifts in the state brought about retrenchment in many of the state's housing initiatives with great uncertainty about their future.

The housing situation of Boston-area Latinos that is presented in the following sections reflects the situation in the middle of the 1980s, based on the most recent data available prior to the fall of 1991. The picture that is painted is at a point in time when some of the forces and factors mentioned here had not yet fully manifested themselves. It is also well before the onset of the recession, which has been particularly long and deep in Massachusetts and particularly hard on Latinos. In this respect it is a conservative picture of the housing problems confronting Latinos in this region.

Latino Households and Their Housing

Latino households in metropolitan Boston are, on average, younger, larger, more likely to be headed by women, much more likely to be renters, and much poorer than are other households. Latino renters have slightly lower average housing costs than other renters, but much lower incomes; and they are more likely to live in housing with physical deficiencies. A high proportion receive housing subsidies but are thereby vulnerable to potential losses of the subsidies. The small proportion of Latinos who are homeowners for the most part have incomes much higher than Latino renters. Their incomes are, on average, not substantially lower than other homeowners. Their housing costs, on the other hand, are somewhat higher as most of them are fairly recent homebuyers. It is useful to examine some aspects of Latino households and their housing situations before delving in detail into the affordability problem.

The two principal types of Latino households in the Boston region are nonelderly, married-couple families and nonelderly, female-headed, single-parent families. More than one-third are female-headed, single-parent households, compared with just one out of eight among all households in metropolitan Boston, and one out of five among Latinos nationally. Latino married-couple families consist of two distinct subgroups, one of middle income, not very different economically from non-Latino, married-couple families, and the other of very low income. The single-parent families are overwhelmingly of very low income.

Four out of five Latino households in greater Boston are renters, compared with a little over two out of five among all households in the region. Nationally, three out of five Latino households rent their homes. The very low homeownership rate among Boston-area Latinos is largely a reflection of the low prevailing incomes of Latinos as well as the very high prices of houses over the past two decades, during which time the region has experienced the large influx of

Latinos. This does not necessarily mean, however, that housing market discrimination has not also played some role.

The median income of metropolitan Boston Latinos in 1985 was about $14,000, barely half the median of all households. Nationally, the median income of Latinos in that year was $16,500, fully three-quarters the median income of all households. By 1989 the median income of metropolitan Boston Latinos had risen to nearly $20,000, but was still only 56 percent of median of all households in the region and $1,000 below that of Latinos nationally. That is, Latino households in the Boston area have a particularly large income gap in relation to other households because they are both poorer, on average, than Latinos elsewhere in the United States and reside in a region that has prevailing incomes higher than the national average. Furthermore, nationally the median income of Latinos is about 25 percent higher than that of blacks, but in the Boston area it is about 25 percent lower.

This general pattern masks considerable diversity and complexity among Boston-area Latinos. About half of all Latino households in greater Boston have very low incomes and consequently are likely to have severe housing affordability problems. A slight majority of these very low-income households are female-headed, single-parent families, about a quarter are married couples, and the balance are nonelderly singles and elderly households. On the other side, about 40 percent of Latino households have moderate to middle incomes, comparable to the incomes of non-Latinos of similar household type. About two-thirds of this group are married-couple households. The remaining 10 percent or so of Latino households are a transitional group, whose affordability situations depend upon their individual constellations of income, housing cost, and household size.

The median income of Latino renters in metropolitan Boston in 1985 was $10,700, only 58 percent of the median of all renters in the region. Nationally, Latino renters had a median income of $12,600, 87 percent that of all renters. Latino homeowners in the Boston region had a median income in 1985 of over $34,000, only slightly lower than the $37,000 median income of all homeowners in the region, but nearly $8,000 higher than the median of Latino homeowners nationally. Only one Latino homeowner in eight in metropolitan Boston had an income of under $15,000, compared with one out of four nationally.

In 1985 the median monthly housing cost of Latino renter households was $411, compared with $458 for all renter households. Among homeowners, Latinos had a median cost of $673 versus $499 for all.

In 1985, 38 percent of Latino renters in metropolitan Boston were receiving housing subsidies, 50 percent of these subsidized households residing in public housing developments and the other half receiving rental assistance in privately-owned developments or units. Among all renter households in metropolitan Boston, a little under 20 percent were subsidized in 1985. Low-income Latinos are more likely than non-Latinos to be receiving housing subsidies. This pattern is probably primarily a result of low-income Latinos being predominantly younger families with children, while other low-income renters consist of a higher proportion of smaller, elderly households.

By 1989 the number of Latino renters receiving housing subsidies had increased somewhat, but the proportion had fallen to 32 percent, reflecting the nearly 30 percent growth in the total number of Latino renter households between 1985 and 1989. In 1989, 44 percent of Latino renters receiving subsidies were in public housing, 34 percent were receiving federal rental assistance in private housing, and 22 percent were receiving state rental assistance in private housing.

The distributions of housing subsidies reveal that Latinos are less likely than other households to be able to obtain unsubsidized, low-rent apartments. This finding could possibly be an indication of housing-market discrimination, particularly among owner-occupant landlords who tend to have the lowest rent, unsubsidized apartments. In both white ethnic and black neighborhoods, long-term owner-occupants of two-family to four-family houses typically obtain tenants from within their own communities and are able to charge below-market rents because of their low mortgage costs. Since there is not such a comparable population of long-term Latino homeowners, Latino renters are less likely to have such apartments available to them from within their own community.

Nationally, 18 percent of Latino renters received housing subsidies in 1985, a little less than half the rate in metropolitan Boston. The higher metropolitan Boston rate of housing subsidy by income among Latino renters is due primarily to the availability of state-aided rental assistance and public housing in Massachusetts in addition to the federal programs. Very few other states have such state-supported housing subsidy programs.

In 1985, 4.5 percent of Latino households in the Boston area reported that they had severe problems with their units, compared with 1.3 percent of all households in the region and 4.1 percent of Latinos nationally. As for moderate problems, the rates were 4.5 percent of metropolitan Boston Latino households, 3.4 percent of all area households, and 13.6 percent of Latino households nationally. (See U.S. Bureau of the Census, 1989, App-14, for the definitions of "severe" and "moderate" physical problems.)

With fewer than 10 percent of Latino households reporting severe or moderate physical problems, the impression could be that this is not a major difficulty. However, disaggregating by income reveals a more troubling situation. About half of Latino households with incomes of under $10,000 who reside in unsubsidized rental housing have physical problems with their units, and most of these problems are severe. About 40 percent of all Latino households in metropolitan Boston have incomes of under $10,000, and nearly 60 percent of these households are female-headed, single-parent households. While it is not known precisely what proportion of households of this type are in subsidized housing, the majority of those who do not receive housing subsidies are apparently living in substandard housing. Not only are a significant proportion of Latinos as a whole faced with bad housing, but female-headed, single-parent families are clearly the Latino subgroup disproportionately forced to endure physically inadequate housing conditions as well as the other consequences of their very low incomes and the stigmatized social status of being a single parent.

A New Affordability Standard

I have developed a measure of housing affordability that is more realistic than both the traditional 25 percent-of-income and the more recent 30 percent-of-income standards. Instead of a constant percentage of income, the alternative shelter-poverty measure is a sliding scale, with the maximum affordable percentage varying with income and household size and type.

The sliding scale arises from the recognition that housing costs generally make the first claim on a household's disposable income, with nonhousing expenditures having to adjust to what is left. That is, when we say that a household is paying more than they can afford for housing, what we mean is that after paying for their housing they are unable to meet their nonhousing needs at some specified minimum level of adequacy. Since small households, on average, can meet their nonshelter needs for less than larger households, they can reasonably afford a higher percentage of income for housing than larger households of the same income. Since lower- and higher-income households of the same size and type would on average need comparable resources to meet their nonshelter needs at a minimum level, lower-income households reasonably can afford a smaller percentage of their income for housing than similar higher-income households. On this basis, it turns out that some households can afford less than the traditional 25 percent-of-income; indeed, some can afford nothing for housing, while others can afford more than 25 percent and even more than 30 percent without hardship. Households paying more than they can afford on this scale of affordability are "shelter poor," meaning that the squeeze between their incomes and housing costs leaves them unable to meet their nonshelter needs at even a minimum level of adequacy. (Fuller explanation of the logic and methodology of the shelter-poverty concept of affordability, as well as actual dollar and percent-of-income affordability levels under this measure, can be found in Stone, 1990a, 1990b, 1991, and, most comprehensively, 1993.)

For example, on the shelter-poverty standard a married-couple family of four with a gross income of $20,000 on average could afford only $160 a month (10 percent of their income) for shelter, including utilities, in greater Boston in 1988-89 if they were to be able to satisfy their nonhousing needs at the minimum of adequacy. Indeed, if their income was under $17,000 they could not afford anything for shelter and still meet their nonshelter necessities at the minimum level. However, if their income was over $26,000, they could afford to spend a maximum of 25 percent of their income on housing, and if their income was $29,000 or more, 30 percent of their income.

An employed, single parent with two children and an income of $14,000 could afford only $100 a month (9 percent of her income) for housing in the Boston area in 1988-89. But if she was unemployed and on public assistance, she could afford nothing for housing, even in a state with higher than average Aid to Families with Dependent Children benefit levels and even with food stamps and Medicaid.

The following section presents an analysis of the scope of the housing affordability problem among Latino renters in metropolitan Boston. Because of the small number of Latino homeowners in the Boston metropolitan area, it was not possible to compute statistically significant estimates of the affordability problem for such households. Shelter poverty is compared with affordability based on the conventional percent-of-income measures. Boston-area Latinos are compared with non-Latinos in the region and with Latinos nationally. (For more detailed results see Stone, 1991.)

Latino Housing Affordability Burdens

A majority of Latino renters in the Boston region have housing affordability problems, regardless of the measure used (see table 1). The incidence of affordability problems among Latino renter households in metropolitan Boston is about 20 percentage points higher than among other renters, but only marginally higher than among Latinos nationally.

The shelter-poverty approach does not reveal a more serious problem than the conventional measures, but it does suggest a somewhat different distribution of the problem. It is particularly valuable in helping to identify realistically which subgroups face the most severe affordability burdens. Specifically, the shelter-poverty standard shows that the problem is more serious among the lowest income households than the conventional percent-of-income standards imply. It also reveals that among moderate- and middle-income households the affordability problem is more serious among large households and less serious among small households than the traditional approach suggests.

SHELTER POVERTY

In 1985, 60 percent of Latino renter households in the greater Boston region were shelter poor; after paying for their housing they did not have enough money left to meet their nonshelter needs for food, clothing, medical care, transportation, and so forth, at even a minimum level of adequacy. These shelter-poor renters are nearly half of all Latino households in metropolitan Boston.

The incidence of shelter poverty varies strongly with income. The median income of shelter-poor Latino renters was about $7,400 in 1985, 70 percent of the median of all Latino renters. Nearly three-quarters of those who are shelter poor have incomes below $10,000, and nearly nine-tenths have incomes below $15,000.

The incidence of shelter poverty generally increases with household size, rising to 83 percent among households of six persons or more. For every size household, except two-person, the median income of those shelter poor ranges between $7,000 and $8,500. By contrast, the median income of those two-person renters who are shelter poor is only $2,800. These households are almost entirely young Latina women with children, living in absolute poverty as well as shelter poverty.

Of the Latino renter households who are shelter poor, three-quarters can afford nothing for housing, and further, even if their housing were free, they still would have insufficient income to be able to pay for their nonshelter necessities at a minimum level of adequacy.

Finally, because shelter poverty is more severe for larger than for smaller households, the percentage of persons living in shelter poverty is higher than the percentage of households who are shelter poor. Specifically, 67 percent of the *people* residing in renter households with a Latino householder were shelter poor in 1985, compared with 60 percent of the *households* with a Latino householder (see table 1).

CONVENTIONAL AFFORDABILITY VERSUS SHELTER POVERTY

The incidence of Latino renter households paying 25 percent or more of their incomes for housing is 61 percent; and of those paying 30 percent or more, it is 51 percent, compared with 60 percent shelter poor (see table 1). Thus the shelter-poverty approach cannot be said to exaggerate the affordability problem, even though it implies that some households realistically can afford nothing for housing. The resolution of this apparent contradiction is to be found in the different distributions of the problem implied by the different affordability standards.

In general, the conventional standards reveal a problem somewhat less severe among very low-income and large households and more severe among small households and those of higher income. Consider the following:

Among one-person Latino households, nearly all of those shelter poor have incomes of less than $15,000. By contrast, nearly a third of those paying 25 percent or more have incomes of $15,000 or more; on the 30 percent standard, a quarter are above $15,000. The reason for this sharp difference is that the shelter-poverty concept says that most one-person households with incomes above $15,000 can afford more than 25 percent and even more than 30 percent of their incomes without hardship, so that the problem is really concentrated on the very poorest people living alone.

Among two-person households, the conventional approach perceives an affordability problem all the way up to $30,000, while shelter poverty is almost entirely concentrated among those with incomes below $15,000. Also, below $10,000 virtually all such households are shelter poor, even those who are receiving housing subsidies.

Latino households of three persons similarly appear to have substantial conventional affordability problems up to $30,000, especially on the 25 percent-of-income standard. Shelter poverty, by contrast, reaches only up to $20,000, but below this income it afflicts a higher percent of households than the conventional measures of affordability.

Households of four persons are the transition where the income distribu-tions of different affordability approaches are least disparate. Below $20,000, shelter poverty is considerably more severe than the percent-of-income measures of the problem, but all of the measures do not show great differences at higher incomes.

Among Latino households with five persons or more, the shelter-poverty measure shows a substantially more severe problem than the conventional approaches for all incomes up to $30,000. The disparity is most striking in the $20,000 to $30,000 range. Here we see the opposite phenomenon from the situation of one-person households; these very large households cannot afford as much as 25 percent or 30 percent of their incomes for housing unless their incomes are well above $30,000.

These findings suggest quite strongly why an adequate understanding of the housing affordability problem among Latinos must be built on an examination of the distribution of the problem, taking into account the implications of differences in household size as well as income.

SHELTER POVERTY AMONG ALL HOUSEHOLDS VERSUS LATINO HOUSEHOLDS

In metropolitan Boston in 1985, 41 percent of all renter households were shelter poor in comparison with 60 percent of Latino renter households. Renter households with a Latino householder accounted for a reported 4.3 percent of all renter households in the region, but they accounted for 9.9 percent of all persons living in shelter-poor renter households. This difference is due not only to the higher overall incidence of shelter poverty among Latino households, but also to the much greater concentration of shelter poverty among large Latino households; the median size of all shelter-poor renter households is just 1.7 persons, compared with a median of 3.3 persons among shelter-poor Latino renter households.

What accounts for the higher incidence of shelter poverty among Latino households in comparison with others? Is it lower incomes, larger household size, or price discrimination? A formal statistical analysis has been carried out to test the hypothesis that Latino and non-Latino households of a given income and household size are equally likely to have an affordability problem. The results are unequivocal: For every income and household-size class there is no significant difference between Latinos and non-Latinos based on the shelter-poverty, 25 percent-of-income, and 30 percent-of-income standards. That is, income and household size are the only predictors of the likelihood of a household paying more than it can afford for housing, regardless of which affordability standard one uses. Latino renters have a higher rate of shelter poverty because they are poorer and have more persons per household, on average, not because they pay more.

Does this conclusion mean that there is no housing-market discrimination against Latinos in the metropolitan Boston area? Not at all. The earlier discussion of the physical condition of housing occupied by Latinos showed that low-income Latinos in the private rental market are significantly more likely to live in substandard housing. Combining those findings with the conclusions about affordability suggests that while Latino renters of a given income do not, on average, pay more for housing than non-Latinos of the same income, a significant proportion do get poorer quality housing for their money. Better quality housing does exist at the same price they are paying, but, for whatever reasons, they do not have access to it. This is price discrimination, since it implies that a Latino household would have to pay more on average than non-Latinos of the same income to obtain comparable quality housing. Income and household size determine whether a Latino household has an affordability problem, but if they are poor and in unsubsidized housing, their ethnicity determines the condition of the housing they get for what they are paying.

SHELTER POVERTY AMONG LATINOS IN THE UNITED STATES VERSUS METROPOLITAN BOSTON

The incidence of shelter poverty among Latino renters in the United States was

58 percent in 1985, virtually no different than the 60 percent rate in metropolitan Boston. Similarly, on the 25 percent-of-income standard there is no difference (60 percent nationally versus 61 percent in the Boston region), and on the 30 percent-of-income standard as well (50 percent nationally versus 51 percent in the Boston area). Comparing the incidence of shelter poverty by income, there is also little difference between the national and Boston-area rates among Latino renters.

Examining the rates of shelter poverty by household size does, however, reveal some important differences. Consider the following:

Among one-person Latino renter households, 42 percent nationally are shelter poor compared with 34 percent in metropolitan Boston. Nationally, a much greater proportion of single Latinos are elderly, especially elderly women, with a high rate of shelter poverty (Stone, 1990b, Chapter 5). Very low-income Latino singles in Boston have a higher rate of shelter poverty than they do nationally, but these very poor households are a smaller share of the total population of Latino singles in the Boston area compared with the relatively greater proportion of younger, moderate- to middle-income Latino singles.

Among two-person and three-person households, the national rates of shelter poverty are significantly lower than those in the Boston area; for two-person households, 49 percent nationally versus 60 percent in metropolitan Boston; for three-person households, 58 percent versus 66 percent. It is the greater concentration of such households at very low incomes in the Boston area, specifically the high proportion of extremely poor, female-headed, single-parent households, that explains most of this difference.

Among four-person Latino renter households, 69 percent nationally are shelter poor in contrast with 54 percent in the Boston region. The explanation is that Latino renter households of four persons have a much lower median income nationally than in the Boston area and do not have the same sharply bimodal income distribution.

Among households with five persons or more, there is virtually no difference between the overall incidence of shelter poverty nationally and in the Boston area. Looking more closely by income, though, it is found that the median incomes of very large Latino renter households are considerably higher nationally than in Boston, and the same is true of those shelter poor; among the shelter poor the respective gaps are about $5,000. This means that while the rates of shelter poverty are comparable, the depth of economic deprivation experienced by a large, shelter-poor Latino household nationally is, on average, considerably less than in the Boston area.

In sum, the aggregate incidence of shelter poverty among Latino renters in greater Boston is very close to the national rate. However, those who are shelter poor in the Boston region are, on average, considerably poorer than shelter-poor Latinos nationally. This means that not only do they face higher housing costs, on average, and higher costs for nonshelter items, but they have less income available to pay for their necessities. The gap between what they have and what they need is thus much wider.

Implications and Recommendations

The nature and severity of housing affordability problems confronting Latinos in greater Boston are the result of processes on both the income side and the housing side of the relationship. They also reflect the interaction between structural features of the labor and housing markets, on the one hand, and the distinctive circumstances of Latinos, on the other (for analyses of the structural flaws in the housing system, see the essays in Bratt, Hartman, and Meyerson, 1986; and Stone, 1990a, 1993). This complexity of the problem means that significant progress in overcoming shelter poverty among Boston-area Latinos will require strategies and policies addressing all of these dimensions, namely: recognizing the decisive importance for Latinos of having affordable housing in order to achieve social and economic well-being, yet also having adequate and secure incomes to be able to obtain and retain decent housing; recognizing the necessity of mobilizing the Latino community to redress the inequities Latinos are confronting in housing and other arenas, and also the necessity for building alliances beyond the community in order to confront the fundamental sources of the affordability problem.

The danger in such a realization is that it might be concluded that nothing can be done unless everything is done. Such a conclusion would certainly be unwarranted and unfortunate. There are numerous avenues for action, and many should be taken; some are more appropriate and efficacious than others, and therefore more worthy of pursuit. A comprehensive agenda and strategy is necessary, but progress is possible even though a complete solution is not at hand.

This chapter obviously has not been focused on the dimensions and determinants of the incomes of Latinos in the Boston area. Other chapters in this book have made comprehensive examination of these issues, and income policies are most appropriately explored in relation to that work. Nonetheless, the analysis presented here does add several dimensions that are worth noting for their policy relevance. First, the shelter-poverty standard provides a basis for determining income adequacy that is far superior to the conventional poverty standard, both conceptually and in its ability to reflect regional differences in living costs. For example, it would suggest that in 1991, a four-person family in the Boston region would need an after-tax income of at least $22,000 to be able to meets its needs at a minimum level of adequacy, including an extremely conservative standard for housing costs. This compares with a national average of about $19,000, and the official poverty level of about $13,000.

Second, as we have seen, application of the shelter-poverty standard to the actual situation of Latinos in the Boston area demonstrates that over 40 percent of all Latino households and nearly 50 percent of Latino renters can afford nothing for housing. These figures are about 10 percentage points higher than for Latinos nationally and 30 percentage points higher than for non-Latinos in metropolitan Boston, reflecting both the very low incomes of Latinos and the higher cost of nonshelter necessities in the Boston area.

Thus, even though it is not appropriate to explore income strategies more fully in this chapter, these findings do suggest that such strategies must be seen as an essential component of an adequate response to the affordability situation of Boston-area Latinos. In terms of the analysis presented here, such strategies might be most appropriately framed in relation to the following goal: assurance to all households of adequate and secure incomes through gainful employment for all those able to participate in the paid labor force and through appropriate income supports for those who cannot obtain adequate income through employment. Standards of income adequacy should reflect realistically the cost of housing and nonshelter necessities. Income supports should consist of housing affordability assistance based upon the shelter-poverty standard, as well as supplemental aid to the very lowest income households who would still be unable to meet their nonshelter needs at a minimum level even if their housing costs were fully subsidized.

Moving to the housing side of the issue, the findings of this research suggest that attention should be focused most particularly on the needs of Latinos who are in one or more of the following categories:

Renter households,
Very low-income households,
Large households,
Female-headed, single-parent households, and
Households in substandard housing.

Combining this recognition with the strategic framework presented in the opening paragraph of this section, I would recommend that Latino communities, leaders, and supporters direct their energies in the housing area primarily toward strategies and policies framed in terms of the following three categories:

Rental assistance and housing opportunity,
Community development and organizing, and
Coalition building and institutional change.

In identifying these as the highest priority areas for housing action, I am suggesting that efforts to expand conventional homeownership among Boston-area Latinos should not be given as high a priority. Despite the understandable emotional and symbolic significance attached to homeownership, it is politically and morally essential to avoid false promises about the possibilities and benefits of conventional homeownership for lower-income households. It is important to recognize that the opportunity to realize conventional homeownership is more a consequence than a cause of upward mobility and economic security. For households with incomes much below $30,000 the risks are significant and too often unacknowledged: Mortgage qualification does not consider the costs of utilities and maintenance and repairs, which are sizable and often unanticipated burdens in older houses; lower-income homeowners are disproportionately victimized by financial scams, as has again become apparent recently; and emotional and financial stress is high, with mortgage defaults and foreclosures not unusual, resulting in loss of home, savings, and even self-esteem.

To be sure, those Latinos who have a sufficient level and stability of income must be assured of full and nondiscriminatory access to housing markets, mortgage credit, and homeownership-opportunity programs. But given the demographic and economic profile of Boston-area Latinos, unless and until there is very substantial improvement in incomes, the most critical Latino housing needs are for deep subsidies, improved housing conditions, and greater security of tenure. With these as priorities, it then becomes reasonable to explore and pursue possibilities for homeownership without speculation (Stone, 1986, 1989; Baker, 1989; Sultemeier, 1989).

RENTAL ASSISTANCE AND HOUSING OPPORTUNITIES

As we have seen, over 80 percent of metropolitan-Boston Latinos are renters, and about one-third of such households received housing subsidies as of 1989 (38 percent in 1985). Massachusetts Latinos therefore have a major stake in subsidized housing and rental assistance, under both federal and state programs. Defending and expanding these programs, reforming the subsidy formulas, and coupling the programs with antidiscrimination efforts are three avenues of action that would have significant benefits for Latinos.

Of the metropolitan-Boston Latinos receiving housing subsidies, about 45 percent are in federal- and state-aided public housing. The rest are in privately-owned housing, some in housing developments, but most in individual apartments with rental assistance certificates and vouchers under the federal Section 8 and state Chapter 707 programs. The Chapter 707 program has been eliminated and replaced with a more limited rental voucher program with fewer eligible households and a lower average level of subsidy per household. This is an area where reversal of cuts and an improved program should be of particular importance to Latinos.

In addition, under state housing-subsidy programs the percentage of net income to be paid in rent by subsidized households increased in mid-1992. Since the existing percent-of-income formulas differ substantially from the shelter-poverty standard, and Latino households are on average larger than other households, most subsidized Latino renters are actually already paying more than they realistically can afford on the shelter-poverty scale and are disproportionately vulnerable to the proposed increases. Thus, a more appropriate and effective strategy than attempting to roll back the increase in the percent of income would be to try to reform the subsidy formula to make it better correspond to genuine affordability. Subsidized households are permitted deductions of $300 for each minor child and for each adult other than the head-of-household who contributes income. If this deduction were raised to $900, or even $600 as a first step, the subsidy formula would move closer to the shelter-poverty standard, and the effect of the increased percentage of net income would be mitigated, most especially for the larger households.

Finally, if the federal and state rental-assistance programs were to be coupled with aggressive antidiscrimination and affirmative marketing efforts, they could be an important vehicle for providing Latinos with increased geographical choice and the opportunity to move out of areas of geographical concentration — for those who so wish. Since Latinos disproportionately live in areas of physically inadequate housing, and subsidized private housing units must meet standards of physical adequacy, affirmatively expanding geographical choice through these programs also increases the chance of Latinos obtaining decent housing.

COMMUNITY DEVELOPMENT AND ORGANIZING

Expanding geographical mobility and housing choice represents one important strategic direction. It is also important to recognize, though, that most Latinos will continue to be relatively concentrated geographically, and hence to pursue strategies that will transform this concentration into a source of strength. Three particularly valuable approaches in this direction are community-based housing development and ownership, creation of housing situations especially responsive to single-parent, female-headed households, and organizing Latino tenants to act collectively on their own behalf.

Massachusetts has one of the greatest concentrations of community-development corporations (CDCs) in the country, including a number in predominantly Latino areas. Inquilinos Boricuas en Accion in Boston's South End is one of the oldest and best known CDCs in the United States. Nuestra Communidad in Boston's Roxbury-North Dorchester section and Coalition for a Better Acre in Lowell are two other successful Latino CDCs within the Boston region; Nueva Esperanza in Holyoke and Brightwood Development Corporation in Springfield are notable examples in western Massachusetts Latino communities.

Nonetheless, there are neighborhoods with great concentrations of Latinos that do not have established community-development corporations and could use assistance in establishing CDCs; in addition, existing CDCs are in need of increased capacity and resources to support their efforts. Furthermore, heavy emphasis on new construction and substantial rehab by most of the CDCs has meant that only a relatively small proportion of households have been reached even in most of the Latino communities that have such organizations. Thus, what is also needed is greater attention to acquisition of existing housing for nonspeculative, community and resident ownership. Such a strategy offers the potential for more widely dispersed benefits at lower per-unit-cost than does exclusive emphasis on more complex and costly major construction endeavors. The HOME Program created by the National Affordable Housing Act of 1990 is potentially an important vehicle for furthering these efforts in Latino communities (Low-Income Housing Information Service, 1990). At the same time, it is also important to recognize the constraints and limitations of CDCs and understand that they need to be coupled with other community housing strategies (Keating, Rasey, and Krumholz, 1990).

Second, the very large proportion of Boston-area Latino women who are single-parent households and the very high incidence of shelter poverty among such households require concentrated attention, not just broader-gauged strategies. Leaders, advocates, and Latina single parents themselves should explore and seek financial and technical assistance for creating shared housing, congregate housing, transitional housing, and alternatively-laid-out individual dwellings responsive to the needs of such households. Integral and complementary to these physical designs should be strategies for supportive services and challenges to the multiple levels of discrimination faced by Latina single parents. The Women's Institute for Housing and Economic Development in Boston would be a valuable resource in developing these kinds of strategies. (See also Hayden, 1984; Birch, 1985; Mulroy, 1988; Franck and Ahrentzen, 1989; Leavitt and Saegert, 1990.)

Finally, even with housing subsidies and expanded community-based housing, for the foreseeable future most shelter-poor Latinos will continue to live in private rental housing without subsidies. Therefore, conscious and deliberate efforts should be made and resources sought to organize Latino tenants so they can act on their own behalf to resist rent increases, improve their living conditions, defend their rights, and build confidence, skills, and solidarity. Ultimately, with adequate resources some groups of tenants might develop the capacity to take control of their buildings under nonprofit or limited-equity ownership. The experience of the community organization City Life/Vida Urbana in working with Latino tenants in parts of Boston's Jamaica Plain and Roxbury demonstrates the exciting possibilities for this strategy (Walker, 1990). Once again, certain caveats are in order: Without sufficient financial resources, organizational development, and stability in other aspects of people's lives, taking over control and ownership of their buildings may leave tenants managing their own exploitation while bailing out the landlords.

COALITION BUILDING AND INSTITUTIONAL CHANGE

As emphasized at the beginning of this section, shelter poverty among Boston-area Latinos reflects structural flaws in the institutions of housing provision in this society, as well as the particular experiences and situations of Latinos themselves. Given the scope of shelter poverty among Latinos, there are substantial benefits to be realized for Massachusetts Latinos through participation in broader housing reform efforts as well as important contributions that Latinos can make to such coalitions.

To date Boston-area Latinos have tended to direct most of their political organizing and advocacy efforts primarily toward improvements in employment, education, and social services, rather than housing — apart, of course, from the several community development corporations mentioned above. In view of the profound significance of housing for social and economic well-being that I have tried to demonstrate here, I would urge Latino organizations not only to give housing a higher priority in their community agendas, but also to become actively involved at the state level in the Massachusetts Affordable Housing Alliance and the Massachusetts HOME Coalition.

At the national level, there are several major organizational links that should be developed to address the kinds of housing problems identified here in a larger context. First, the National Low-Income Housing Coalition is the major progressive housing advocacy and lobbying organization with a significant presence in Washington. It has long had a multiracial constituency but would undoubtedly welcome and benefit from increased Latino participation. Second, the National Council of La Raza has had housing as a major component of its agenda for many years (see, for example, the Foreword by Raul Yzaguirre to Dolbeare and Canales, 1988). While historically La Raza has its roots and most of its local activities in Chicano communities of the Southwest, it has established a significant national presence representative of Latinos throughout the country, with its housing activities providing a potentially valuable point of involvement for Massachusetts Latino organizations and leaders.

Finally, even as problems of shelter poverty among Boston-area Latinos are challenged through specific policies and strategies at the local and state levels and through political participation and alliances in the national arena, Latino activists and leaders from Massachusetts should participate in projecting a vision of housing reform that can resonate within local communities as well as guide state and national policies. As formulated by the Institute for Policy Studies Working Group on Housing (1987, 1989) and introduced to Congress by Representative Ronald Dellums, the principal ingredients of such a long-range comprehensive program are several:

Increasing the amount of housing under various forms of social and nonspeculative ownership with resident control;

Expanding socially-oriented production of housing, including housing produced by community-based developers; and

Financing the production, rehab, and acquisition of nonspeculative housing more frequently through direct public capital grants rather than debt.

Other complementary actions would include progressive reform of the financial system and generating public resources through substantial cuts in the military budget and restoration of a truly progressive income tax. Shelter poverty among Latinos, and shelter poverty in general, cannot and will not be solved by the private market, even with some measure of government assistance. Thus, rather than idealizing the market and serving as the handmaiden of private profit, public policy ultimately must transcend the limits of the market and serve truly social purposes. Shelter poverty may be ameliorated, but it will not be overcome until housing is established as a right. Massachusetts Latinos have an important part to play and compelling reasons to participate in the struggle for a right to housing.

Note

I want to thank Phillip Clay, Edwin Meléndez, and Miren Uriarte for helpful comments and suggestions. Melvyn Colon and Miriam Colon kindly provided some factual information that was useful in preparing the recommendations portion of this chapter.

196 Michael E. Stone

References

Achtenberg, E. P. (1989). Subsidized Housing at Risk: The Social Costs of Private Ownership. In Rosenberry, S. and C. Hartman (Eds.), *Housing Issues of the 1990s*, pp. 227-267. New York: Praeger.

Achtenberg, E. P. (1990, July/August). Preserving Expiring Use Projects: A Political and Economic Perspective. *Boston Bar Journal*, 17-21.

Baker, A. (1989 February/March/April). Community Land Trusts: Preserving Affordability. *Shelterforce*, 15-17.

Birch, E. L. (Ed.). (1985). *The Unsheltered Woman*. New Brunswick, NJ: Center for Urban Policy Research.

Bratt, R. C. Hartman, C., and Meyerson, A. (Eds.). (1986). *Critical Perspectives on Housing*. Philadelphia: Temple University Press.

Clay, P. L. (1987, May). *At Risk of Loss: The Endangered Future of Low-Income Rental Housing Resources*. Washington, DC: Neighborhood Reinvestment Corporation.

Congressional Budget Office. (1988, December). *Current Housing Problems and Possible Federal Response*. Washington, DC: Government Printing Office.

Darden, J. T. (1986). Accessibility to Housing: Differential Residential Segregation for Blacks, Hispanics, American Indians, and Asians. In Momeni, J. A. (Ed.), *Race, Ethnicity, and Minority Housing in the United States*, pp. 109-126. New York: Greenwood Press.

Dolbeare, C. N., and Canales, J. N. (1988, June). *The Hispanic Housing Crisis*. Washington, DC: National Council of La Raza, Policy Analysis Center.

Franck, K. A., and Ahrentzen, S. (Eds.). (1989). *New Households, New Housing*. New York: Van Nostrand Reinhold.

Hayden, D. (1984). *Redesigning the American Dream: The Future of Housing, Work and Family Life*. New York: W. W. Norton and Company.

Institute for Policy Studies Working Group on Housing. (1987). *A Progressive Housing Program for the United States*. Washington, DC: Institute for Policy Studies. Summarized in *Institute for Policy Studies Working Group on Housing* (Richard P. Appelbaum). A Progressive Housing Program for the United States. In Rosenberry, S., and Hartman, C. (Eds.), *Housing Issues of the 1990s*, pp. 313-331. New York: Praeger.

Institute for Policy Studies Working Group on Housing (with Dick Cluster). (1989). *The Right to Housing: A Blueprint for Housing the Nation*. Washington, DC: Institute for Policy Studies.

Joint Center for Housing Studies of Harvard University. (1990). *The State of the Nation's Housing 1990*. Cambridge: Joint Center for Housing Studies of Harvard University.

Keating, W. D., Rasey, K. P., and Krumholz, N. (1990). Community Development Corporations in the United States: Their Role in Housing and Urban Development. In van Vliet, W. and J. van Weesep (Eds.), *Government and Housing: Developments in Seven Countries*, pp. 206-218. Newbury Park, CA: Sage Publications.

Krivo, L. J. (1982). Housing Price Inequalities: A Comparison of Anglos, Blacks, and Spanish-Origin Populations. *Urban Affairs Quarterly, 17*(4), 445-462.

Lazere, E. B., and Leonard, P. A. (1989, July). *The Crisis in Housing for the Poor: A*

Special Report on Hispanics and Blacks. Washington, DC: Center on Budget and Policy Priorities.

Leavitt, J. and Saegert, S. (1990). *From Abandonment to Hope: Community-Households in Harlem.* New York: Columbia University Press.

Lopez, M. M. (1986). Su casa no es mi casa: Hispanic Housing Conditions in Contemporary America, 1949-80. In Momeni, J. A. (Ed.), *Race, Ethnicity, and Minority Housing in the United States,* pp. 127-145. New York: Greenwood Press.

Low-Income Housing Information Service. (1991, January). *Briefing Materials on the National Affordable Housing Act of 1990.* Washington, DC: Author.

Massey, D. S., and Denton, N.A. (1987, December). Trends in Residential Segregation of Blacks, Hispanics, and Asians. *American Sociological Review, 52,* 802-825.

Massey, D. S., and Denton, N. A. (1989, August). Hypersegregation in U.S. Metropolitan Areas: Black and Hispanic Segregation Along Five Dimensions. *Demography, 26*(3), 373-391.

Mulroy, E. A. (Ed.). (1988). *Women as Single Parents: Confronting Institutional Barriers in the Courts, the Workplace, and the Housing Market.* Dover, MA: Auburn House.

Stone, M. E. (1986, November/December). Homeownership Without Speculation. *Shelterforce,* 13-15.

Stone, M. E. (1989). Shelter Poverty in Boston: Problem and Program. In Rosenberry, S. and Hartman, C. (Eds.), *Housing Issues of the 1990s,* pp. 338-378. New York: Praeger.

Stone, M. E. (1990a). *One-Third of a Nation: A New Look at Housing Affordability in American.* Washington, DC: Economic Policy Institute.

Stone, M. E. (1990b). *Housing Affordability and the Elderly: Definition, Dimensions, Policies.* Boston: University of Massachusetts, Gerontology Institute.

Stone, M. E. (1991). *Shelter Poverty Among Latinos in Greater Boston.* Boston: University of Massachusetts, Mauricio Gastón Institute for Latino Community Development and Public Policy.

Stone, M. E. (1993). *Shelter Poverty: New Ideas on Housing Affordability.* Philadelphia: Temple University Press.

Sultemeier, D. (1989, May/June). Mutual Housing: Resident Control Without Ownership. *Shelterforce,* 7-9.

Turner, M. A., Struyk, R. J., and Yinger, J. (1991, August). *Housing Discrimination Study: Synthesis.* Prepared for the Office of Policy Development and Research, U.S. Department of Housing and Urban Development by the Urban Institute and Syracuse University. Washington, DC: The Urban Institute.

U.S. Bureau of the Census, and U.S. Department of Housing and Urban Development. (1988, December). *American Housing Survey for the United States in 1985.* Current Housing Reports, H-150-85. Washington, DC: Government Printing Office.

U.S. Bureau of the Census, and U.S. Department of Housing and Urban Development. (1989, August). *American Housing Survey for the Boston Metropolitan Area in 1985.* Current Housing Reports, H-170-85-3. Washington, DC: Government Printing Office.

U.S. Bureau of the Census, and U.S. Department of Housing and Urban Development.

(1991, October). *American Housing Survey for the Boston Metropolitan Area in 1989.* Current Housing Reports, H-170-89-3. Washington, DC: Government Printing Office.

van Vliet, W., and van Weesep, J. (Eds.). (1990). *Government and Housing: Developments in Seven Countries.* Newbury Park, CA: Sage Publications.

Walker, A. (1990, November 19). Staking Their Claim: Tenants Make Jamaica Plain Building Their Own. *Boston Globe.*

Woolbright, L. A., and Hartmann, D. J. (1987). The New Segregation: Asians and Hispanics. In G. A. Tobin, (Ed.), *Divided Neighborhoods: Changing Patterns of Racial Segregation,* pp. 138-157. Newbury Park, CA: Sage.

Table 1

Percentage of Latino Renter Households with Affordability Problems, Metropolitan Boston, by Income and Household Size, 1985

Household Size	Less than $5,000	$5,000 to $9,999	$10,000 to $14,999	$15,000 to $19,999	$20,000 to $29,999	$30,000 to $39,999	$40,000 or More	Total Under $10,000	Total Under $15,000	Total All Incomes	Median Income	Percent of Persons
Shelter Poor												
1 - Person	91.4%	72.5%	23.9%	9.8%		100.0%	0.0%	78.4%	59.0%	34.6%	$8,510	34.6%
2 - Person	98.2%	99.5%	47.6%	24.4%	4.5%	0.4%	0.0%	98.2%	89.7%	60.2%	$2,900	60.2%
3 - Person	94.3%		93.0%	68.1%		0.1%	0.0%	97.7%	96.8%	65.7%	$7,710	65.7%
4 - Person		88.9%		87.1%	32.0%	4.5%	0.1%	88.9%	88.9%	54.1%	$8,390	54.1%
5 - Person	82.1%	83.2%	82.0%		71.7%		1.7%	82.4%	82.2%	69.1%	$7,040	69.1%
6 + Person	79.2%	89.9%	87.7%				4.6%	88.6%	88.3%	83.0%	$8,250	83.0%
Total	92.0%	90.1%	66.7%	44.2%	22.3%	2.9%	0.7%	90.8%	85.5%	59.7%	$7,430	66.7%
Paying 25% or More												
1 - Person	78.9%	72.8%	69.2%	61.6%	26.5%	0.0%	16.9%	74.7%	72.8%	58.2%	$10,700	58.2%
2 - Person	86.9%	84.1%	59.9%	76.6%	34.9%	6.7%	16.9%	86.9%	82.4%	66.9%	$3,640	66.9%
3 - Person	88.1%		84.7%	80.3%	73.7%	1.1%	9.4%	85.5%	85.3%	63.7%	$8,210	63.7%
4 - Person		66.5%		68.8%	37.9%	11.9%	16.5%	66.5%	67.0%	46.5%	$8,890	46.5%
5 - Person	79.4%	54.6%	80.0%		38.0%		17.5%	74.4%	76.1%	63.5%	$6,420	63.5%
6 + Person	67.2%	77.7%	61.9%				15.0%	76.3%	72.6%	71.0%	$8,230	71.0%
Total	83.8%	76.0%	72.9%	76.1%	38.5%	6.0%	14.0%	79.0%	77.6%	61.3%	$8,380	62.5%

Table 1 (Cont)

Paying 30% or More

1 - Person	71.7%	62.2%	55.6%	38.4%	11.1%		8.3%	65.2%	61.8%	44.3%	$9,650	44.3%
2 - Person	80.3%		51.9%	51.7%	17.2%	4.9%	8.5%	80.3%	75.5%	56.8%	$3,340	56.8%
3 - Person	84.0%	76.4%	66.7%	53.0%	24.0%		4.8%	79.0%	76.7%	53.3%	$7,600	53.3%
4 - Person		59.5%		50.2%	19.3%	9.4%	7.8%	59.5%	59.5%	37.2%	$8,490	37.2%
5 - Person	78.1%	40.5%	66.6%		19.1%		8.8%	70.4%	69.3%	53.6%	$4,510	53.6%
6 + Person	60.2%	70.3%	52.7%				7.6%	69.1%	64.9%	61.6%	$8,070	61.6%
Total	78.9%	67.8%	59.3%	50.0%	16.9%	4.3%	7.0%	72.0%	69.2%	50.6%	$7,680	52.5%

SOURCE: Derived from data in U.S. Bureau of Census and U.S. Department of Housing and Urban Development. (1989, August). *American Housing Survey for the Boston Metropolitan Area in 1985*. Current Housing Reports, H-170-85-3. Washington, DC: Government Printing Office.